THE TRANSFORMATION OF THE SUPREME COURT OF CANADA

DONALD R. SONGER

The Transformation of the Supreme Court of Canada

An Empirical Examination

UNIVERSITY OF TORONTO PRESS
Toronto Buffalo London

ISBN 978-0-8020-9689-0

Printed on acid-free paper

Library and Archives Canada Cataloguing in Publication

Songer, Donald R.
The transformation of the Supreme Court of Canada / Donald R. Songer.

Includes bibliographical references and index.
ISBN 978-0-8020-9689-0

1. Canada. Supreme Court. 2. Judicial review – Canada. 3. Political questions
and judicial power – Canada. I. Title.

KE8244.S65 2008   347.71'035   C2008-906539-5
KF8764.ZA2S65 2008

This book has been published with the help of a grant from the Canadian Federation for the Humanities and Social Sciences, through the Aid to Scholarly Publications Programme, using funds provided by the Social Sciences and
Humanities Research Council of Canada.

The University of Toronto Press acknowledges the financial assistance to its publishing program of the Canada Council for the Arts and the Ontario Arts Council.

University of Toronto Press acknowledges the financial support for its publishing activities of the Government of Canada through the Book Publishing Indus-
try Development Program (BPIDP).

Contents

Tables and Figures

Tables

Figures

Acknowledgments

The author gratefully acknowledges the support of the National Science Foundation of the US and the Canadian Embassy to the United States for their support, which made this research possible. The interpretations of the data and the conclusions are of course the author's and are not endorsed by either the National Science Foundation or the Canadian Embassy. Support from the Canadian Studies Grant program enabled the author to make several trips to Canada to interview justices of the Supreme Court of Canada and several judges on the Court of Appeal in several provinces. Much of the statistical analysis in this book was based on the High Courts Judicial Database (HCJD). The HCJD is a public access database created by Stacia L. Haynie, Reginald S. Sheehan, Donald R. Songer, and C. Neal Tate with the support of grants provided by the Law and Social Science Program of the National Science Foundation (NSF). These data were collected under two grants funded by the National Science Foundation: 'Collaborative Research: Fitting More Pieces into the Puzzle of Judicial Behavior: A Multi-Country Database and Program of Research,' SES-9975323; and 'Collaborative Research: Extending a Multi-Country Database and Program of Research,' SES-0137349, C. Neal Tate, Donald R. Songer, Stacia Haynie, and Reginald S. Sheehan, Principal Investigators. It is available for public use and download at http://sitemason.vanderbilt.edu/site/d5YnT2/data_sets. This book has been published with the help of a grant from the Canadian Federation for the Humanities and Social Sciences, through the Aid to Scholarly Publications Program, using funds provided by the Social Sciences and Humanities Research Council of Canada. Finally, I would like to express my appreciation to my colleague, Professor Susan Johnson at the University of North Carolina, Greensboro, for all of her assistance to help make this project a reality.

THE TRANSFORMATION OF THE SUPREME COURT OF CANADA

1 Introduction: The Changing Role of the Supreme Court in Canadian Politics

On 28 June 1971, the Supreme Court of Canada handed down decisions in four separate cases, all by unanimous vote of the five justices participating in each case. In *Schwartz v. Schwartz*[1] the Court settled an inheritance dispute among five children arising from ambiguous language in their deceased father's will. In *City of Victoria v. University of Victoria*[2] the city appealed from a decision by the Court of Appeal denying its tax claim against the university for taxes levied against a commercial building situated half on land left to the university in a will and half on property privately owned. The Court dismissed the university's appeal. In *Canadian General Insurance Company v. Western Pile and Foundation, Ltd.*,[3] the Court wrestled with complex factual issues over liability for damages caused by the collapse of a dam. And in *Phillips v. Samilo*,[4] the Court had been asked to decide which of several heirs was responsible for the tax liability of the deceased father, who had defrauded the government out of $300,000 in taxes owed from his various business schemes. It is probable that no reader of this book has ever heard of any of these cases, and the decisions of the Court were widely ignored even in 1971. These decisions do not appear in any history of Canadian politics or society, and even the leading newspapers of the day ignored them. For example, none of the decisions was even reported by the *Globe and Mail* the next morning.

In contrast, many of the Supreme Court's decisions over the past two decades have generated extended media coverage and heated political controversy. The Court began the new century by announcing, on 26 January 2001, a controversial decision that upheld in part a constitutional challenge to provincial law prohibiting child pornography. In *R. v. Sharpe*,[5] the accused was charged with two counts of possession of child pornography under s. 163.1(4) of the Criminal Code. Prior to his trial, the accused brought a preliminary motion challenging the constitutionality of the act, contending that it violated his constitutional guarantee of freedom of expression. The Crown conceded that the prohibition of possession of child pornography infringed s. 2(b) of the Canadian Charter of Rights and Freedoms but argued that the infringement was justifiable under s. 1 of the Charter. Both the trial judge and the majority on the British Columbia Court of Appeal ruled that the prohibition of the simple possession of child pornography as defined under s. 163.1 of the Code was not justifiable in a free and democratic society.

In a divided decision (L'Heureux-Dubé, Gonthier, and Bastarache dissenting), the Court upheld the constitutionality of the prohibition of child pornography but limited its reach, allowing some private possession of child pornography. Specifically, the Court said that the law should be read as though it contained an exception for the following: (1) any written material or visual representation created by the accused alone, and held by the accused alone, exclusively for his or her own personal use; and (2) any visual recording, created by or depicting the accused, provided it does not depict unlawful sexual activity and is held by the accused exclusively for private use. The public reaction was swift, and the media coverage was extensive. The decision attracted the attention of all the major television news broadcasts and was a major focus of leading newspapers throughout Canada. The *Globe and Mail* alone ran six separate stories highlighting different aspects of the case. A page one article was headlined: 'Top Court Rules 9-0: Child Porn Law Stays.' The same day, other stories were featured on page one of the *Globe* and on pages A4 and A5 under headings such as these: 'Activist Days Long Gone for Deferential Court'; 'Both Sides Claim Victory'; 'BC Defendant Unrepentant after Court Ruling'; and 'McLellan[6] Welcomes Balanced Judgment.' In all, the *Globe and Mail* devoted more than 120 column inches to the decision and to political and personal reactions to it, and that was just the first day after the decision was announced.

Other cases besides that one have elicited fierce public reaction and extensive media coverage. When the Court reversed a pre-Charter precedent to legalize abortion,[7] the reaction from the public was intense and heavily chronicled in the media. Once again, the Court's decision was literally front page news. The day after the *Morgentaler* decision was announced, the headline covering the entire top of page one of the *Globe and Mail* declared 'Abortion Law Scrapped, Women Get Free Choice.' Front page coverage in the *Globe and Mail* also featured passionate responses from both supporters and opponents of the decision. Under the heading 'Jubilant,' the paper reported that 'feminists across the country rejoiced yesterday, calling the Supreme Court's rejection of Canada's abortion law the most important for women since they won the vote.'[8] In a parallel story headed 'Defiant,' a Roman Catholic cardinal was quoted as saying, 'The Supreme Court decision is a disaster ... It is uncivilized.'[9] The political reaction to the decision was covered in great detail – for example, in a long feature headed 'Pro-Choice Supporters Celebrate as Anti-Abortionists Mourn.'[10] The text of the decision also received detailed coverage.[11] Follow-up stories focused on the reaction of women's groups around the country, on the personal life of the doctor at the centre of the case, on the legal history of the battle over abortion, and on the responses of government officials to questions about how they were going to implement the decision.

More recently, the Court again created political controversy when it provided official sanction for advocates of gay rights. In *Vriend v. Alberta*[12] the Court ruled that the Charter of Rights and Freedoms prohibited discrimination on the basis of sexual orientation. In 1990, in response to an inquiry by the president of the college at which he worked, Vriend disclosed that he was homosexual. Shortly thereafter, the college president requested his resignation. When Vriend refused to resign, the college terminated his employment. The sole reason given was his non-compliance with the college's policy on homosexual practices. When Vriend attempted to file a complaint with the Alberta Human Rights Commission on the grounds that his employer had discriminated against him because of his sexual orientation, the commission advised him that he could not make a complaint under the Individual's Rights Protection Act (IRPA), because that act did not include sexual orientation as a protected ground. The trial judge found that the omission of protection against discrimination on the basis of sexual orientation was an unjustified violation of s. 15 of the Charter of Rights. She ordered that the words 'sexual orientation' be read into the IRPA as a prohibited ground of discrimination. The majority on the Court of Appeal allowed the Alberta government's appeal; then, in a split decision, the Supreme Court overturned the Court of Appeal, insisting that protection against discrimination on the grounds of sexual orientation was protected by the Charter even though it was not explicitly mentioned in the Charter. The media reaction was again extensive. For example, the *Globe and Mail* ran half a dozen articles on the decision, supplemented by an editorial and lengthy quotes from the actual opinions of the justices. One article noted that radio talk shows throughout Canada were being swamped by people calling in to express both support and outrage over the decision.[13]

These cases from 1971 and the Charter period illustrate that for much of its history the Supreme Court of Canada toiled in obscurity, well out of the limelight of political controversy. As recently as 1966 the Court was described as the quiet court in the unquiet country' (McCormick 2000, 1). But with the advent of the Charter of Rights and Freedoms, that all changed. Indeed, a major national newspaper recently asserted that the Supreme Court was of profound importance in the Canadian political system because 'the court's rulings have far-reaching effects, particularly in the age of the Charter of Rights and Freedoms.'[14] Another writer asserted that Canadian politics as a whole had been 'transformed' by the Charter (Morton and Knopff 2000, 13) Few now doubt that the Charter has placed the Court at centre stage in some of Canada's most dramatic policy debates. Given this transformation, it is increasingly important to examine how the Court rose to its current prominence. Many commentaries, both scholarly and popular, have critiqued the normative implications of the Court's recent role (see Morton and Knopff 2000; Mandel 1989 1994; Manfredi 1993; Russell 1983). Much less, however, is known about how the Court actually operates and about the empirical realities of its decision-making trends. This book attempts to fill those gaps by providing the most comprehensive empirical analysis to date of continuity and change on the Court in terms of its shifting agenda, the litigants appearing before it, and its patterns of decisions. The focus of the analysis is the period 1970 to 2003.

Over the past half century, the Supreme Court of Canada has undergone two institutional changes. Both have had a profound impact on its role in national life. In 1975 the Court gained substantial control over its docket. Specifically, cases coming before it as appeals 'as of right' were sharply limited; and an expansion of the 'leave to appeal' process provided it with it greater control over which cases it would hear. The second change came in 1982 with the adoption of the Charter of Rights and Freedoms, which transformed the nature of the questions coming to the Court, thereby greatly increasing the Court's role in politically important issues. The time period examined in this study has been chosen to permit an analysis of the impact of these two significant institutional changes. The analysis begins five years before the Court acquired its enhanced agenda control. This is so that the Court *before* the changes can be compared with the Court *after* the changes. The analysis then continues until close to the present time.

Understanding the Transformation of the Supreme Court: Four Themes

Four themes emerge from the detailed analysis that follows. First, the Supreme Court's role in Canadian law and politics has been transformed, largely as a result of the *Charter*. Second, while it is still fashionable to think of the work of courts as divorced from the often disdained world of politics, to properly understand the current Court one must understand it as a court of law *and* a political court. Third, Canada's Supreme Court is clearly a political court, yet compared to many courts in the common law world (including the Supreme Court of its southern neighbour), it is politically moderate. Fourth and finally, almost by definition, courts in a country that has a strong attachment to the rule of law are staffed by people who may fairly be categorized as among the elite of the nation. Nevertheless, compared to many top appellate courts, the Supreme Court of Canada appears to be a rather 'democratic' court, one that largely reflects Canada's diversity.

Regarding the first theme, Canada adopted the Charter in 1982, yet the first case involving it did not reach the Supreme Court until 1984; hence evidence of the effects of the Charter on the Court do not begin to appear until 1984. Since that year, the Court's agenda has undergone a radical revision. As the examples at the beginning of this chapter illustrate, in the early 1970s the Court was still focusing largely on resolving disputes in private law. Since 1984, however, there has been a dramatic increase in the number of criminal appeals and a proportionately large increase in attention to challenges brought by rights claimants (see chapter 3). In addition, the agenda is now dominated by questions of constitutional and statutory interpretation – questions that have potentially widespread effects on society as a whole. This agenda change has taken place at roughly the same time that there has been a significant change in the composition of the Court, most notably with the addition of female justices. Since 1982 more women have served on the Supreme Court of Canada than on the highest courts of

Australia, the United Kingdom, and the United States combined. Also, decision-making processes have changed: the rapid increase in the number of cases has drawn the participation of interveners and resulted in a larger proportion of cases being decided by the full Court or by panels of seven justices (i.e., instead of five).

Regarding the second theme, the Supreme Court is of course the institution tasked with resolving the most perplexing legal issues facing the country. Law and precedent therefore loom large in the justices' deliberations. But the Court cannot be adequately appreciated unless it is understood as both a political and a legal institution. To begin with, the Court has played a major role in the resolution of many of the politically most controversial issues of public policy, especially since the adoption of the Charter (see chapter 6). Thus the Court produces politically important outputs regardless of the justices' preferences. The Court's agenda – in particular, the nature of the issues brought to it by politically motivated individuals and groups – guarantees that no matter who is on the Court, it will be intimately involved in the political process. Moreover, the Court is political in another sense (see chapter 7). The evidence is strong that in a substantial number of politically significant cases, the justices' private political attitudes and preferences influence their decisions. In this respect, the role played by the Supreme Court of Canada does not appear to be fundamentally different from the political role played by the top appellate courts in other common law countries such as the United States, the United Kingdom, Australia, and India, or from the role played by top civil law courts in most of modern Europe. Nevertheless, the evidence suggests that the *magnitude* of the influence of the justices' political attitudes may be more modest than in the United States and Australia.

Regarding the third theme, once one concludes that politics plays a role in judicial decision making, it is important to ask what the political consequences of that role are. It is not possible to give a completely objective answer to this question,[15] and a series of normative analyses of the Supreme Court of Canada have arrived at diverse conclusions, but to an outside observer with no attachments to any faction in Canadian politics, it appears that a good case can be made that overall, the Supreme Court has generally been politically moderate. The evidence for this is drawn from several of the chapters below. First, there have been relatively modest swings over time in the proportion of decisions favouring liberal versus conservative outcomes as a function of changes in the political composition of the Court (as measured by the party of the appointing prime minister; see chapters 6 and 7). For example, changes brought about by changes in party control have been much smaller than in the United States. Journalists writing for Canada's national newspapers concur that most Supreme Court justices have been moderate (see chapter 2). Indeed, the justices themselves sense that most of their colleagues are not interested in pushing ideological agendas and that they are largely willing to compromise (see chapter 5). Finally, over the past third of a century the Court has reached a unanimous decision in the large majority of its cases. Chapter 8 of this book will suggest that political ideology plays little if any role when the Court is unanimous.

Finally, regarding the fourth theme, the Supreme Court of Canada can be understood as relatively 'democratic' compared to many other courts around the world. The justices in the courts of all industrially advanced modern nations are of course more highly educated and tend to be recruited from national elites. But compared to courts in many countries, the Canadian justices appear to be less elite. As noted, Canada has been appointing female justices for decades. Its justices are regionally diverse and have been drawn from a variety of Canadian universities and law schools. Both of Canada's main religious groups have always been represented. Moreover, the Court has long been open to a broad spectrum of the population. And finally, compared to most other common law courts, individuals win relatively often compared to the representatives of entrenched institutionalized power.

Evidence in support of each of these four themes is presented throughout the analysis that follows. However, to provide a descriptive account of the Court that flows more logically, the remainder of this book is organized according to more traditional notions of the functions of courts. The account starts in chapter 2, with a look at the justices who have served on the Court since 1970: how they are selected, what criteria are used in selection, and what types of men and women have been selected. Next, chapter 3 examines the Court's agenda. The process of determining which cases reach its docket is examined; the focus then turns to the nature of those cases. For both questions, a central concern is changes over time in processes and results. Chapter 4 examines the litigants. The first orienting question relates to who participates. That is, who brings cases to the Court? And who is defending their gains in the courts below? In the second half of the chapter, the focus shifts to who wins and who loses in the Supreme Court. Once again, both the overall pattern and changes over time are examined. In chapter 5 attention turns to the Court's internal processes. Much of this chapter is derived from a set of interviews with the justices and some of their former clerks. In chapter 6, trends in policy making are examined. That is, the Court's decisions are examined in aggregate. Instead of asking which individuals (or litigants) win and lose, the analysis explores which policy positions have been favoured and how those trends have changed over time. In chapter 7 the focus remains on the Court's decision making, but the focus shifts to an individual level of analysis. Evidence of attitudinal decision making is explored, and so is the nature of the cleavages on the Court. Most of the analysis in that chapter focuses on the Court's divided decisions. The final substantive chapter, chapter 8, shifts attention from the divided decisions of the Court to the decisions in which it was unanimous. Particular attention is devoted to whether the justices' policy preferences have driven these unanimous decisions. Chapter 9 then summarizes and discusses this study's major findings in terms of the four themes outlined above.

An Outsider's Perspective and an Empirical Analysis

Two things stand out about the analysis that makes this book different from most writing on the Supreme Court of Canada. First, it is written from the perspective of an 'outsider'; second, it presents an empirical rather than a doctrinal or normative analysis of the Court. The author is an outsider in at least three senses. First, I have no special insider connection to the Supreme Court or to any of the present or former justices. Nor have I participated in any of the legal or political battles in which the Court has been involved. Second, I am a social scientist rather than a lawyer or law professor. I am not primarily concerned with the evolution of legal doctrine or even in the precise nature of the precedents spelled out in key decisions of the Court. This book is not in any sense an examination of Canadian law. Rather, my interest is in the role of the Court in Canada's political and legal system and in the similarities and differences in that Court's role compared to the roles played by appellate courts in other countries. Finally, I am an outsider in the sense that I am not a Canadian. I am a political science professor at a university in the United States who embarked on a study of the Supreme Court of Canada out of a broad interest in the comparative analysis of courts in the common law world. I hope that my status as an outsider has enabled me to gain a perspective that may be somewhat different from those of 'insiders' and thus help to cast new light on some recurring themes in discussions of the Supreme Court of Canada.

There is by now a fairly large literature on the Supreme Court of Canada. In part, that is the result of increased public interest in the Court since the Charter of Rights was adopted. But most of that literature does one of two things. A number of scholarly works present a doctrinal account that carefully examines the legal doctrines enunciated by the Court and that traces the evolution of those doctrines over time. Other works provide a normative critique of the Court and its decisions. Many of the Supreme Court's decisions, especially since the adoption of the Charter, have evoked intense political passions. Out of those passions, both defenders and detractors of the Court have provided searing accounts that either justify or attack the Court from a variety of political perspectives. The current account does neither. Instead, it attempts to provide an empirical account that examines as objectively as possible both continuity and change on the Court since 1970. Wherever possible, quantitative and statistical analyses are employed both to provide a descriptive account and to test empirical hypotheses about the Court.

The analyses presented below are the first to combine the insights gained from in-depth interviews with the justices with a series of quantitative analyses of judicial decisions. No other studies of decision making in the top courts of Canada, the United States, or Britain contain such a rich combination of quantitative analysis and insights from judicial interviews. The study utilizes two main sources of data: a set of in-depth interviews with the Supreme Court justices, and the most comprehensive database of Canadian decisions spanning more than three decades, paying particular attention to decisions handed down by the Court in three pivotal issue areas: criminal law, Charter rights and liberties, and economic disputes.

Much of the research was made possible by a pair of grants from the National Science Foundation of the United States and Canadian Studies Grant program of the Canadian Embassy in Washington.[16] This support enabled the author to code all of the published decisions of the Supreme Court from 1970 through 2003. All decisions published in the *Supreme Court Reporter* have been coded. For each case, detailed information has been recorded regarding the nature of the issues, the litigants, the interveners, the votes of the justices, and the outcome of the

Court's decision, along with the history of the case before it reached the Supreme Court. In all, detailed information on more than seventy variables has been collected for each case.

The author also interviewed ten of the current or recent justices of the Supreme Court and four former law clerks to the justices. All of the interviews with the justices were held in the offices of the justices in the Supreme Court building in Ottawa on one of several trips the author made to Ottawa between 2001 and 2007. All interviews were conducted under the following ground rules: the comments of the justices would not be attributed to any justice, nor would any descriptive information about the justices be linked to the comments that would allow anyone familiar with the justices to make such attributions. Thus, accounts of the interviews refer to the justices only as 'Justice A,' 'Justice B, and so on. All justices are referred to using a male pronoun regardless of the actual gender of the justice. The interviews were opened ended, and the justices were encouraged to elaborate on their answers to all questions. Most interviews lasted between an hour and an hour and fifteen minutes. A copy of the interview schedule is provided in the Appendix.

An Overview of the Analysis

There have been plenty of studies defending or attacking Canada's Supreme Court on normative grounds. Less is known about how it operates. Indeed, one prominent scholar maintains that the 'internal decision making process of the Supreme Court of Canada has been shrouded in secrecy' (Baar 1988, 70). In this book an attempt is made to lift that veil and cast some light on the main features of the Supreme Court's decision-making process over the last third of a century. Interviews with the justices and with some former clerks on the Supreme Court explore how cases get to the Court, who determines which judges will hear the appeal, how the justices prepare for the hearing, what happens in conference, and why the negotiations surrounding the actual writing of the opinion are so crucial.

These interviews are supplemented with a quantitative analysis of all of the published decisions of the Court since 1970. Besides tracing changes in the characteristics of the lawyers appointed to the Supreme Court, trends in the agenda of the Court, variations in who participates, and variations in who wins appeals to the Court, the book devotes four chapters to the justices' decision making. First, interviews with the justices are used to provide new insights into that process. Then the Court's decisions are analysed in aggregate so as to explain changes in trends in the Court's decisions. The focus then shifts to the individual voting decisions of the justices and the bases of divisions in the Court. Finally, the analysis focuses on the unanimous decisions of the Court, in order to integrate the perspectives of the justices with an empirical analysis that probes whether those unanimous decisions are consistent with an attitudinal explanation of judicial behaviour or, rather, reflect collegiality and compromise.

2 The Changing Profile of Justices on the Supreme Court

In chapter 1 it was noted that the Supreme Court of Canada has for more than a century been involved in the resolution of some of the most important political issues of the day. The extent of its impact and the visibility of its actions have increased dramatically since the adoption of the Charter of Rights and Freedoms. To begin to understand the Court's role in Canadian politics, one might ask who the judges actually are and how they reached the pinnacle of judicial power in Canada. Those two questions are the focus of the current chapter.

The Selection of the Justices

In the past few years, there has been more debate and controversy over the methods for selecting justices to the Supreme Court than at any other time in anyone's memory. This debate led to a modest change in the process when Abella and Charron were selected as justices in 2004 and to further modifications leading up to the appointment of Rothstein in 2006. At the time of this writing there are doubts whether the most recent 'reforms' will persist. No one can say what the future will hold for the process of selecting Supreme Court justices.

Prior to these recent changes, the formal contours of the process were widely understood, yet surprisingly little was known about the actual informal workings of the process for selecting Supreme Court justices. In most important ways, that statement still holds. As Sharpe and Roach recently put it, the 'actual appointment process is shrouded in mystery' (2003, 297). Formally, like all other federal judges, the justices are appointed by Cabinet, with a major role played by the Minister of Justice. The only formal criterion for selection is that the nominee must have been a member of the bar for at least ten years. In practice, this has meant that the appointment of a new justice to the Supreme Court has been the unfettered, unilateral choice of the prime minister; the same with the choice of chief justice (McCormick 1994a). This is confirmed by the members of the Court. In the interviews conducted for this study, none of the justices seemed to know why they had been selected. And according to one former justice, there is not even any requirement that members of the bar or the judiciary be consulted; simply put, the prime minister names the justice (L'Heureux-Dubé 1991). As one study of the appointment process summarized the situation, the system 'offers no checks and balances either before or after appointment, no representation from the bar or the public, no formal procedures or criteria of selection other than experience at the bar' (Weinrib 1990, 114).

So there is no requirement for consultations. However, anecdotal accounts suggest that with at least some nominations, either the justice minister or the prime minister consulted fairly extensively with either senior judges or leading members of the bar. Early in Brian Dickson's term as chief justice, there did not appear to be any consultations with the bench or the bar. However, Brian Mulroney, once he became prime minister, established a regular practice of consultations for Supreme Court appointments. Dickson described it this way: 'The minister of justice or the prime minister would usually get in touch, not for nominations, but simply to say, "We are considering so-and-so or so-and-so, and what would be the reaction of the Court?"' Dickson would then share the information with the rest of the justices and report their reactions (Sharpe and Roach 2003, 298).

Since the prime minister has so much control over the selection of the justices, it is important to know what different holders of that office have looked for when appointing new justices. Unfortunately, there is little information about this in the record. There is a fairly extensive literature about judicial appointments. Most such studies conclude that the pre-2004 system was flawed and then suggest reforms (see Beatty 1990; Weinrib 1990; L'Heureux-Dube 1991; Ziegel 1987; Ziegel 1994). Yet few studies have probed the actual reasons for appointments. A constant theme of reform proposals is the need to take partisan and ideological considerations out of the selection process – this, even though there is little clear evidence that such factors are important in the current system. Indeed, there is some evidence that the judges themselves do not think that either partisanship or ideology plays a central role. For example, in a survey of appellate judges, Miller (1998) reported that the judges prided themselves on not having been chosen for their politics. Several noted that they had been appointed to the trial court by a government of one party and then elevated by a different party. And when asked to state the main difference between judges in the United States and those in Canada, almost all the Canadian judges interviewed said that the biggest difference was the political nature of judicial selection in the United States (ibid., 264). A similar view was expressed in recent interviews with six Supreme Court justices. All stressed that partisan politics no longer plays a role in appointments to the Supreme Court, though none professed to know exactly which criteria were important to the prime minister doing the selecting (Greene et al., 1998). Nevertheless, three of the ten justices interviewed for the current project indicated that while they had no direct knowledge of the criteria applied by the government that appointed them, they agreed with the sentiment expressed by Justice J that 'any government can be expected to appoint justices who in at least a broad sense identify with the government's policies.'

Prior to 2004 it was widely recognized and accepted that the prime minister had nearly complete discretion as to the criteria or qualifications deemed essential for appointment and that any debate or consultations on potential candidates took place behind closed doors. Usually, the first thing anyone outside the government heard about the process was when the prime minister's choice was formally announced. The process seemed at first to be the same when two vacancies from Ontario arose in 2004. Whatever consultations took place in the Liberal government took place behind closed doors. However, after selecting two judges from the Ontario Court of Appeal as its 'nominees,' the government announced that the justice minister, Irwin Cotler, would appear before an ad hoc committee of seven MPs and two members of the bar and answer questions about the process as well as the qualifications of the nominees (Hogg 2006). The nominees, however, did not appear before the committee. The minister's presentation generated spirited debate within the committee – debate that included sharp attacks from both Conservative members. According to news accounts of the hearings, 'Conservative MPs angrily described yesterday's unprecedented hearing into two new Supreme Court of Canada appointments as a "rubber stamp" and both Conservative Party members of the committee refused to endorse either candidate' (Naumetz 2004; Lunman 2004). Nevertheless, two days later the government issued a statement confirming the names of the new justices in which Cotler said, 'I am delighted that the ad hoc committee recognizes and acknowledges that Madam Justice Rosalie Abella and Madam Justice Louise Charron are "eminently qualified" for appointment to the Supreme Court of Canada.'

The reaction to the process used to select the justices in 2004 was mixed, breaking along party lines to some extent. Meanwhile, there was considerable disappointment among those in the public who had been led to expect a more transparent, merit-based process, one that would end any taint of partisanship. Some went so far as to call the process a 'sham.'[1] One *Globe and Mail* columnist described the hearing as 'a good day's work and a valuable lesson for democracy' (Ibbitson 2004). Yet in the same edition of that paper, the lead editorial described the process as a 'sham' that had prevented the public from enjoying an objective examination of the views of the nominees (*Globe and Mail* 2004a). A *National Post* writer went even further, declaring that 'this is the first time I can recall that a judicial appointment has been used as a political weapon, in the most partisan sense of the word' (Coyne 2004).

In response to such criticisms and to ongoing dissatisfaction with the selection process, when Justice Major retired in 2005 the government moved quickly to create a new and more elaborate process. After Paul Martin's Liberal government completed its own private consultations about possible candidates, the government announced that it would send a short list of about eight candidates to an advisory committee composed of an MP from each party, a nominee of the provincial attorneys general, a nominee of the provincial law societies (i.e., the organized bar), and two prominent Canadians who were neither lawyers nor judges (Hogg 2006). The committee would examine the qualifications of each nominee in a confidential process and then narrow that list from eight names to three. The government pledged that it would appoint one of those final three to the Supreme Court.

The advisory committee apparently functioned as anticipated, examining the professional backgrounds of each candidate as well as their writings and speeches. However, before Cabinet could meet to discuss the three candidates, the government was defeated in Parliament and forced to hold new elections. In those elections, held on 23 January 2006, the Liberals were defeated and replaced by the Conservatives. The new prime minister, Stephen Harper, decided that he would select the new Supreme Court justice from the list of three names already submitted to the previous Liberal government by its Advisory Committee. He acted quickly, on 10 February 2006, just four days after taking office, calling Judge Rothstein of the Federal Court of Appeal to ask him to be the government's nominee for the Supreme Court, but requiring that he first appear before a Parliamentary Committee to answer its questions. Rothstein immediately began preparing for the hearings, examining the transcripts of the confirmation hearings of Justice Roberts before the U.S. Senate and brainstorming with his clerks and others about possible questions that might be asked and how to respond. He was assisted in his preparations by the noted constitutional scholar Peter Hogg as well as by George Thompson, a deputy justice minister.

The government then created an unprecedented Ad Hoc Committee to Review a Nominee for the Supreme Court of Canada, composed of twelve MPs, with each party represented according to its strength in the House of Commons. On 24 February the government announced that Rothstein was its nominee; three days later the committee held a three-hour televised hearing. Members of the Ad Hoc Committee were supplied with Rothstein's curriculum vitae, a list of all his decisions, four sample decisions in full, a list of all his publications, and four of those publications in full. The committee had only three days to review this material; however, several members of the Ad Hoc Committee had earlier been members of the Advisory Committee that had examined Rothstein's record in much greater depth.[2]

During the hearing, Rothstein was asked sixty or so questions; of these, he refused to answer about a dozen. As one observer put it: 'Employing a blend of common sense, humour and a down-to-earth touch ... the judge sailed through the historic hearing' (Tibbetts 2006a, A1). The judge 'charmed the committee' and was clearly the star of the proceeding (Ziegel 2006, 549). At the end of the hearing the committee was not asked to issue a formal report; no vote was taken on the nominee. Instead, members were simply asked to communicate individually to the justice minister. Two days after the hearing, the government formally appointed Rothstein to the Court.

The reaction to the new process for selecting Supreme Court justices has been mixed. Most of the comments, both pro and con, focus on the public hearing for the nominee rather than on the resort to an Advisory Committee to provide a list of three nominees from which the prime minister must pick. Some believe that the public hearings act as a deterrent to a government that is considering making a partisan appointment of a poorly qualified nominee (Hogg 2006, 533). (It is less clear whether a government would be deterred from making an appointment for partisan or policy reasons of an otherwise well qualified nominee.) Others argue that while the process may not be perfect, it helps ensure that a nominee will be 'preeminently qualified, intellectually and otherwise' (Ziegel 2006, 554).

Others responded to opponents' fears that the public hearings would turn into a circus, like the confirmation hearings in the United States. One said that 'after Monday it seems silly to worry that hearings on candidate justices might degenerate into partisan chaos' (Cash 2006). Prominent law professor Patrick Monahan (2006, A21) wrote that asking nominees to appear before a parliamentary committee 'shines a much needed spotlight' and is 'an important step towards greater transparency and accountability in the appointments process.' On the same day, the *Globe and Mail* editorialized that the public appearance of the nominee was a 'worthy step' towards more openness and accountability (Editorial 2004b).

Yet not everyone shared this rosy evaluation. One columnist called Rothstein the perfect nominee; nonetheless, he doubted the utility of the hearing, asking rhetorically, 'But political transparency? Judicial accountability? Nothing of the sort was accomplished by the committee' (Martin 2006). Similarly, Andrew Coyne (2006) opined in the *National Post* that 'to listen to either side, pro and con, you'd think the judge's appearance before an all-party Commons committee was a revolution ... All this over a process that could have nothing to do with the actual outcome.' Similar sentiments were voiced in the *Globe and Mail*: 'The new process cannot override the constitutional reality that judicial appointments are the prerogative of the prime minister ... How do you imagine this nonsense will prevent prime ministers from veering down the path of partisanship?' (McKenty 2006). And opposition to having nominees appear before parliamentary committees continued in legal circles. After noting that the Canadian Bar Association remained opposed to these hearings, the *Ottawa Citizen* quoted retired Supreme Court justice John Major: 'But despite the advantages, bringing the appointment process into the public arena sets a dangerous precedent that will inevitably degenerate into political warfare' (Weeks 2006).

For others the key issues in the making of appointments are not the 'qualifications' or 'merit' of the nominee, but the political policy preferences of the nominee, because 'we have no transparently objective way of determining which candidate is truly "best"' (McCormick 2006, 541). 'Judges matter ... Every time the Supreme Court hands down a 5–4 decision, it makes the point for me. And there have been some very important 5–4 decisions recently' (ibid., 539).

There is also scepticism about whether the process used to select Justice Rothstein has actually eliminated politics from the process. One observer of a number of Supreme Court appointments notes that the parties are divided over some social issues, especially gay rights, and that Prime Minister Harper has often railed against 'activists' on the Court.[3] Indeed, the Conservative Party's campaign platform reflects the prime minister's desire to appoint judges who will have a more pro-prosecution orientation to criminal process. From this perspective, the selection of Justice Rothstein might be interpreted as a pick designed to further the policy preferences of the Harper government. Media accounts suggest that Rothstein was the least liberal of the three candidates on the short list considered by Harper and that in the past he had taken clear stances against judicial activism (e.g., see Gunther 2006; Tibbetts 2006b). Rothstein himself confirmed those perceptions.[4] Furthermore, during the election campaign, the Liberal leader Paul Martin accused the Tories of planning to 'stack' the Supreme Court with conservative judges (Tibbetts 2006b). Such allegations, of course, do not prove that Rothstein was picked because he agreed with the government on policy. They are, however, enough to suggest that even with a process that emphasizes evaluating the merit of potential Supreme Court justices, it is possible for prime ministers to obtain policy agreement *as well as* candidates who are highly meritorious in a traditional legal sense. McCormick agrees, asserting that governments will always try to create a court that reflects their own values and priorities and that even under the new process, 'all the bells and whistles ... are in the hands of the prime minister, who is only as constrained as he wants to be (but no more)' (2006, 542).

It is uncertain whether a process similar to the one used to appoint Justice Rothstein will become the norm, in part because there is no statutory or constitutional provision that compels the prime minister to hold public hearings when choosing justices. Hogg thinks that in the future it will be difficult 'for a federal government to revert to a wholly confidential process' (2006, 531). This sentiment is echoed by others who have followed Supreme Court appointments for a number of years, including Janice Tibbetts of the *Ottawa Citizen*.[5]

Whether the 2006 reforms' are retained or not, remember that the recent changes have left untouched some aspects of the selection process. Geographical representation is important when justices are being appointed. By law, at least three justices must be from Quebec, and by convention, three are from Ontario, which has roughly 40 per cent of Canada's population. Of the remaining three justices, two are generally from the Western provinces and one from the Atlantic provinces. Regarding the Western provinces, there seems to be an unwritten rule that no province will have both 'Western' justices. For example, when discussing the retirement of Justice Major (from Alberta), justices on the Court of Appeal of British Columbia all agreed that as long as Chief Justice McLachlin (a former Court of Appeal justice from BC) remained on the Court, none of them would be considered for elevation. Rather, it was now the 'turn' for either Manitoba or Saskatchewan to receive an appointment.[6]

This regional representation has provided the Court with ethnic, linguistic, and religious diversity. In the past, by convention, one of the justices from Quebec was always an anglophone; the current practice is that all three Quebec justices are francophones (Baar 1988, 62). No francophone from outside Quebec had been appointed to the Supreme Court until Gerard Le Dain, from Ontario, was selected in 1984; it seems that there is no longer an impediment to the appointment of francophones from outside Quebec.[7] Most Quebec justices have been Roman Catholic, and most from outside Quebec have been Protestant Christians, which guarantees religious diversity on the Court as well. Yet that pattern, too, seems to be changing – three of the past five justices appointed to the Court have been Jewish. It has also been suggested that regional diversity helps legitimize a policy-making court in a country where politics have long been heavily influenced by region (McConnell 2000, 65).

Some have suggested that as an informal tradition, chief justices have alternated between anglophone and francophone. However, McConnell (2000, 66) reports that Justice Louis-Philippe Pigeon studied the record and found no historical evidence for it. Justice Pigeon maintained that the selection of the chief justice, like the appointment of the justices, has been solely the prerogative of the prime minister.

There are no formal age requirements; in practice, though, no one is appointed without having established a strong presence in the legal community, so justices are typically not young. Supreme Court justices during the Charter period have ranged in age from fifty-three to seventy-four, with an average in the sixties (Greene et al. 1998 report that the average age was sixty-three in 1989 and sixty-five in 1996).

There have never been any formal gender restrictions related to Supreme Court appointments, but for more than one hundred years only men were appointed. Currently, four of the nine justices are women – including the Chief Justice – and there has been at least one female justice on the Court since Bertha Wilson was appointed in 1982. Most of the justices served on provincial Courts of Appeal immediately before being appointed to the Supreme Court. Traditionally, though, one justice has been appointed directly from private law practice and one from the Federal Court (Greene et al. 1998, 101).

A look at appointments to *all* federal judgeships over the past century brings to light the importance – some would say dominance – of partisan considerations. A study of Mulroney's judicial appointments found that just under half those chosen had clear links to the Conservative Party – which made the patronage practices of the Mulroney government very similar to those of Trudeau's Liberal government (Russell and Ziegel 1991). Party politicians who have lost bids for re-election have often been consoled with judicial appointments. This fact of political life has led to the oft repeated if tongue-in-cheek comment that 'to become a judge in the United States, you must be elected; to become a judge in Canada, you must be defeated' (Baar 1988, 61). Even with the Supreme Court, partisanship was a significant factor in the early days, though this seems to have changed over the past half century. Before 1949, 55 per cent of the justices had at some point in their career been elected politicians; between 1949 and 1987, only one of the twenty-two Supreme Court justices had this sort of partisan background, and only one other had been defeated in a bid for elected office (Russell 1987, 115). That said, Russell notes that many lawyers appointed to the bench at all levels have been 'behind the scenes' supporters of the government party, and this less overt patronage may still be a strong factor in judicial appointments.

The partisan nature of appointments, especially to the lower federal courts, has been heavily criticized. Even so, one thorough study of judicial selection has pointed out that the selection process itself is to blame, not the deplorable actions of a few irresponsible cabinet members. After all, any appointment process that is left solely to the discretion of politicians will be partisan unless specific constraints are built into the system (Weinrib 1990). Among Court watchers there seems to be a consensus – though apparently little concrete evidence – that at least during the Charter era, patronage has declined as a strong factor in Supreme Court appointments, and that group representation and ideological compatibility have become more important (Morton 2002a, 120).

It is difficult to tell which criteria have had the strongest impact on prime ministers' choices, but it is clear that recent prime ministers have been lobbied heavily by interest groups and party factions. Morton traces these ideologically oriented attempts to influence the prime minister back to the appointment of Bora Laskin in 1973. At the time, civil rights activists were harshly criticizing the Court for its cautious interpretation of the 1960 Bill of Rights. Justice Laskin had been the foremost civil libertarian on the Court since his selection in 1970 and thus was the choice of rights activists. He was elevated to chief justice; however, there is no solid evidence that ideological lobbying on his behalf played an important role in Trudeau's choice. Similarly, the second *Morgentaler* decision,[8] which legalized abortion, led to intense lobbying by pro-life groups and conservative MPs to secure the appointment of more conservative justices. More recently it has come to light that EGALE, Canada's leading gay rights advocacy group, mounted an intense lobbying campaign in 1997 to influence the Chrétien government's Court appointments. As a final example, LEAF (Women's Legal and Education Action Fund) has lobbied actively for the appointment of compatible justices since the retirement of Bertha Wilson in 1990 (Morton 1997).

One might ask whether it actually *matters* who is appointed to the Supreme Court. Both the academic literature reviewed below and this book's analysis of justices' decision-making patterns (see chapter 7) provide a resounding 'yes.' When those who select justices are unconstrained by political forces or legally imposed criteria, the potential exists for justices to be chosen on the basis of the values of the one doing the selecting, in order to impose 'ideological or behavioural criteria' on judicial selection. This is not necessarily an insult to either the prime ministers making the selections or to the justices selected; it is simply 'a matter of common sense, blindingly obvious once it is pointed out' (McCormick 1994a, 108).

Picking justices on the basis of their political values is especially easy with regard to those being elevated from provincial appeal courts. Appeal court judges' reasons for their decisions are readily available to anyone who takes the time to look them up, and those decisions indicate how they will tend to exercise their discretion. This 'stacking' of the Court does not necessarily reflect compromised standards; rather, a prime minister may select 'from among the ranks of qualified individuals those whose values match those of the appointer' (McCormick 1994a, 108). In fact, the potential exists for a prime minister to make much more 'political' selections than have been made by presidents in the United States, where the political nature of the selection process has received so much comment. After all, the Canadian prime minister faces no constraints analogous to the U.S. president's requirement to face Senate confirmation hearings regarding his choices for the Supreme Court. Yet it is difficult to ascertain whether such political concerns have in fact dominated the selection of Supreme Court justices 'because the process has not been open to public view' (Weinrib 1990, 115).

All of that aside, none of the justices interviewed for this book thought that politics – whether it involved patronage or policy 'cosiness' – was a factor in their selection. In this regard, though the process had been adjusted slightly, the views of the three most recently appointed justices were not substantially different from those of the justices appointed before them. In addition, several anecdotal accounts debunk the idea that politics influenced the selection. A biographer of Justice McIntyre notes that he had only the most tenuous ties to the Liberal Party when he was appointed by a Liberal government. The same account quotes Justice Wilson's conclusion that appointments to the Supreme Court were not political (McConnell 2000, 68). However, the justice minister who recommended the appointment of Justice McIntyre knew him well personally and thus presumably was aware of his political views.

Some appointments have seemed, at least to outsiders, to be tainted by politics; yet those same choices have been widely viewed as exemplary in terms of legal qualifications. (Presumably, those outsiders had no inside information on the prime minister's actual reasons for the appointment.) Pigeon's appointment in 1968 is one example. He had strong ties to the Liberals, and he seemed to fit Trudeau's policy preferences. Yet Snell and Vaughan report that he was widely respected as a constitutional expert and as a 'lawyer's lawyer' (1985, 216). Similarly, Julien Chouinard, appointed to the Court by Joe Clark, the Conservative prime minister, in some ways fit the stereotype of a patronage appointment. He had served in two Conservative governments in Quebec before running for Parliament as a Conservative and losing. Yet he also had a distinguished record in law school and had been a Rhodes Scholar.

A number of empirical studies strongly suggest that justices' political attitudes influence their decisions, at least when it comes to 'hard' cases with no clear precedent (see chapter 7). But these empirical studies do not generally attribute justices' policy views to deliberate choices by the prime minister to appoint those who share his political philosophy. Heard (1991) concludes that recent prime ministers have tended to pick ideological moderates for the Court. Morton, Russell, and Withey go further, asserting that 'there has thus far been no evidence that the federal government has let ideological criteria influence its Supreme Court appointments' (1992, 46). A follow-up study by Russell (1992) appears to support essentially the same conclusion. Earlier, Russell (1987) had suggested that there is little evidence of conscious ideological selection in federal judicial appointments, though he speculates that the Charter of Rights may make those who control judicial appointments more interested in the policy orientations of the persons they appoint.

Removal of Justices

All Supreme Court justices, like all federally appointed judges, serve during 'good behaviour'; that is they can be removed only for cause. Also, Supreme Court justices must retire at seventy-five. Short of that mandatory retirement, all federally appointed judges – including Supreme Court justices – can only be removed by 'joint address,' a process somewhat like impeachment in which the governor general, acting on behalf of Cabinet, presents a bill of particulars describing the alleged wrongdoing of the judge. That bill is then debated by the House of Commons and the Senate, which may remove the judge by majority vote. On the surface, the procedure seems easy to implement[9] as well as susceptible to partisan manipulation. However, all of the justices interviewed for this study agreed that the political reality is that there is no danger of justices being removed for partisan reasons. Indeed, to date no Supreme Court justice has ever been removed by joint address.

The apparent ease of removal is modified in practice by the statutory requirement since 1971 that before Parliament considers any action of removal, a complaint of misconduct against the judge must be referred to the Canadian Judicial Council. That council is composed of the chief justices and associate chief justices of Canada's Superior Courts. It is chaired by the chief justice of the Supreme Court. Thus it is the judges themselves, rather than politicians, who determine whether a judge may be removed from office. This procedure makes it unlikely that any government will attempt to remove a federal judge for political purposes.

The council receives and investigates complaints of judicial misconduct. If the committee believes that a complaint is not frivolous, the chair appoints an outside attorney as independent counsel to investigate the charges and to present the case to a Committee of Inquiry appointed by the chair.[10] Hearings are conducted in public, and the judge is given adequate notice of the charges against him or her. The judge is entitled to appear before the Inquiry Committee and to retain counsel. The report of the Inquiry Committee goes to the entire council, which may recommend the judge's removal from office or may issue a reprimand. Only if the council recommends removal will Parliament act on a request for the judge to be removed.

Who Are the Justices?

A number of sources provide individual descriptions of the justices who have served on the Supreme Court. Brief, official biographies can be found on the Court's website or in the Court's glossy commemorative book (Supreme Court 2000). Several works go beyond the official biographies, providing an overview of each justice's background as well as some description of how each justice was viewed at the time of appointment and of the political environment at the time. Among the best of those which provide these descriptions are the ones by Snell and Vaughan (1985) and McCormick (2000). In addition, there are biographies of some of the justices that provide much greater detail regarding the subject of their study (e.g., see McConnell 2000 on McIntyre; Anderson 2001 on Wilson; and Sharpe and Roach 2003 on Dickson). The present chapter makes no attempt to repeat those excellent studies. Instead, the focus will be on aggregate descriptions of the types of men and women who served on the Court from 1970 to the end of 2006. Particular attention will be paid to whether the backgrounds of the justices have changed over time and whether there are distinctive patterns in the types of people selected by Liberal versus Conservative prime ministers or differences in the backgrounds of male and female justices.

A Collective Portrait of the Justices

Until the recent past, Canadian Supreme Court justices were drawn from a narrow social elite: middle-aged, upper-middle-class males of

French or British background with at least a formal connection to some Christian religious group. All lived in Ottawa while serving on the Court. Early in the Court's history, all justices were required by law to live within five miles of Ottawa. Eventually, though, Justice Dickson made the point that the five-mile limit made sense only when the justices had to travel to the court 'by sleigh or buggy.' In 1975, amendments to the Supreme Court Act increased the distance from Ottawa within which justices were required to live to twenty-five miles.

Many empirical analyses of judges' decisions in appellate courts around the world have noted the importance of the party affiliations of judges or of those who selected the judges. An examination of whether party adherence is related to judicial decisions in Canada is reserved for chapter 7. The question addressed by the data in figure 2.1 is simply this: Who appointed the justices who served on the Court between 1970 and 2006?[11] The answer is straightforward: the Court has been bipartisan since 1970; no third party has elected a prime minister, and the two dominant national parties have alternated in power often enough that neither has ever had a monopoly on judges on the Court at any time. That said, the division on the Court has not been equal. As figure 2.1 indicates, the Liberals have enjoyed a roughly three-to-two advantage over the Conservatives when it comes to appointing justices to the Court.

As noted earlier, regionalism has been an important factor in the appointment of justices (as in many other aspects of Canadian life). Therefore, no profile of the Court would be complete without a consideration of where its members have come from. It should be no surprise that, given the formal guarantee that there be three justices from Quebec on the Court at all times, and given the strong informal tradition that there also be three justices from Ontario, most of the thirty-seven justices who served during the period examined were appointed from either Quebec or Ontario. The greater number from Quebec simply reflects the fact that the turnover rate among the Quebec justices was greater than among the justices from Ontario. After representation for Quebec and Ontario has been satisfied, there are only three justices on a given court to distribute among the rest of the country. Figure 2.2 indicates that the only Atlantic province that has been represented since 1970 has been New Brunswick. In contrast, there has been a relatively even distribution of justices among the western provinces; there, Alberta and British Columbia lead the way with three appointments each.

Figure 2.1
Justices on the Supreme Court 1970–2006,
by Party of Prime Minister

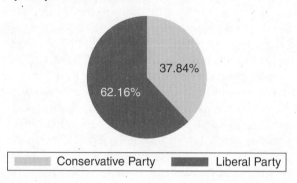

Figure 2.2
Justices on the Supreme Court 1970–2006, by Province
of appointment

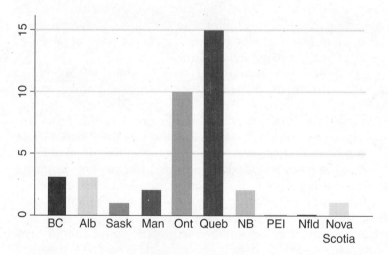

Regionalism has been a factor in the judicial selection practices of a
number of other common law countries. In Britain in recent years there
has been at least one Law Lord from Scotland and one from Northern
Ireland. In the United States, 'allocations' to regions on the Supreme
Court have not been formalized, and no individual state has had a
recognized claim in the past century. There is a general consensus,

though, that presidents have long recognized the political benefits of maintaining regional diversity on the Court. Similarly, in the absence of any formal requirements, Indian prime ministers seem to have recognized the political advantages of maintaining at least a rough regional balance on the Supreme Court.

At least since the appointment of Justice Bertha Wilson in 1982, the gender of Supreme Court justices has become an increasingly salient consideration for Canadians and in their media. As figure 2.3 indicates, seven women were appointed to the Supreme Court between 1970 and 2006. The two most recent appointments of female justices (Rosalie Abella and Louise Charron, both in 2004) brought the proportion for the period since 1970 to approximately one-fifth of all appointments. The current Court[12] has five men and four women.

Canada's Supreme Court stands out among comparable common law courts when it comes to gender diversity. The first woman was appointed to the U.S. Supreme Court at about the same time as Justice Wilson, yet only one other woman has been appointed since then. In England, the first (and only) female Law Lord was not appointed until 2004. In Australia, only one female had been appointed to the High Court before 2005. However, recent appointments have resulted in a High Court with five male and two female justices.

One need not look far around the world to realize that religious differences often explode into political violence. Northern Ireland, Palestine, Iraq, the former Yugoslavia, and India/Pakistan spring immediately to mind, but the list could easily be extended. Given how often religious and cultural groups slaughter non-believers, one might easily conclude that the inclusion of religious diversity in a nation's visible centres of power is vital to democratic stability. In Canada, both the main religious groups have been prominently represented on the Supreme Court for the past third of a century. Indeed, as figure 2.4 indicates, Roman Catholics – a nominal minority – have had a slight majority when it comes to appointments to the Court. Most of the Catholic justices have come from Quebec, which suggests that Catholics have benefited from the statutory requirement that three of the nine justices be from that province. However, even outside Quebec, in heavily Protestant English Canada, 35 per cent of the appointments have gone to Catholics.[13]

Other religious groups were virtually unrepresented on the Court until recently. When Bora Laskin became the first Jewish Supreme Court justice in 1970, there were no other non-Christians on the Court. Over the past five years, three more Jewish justices have been appointed.

Figure 2.3
Justices on the Supreme Court 1970–2006,
by gender

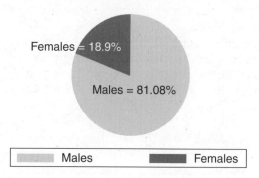

Figure 2.4
Justices on the Supreme Court 1970–2006,
by religion

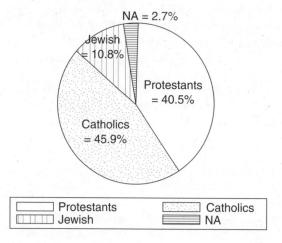

Appellate judges in all industrialized countries are unrepresentative
of the population in terms of education because the job by its nature requires that the incumbents be highly educated. All recent justices have
been university graduates and have received formal legal education.
Thus in terms of the overall level of education, the justices are inevitably part of the elite. One might then ask whether the justices represent
an elite within the country's university-educated workforce. A number

of anecdotal accounts suggest that many of the justices had distin-guished academic records both as undergraduates and as law stu-dents. Unfortunately, no statistics are readily available that would allow a systematic comparison of the university performance of future justices compared to other professionals. We can, though, ask whether the justices were recruited from a small group of elite universities. Tables 2.1 and 2.2 suggest an answer to that question.

In Britain, the criticism has often been levelled that the Law Lords – indeed, all of the country's senior judges – lack diversity. It has been noted for some time that most senior judges in Britain are recruited from just two universities: Oxford and Cambridge. In the United States, the educational backgrounds of Supreme Court justices have sometimes been more diverse. Yet even though there are more than a hundred law schools in the United States, most of the justices have been recruited from the 'top ten.' In fact, six of the nine present justices studied law at Harvard.

In Canada, even though there are fewer law schools, there is sub-stantially less concentration. Canadian justices have graduated from a remarkably diverse cross-section of universities. Table 2.1 indicates that no undergraduate school has sent more than four justices to the Supreme Court since 1970 and that twenty-four different schools have had at least one graduate appointed to the Court. In regional terms, the law schools they come from are spread literally from coast to coast.

If there is less diversity in the law school origins of the justices, it is simply because there are fewer law schools in Canada. Note that the thirty-seven justices came from fourteen different law schools and that no law school produced as many as 15 per cent of the jus-tices. Five schools accounted for at least 10 per cent of the justices (i.e., four or five justices appointed since 1970): the University of Montreal, Osgoode Hall Law School, McGill University, Laval Uni-versity, and the University of Toronto. Moreover, this list of the top five schools and the complete list in table 2.2 together indicate that Canadian Supreme Court justices obtained their legal training primarily within Canada (though some of the justices obtained fur-ther legal or graduate education at foreign universities, mainly in England and the United States). To summarize, the educational training of the Canadian justices is considerably more diverse than that of their British counterparts.

The final table in the 'collective portrait' of the justices serving since 1970 presents a general overview of some of the experiences of the justices prior to their appointment to the Supreme Court. The age

Table 2.1
Undergraduate college or university attended of justices
on the Supreme Court of Canada, 1970–2006

School	No. of justices	% of justices
Toronto	4	10.8
Alberta	3	8.1
Montreal	3	8.1
Saskatchewan	3	8.1
McGill	3	8.1
Laval	2	5.4
Manitoba	2	5.4
Other (1 each)	17	45.9
Total	37	

Table 2.2
Law school attended of justices on the Supreme Court
of Canada, 1970–2006

School	No. of justices	% of justices
Montreal	5	13.5
Osgoode Hall	5	13.5
Toronto	5	13.5
Laval	4	10.8
McGill	4	10.8
Saskatchewan	3	8.1
Alberta	2	5.4
Manitoba	2	5.4
Dalhousie	1	2.7
Cambridge	1	2.7
Oxford	1	2.7
New Brunswick	1	2.7
Paris	1	2.7
Ottawa	1	2.7
None attended	1	2.7
Total	37	

Table 2.3
Average age and experience at appointment of justices on
the Supreme Court of Canada, 1970–2006

School	No. of justices	% of justices	Median
Judicial experience	8	21.6	6 years
None			
1–5 years	9	24.3	
6–10 years	6	16.2	
11+ years	14	37.8	
Age at appointment			57 years
40s	5	13.5	
50s	21	56.8	
60s	11	29.7	
Gender			
Male	30	81.1	
Female	7	18.9	
Subst. private practice	20	54.1	
Law professor	14	37.8	
Prosecutor	3	8.1	

Total number of judges in each comparison = 37

distribution of the justices at appointment reflects the unsurprising finding that they are expected to have amassed a substantial legal career before ascending to the Court. The statutory requirement of ten years at the bar seems to be irrelevant. None of the justices appointed since 1970 was appointed just ten years after completing law school. The youngest justice was age forty-six at appointment, the oldest sixty-five. Most were in their fifties when appointed, the average age being fifty-seven.

More surprising, perhaps, is the considerable variation in the nature and length of prior judicial experience of those appointed to the Supreme Court. More than one-fifth of the justices had no prior experience on any court; they came directly to the Supreme Court from either private practice or a stint as a law professor. Those with past judicial experience typically were elevated from a province's Court of Appeal. But even for those with prior judicial experience, that experience often was not very long. One-third of those with judicial experience had served as a judge for less than six years. At the other end of the spectrum, more than one-third of those appointed to the Supreme Court had more than ten years of prior judicial service.

More than half the justices had substantial experience in private law practice before being appointed to the Court. Such experience was categorized as 'substantial' if it was his or her primary employment since law school. Also, fourteen justices had been full-time law school professors at some point before joining the Court.[14] All but two of those law professors also had some experience on a court of appeal or a trial court before being elevated to the Supreme Court.

Only three of the justices had worked as a federal or provincial prosecutor. Contrast this with the United States, where early experience as an assistant district attorney or service in the U.S. Justice Department is often viewed as an ideal career path for someone with aspirations to a judgeship.

In summary, there has been considerable diversity in the backgrounds of those serving on the Supreme Court over the past thirty-four years. All justices have been highly educated and at least middle-aged. Together, they comprise a wide cross-section of Canada's law schools. The Court is bipartisan and reflects both the dominant religious groups in society. Though most justices have been men, compared to most other common law courts the Supreme Court of Canada has been notable for its gender diversity.

Variation in Judicial Backgrounds by Party, Gender, and Time

The description of the judicial selection system at the beginning of this chapter emphasized the unfettered discretion of the prime minister to decide whom to appoint. Thus the potential exists for considerable variation regarding the types of people selected by different prime ministers. A question then arises: Are there systematic differences between the political parties in terms of who is selected to be a Supreme Court justice? Table 2.4 provides a preliminary answer to that question by breaking out several of the above-mentioned categories in terms of which parties made the appointments.

Party-based preferences regarding age appear to be minor, with a higher percentage of Conservative appointees being over sixty. Recent Republican presidents in the United States – at least, according to media accounts – have made a concerted attempt to find suitable candidates for the appellate courts who are relatively young as part of a

Table 2.4
Party differences in characteristics of justices on the Supreme Court of Canada,
1970–2006

Characteristic	Conservatives (N = 14)		Liberals (N = 23)	
	No. of Con	% of Con	No. of Lib	% of Lib
Judicial experience				
None	3	21.4	5	21.7
1–5 years	4	28.6	5	21.7
6–10 years	1	07.1	5	21.7
11+ years	6	42.9	8	34.8
Age at appointment				
40s	2	14.3	3	13.0
50s	6	42.9	15	65.2
60s	6	42.9	5	21.7
Gender				
Male	12	85.7	18	78.3
Female	2	14.3	5	21.7
Religion				
Catholic	6	42.9	11	47.8
Protestant	6	42.9	9	39.1
Jewish	1	07.1	3	13.0
Subst. private practice	9	64.3	11	47.8
Law professor	6	42.9	8	34.8

Number of Conservatives =14, number of Liberals = 23

deliberate strategy to extend their party's influence over time on the ideological composition of the Court. No analogous trend is apparent in Canada. Both parties have selected mainly justices in their fifties; both have selected nearly identical percentages of justices below fifty.

There are also only minor partisan differences related to religion: the percentage of Catholics appointed by each party is nearly identical. Similarly, there appear to be only minor differences between the parties regarding the prior judicial experience of their appointees to the Supreme Court. A somewhat higher percentage of Conservative than Liberal appointees had more than ten years of prior judicial experience, but this seems to be balanced by the greater percentage of Liberal Party justices coming in with between six and ten years of earlier judicial experience.

Some differences are apparent regarding the propensity to pick candidates with long careers in private practice. Thus, 64 per cent of Conservative justices compared to only 48 per cent of Liberal ones had substantial private practice. Since most of those thus categorized had worked in prestigious corporate law firms, these differences presumably reflect the somewhat close ties the Conservative Party has maintained with the corporate business establishment.

Conclusions about partisan patterns relating to law school–based recruitment are somewhat more subjective, but an examination of the list of the law schools attended by the justices broken down by party[15] reveals no clear pattern of differences. Both parties appointed at least one justice from each of the five law schools most often represented on the Court, and there do not appear to be any concentrations for either party.

Finally, the Liberals may have a greater preference for appointing women to the bench. Five of the seven women to date have been appointed by Liberal prime ministers. However, firm conclusions are difficult both because the number of women appointed to the Court remains small and because neither party appointed any women until 1982.

In sum, the types of people appointed to the Supreme Court by Liberal and Conservative prime ministers appear to be remarkably similar. There may be a slightly greater tendency for Conservatives to appoint lawyers with substantial private practice and for Liberals to appoint women, but even these differences are far from sharp.

Table 2.5 presents a comparison of the characteristics and backgrounds of the women appointed to the Court compared to the analogous characteristics of the male appointees.

First, women may be slightly less likely than men to be appointed once past sixty. However, in this (as in all other comparisons by gender), extreme caution must be exercised in generalizing from the data because so few women have been appointed to date. The gender difference relating to judicial experience seems more pronounced: all of the women appointed to date have had prior judicial experience, and most have had fairly extensive experience. Indeed, the only two justices with at least twenty years of past judicial experience when appointed to the Court were women (Justices Abella and Charron).

Other gender-based differences seem minor. Men and women spent about the same time in private practice before joining the Court.

Table 2.5
Gender differences in characteristics of justices of Supreme Court of Canada, 1970–2006

School	Males (N = 30)		Females (N = 7)	
	No. of men	% of men	No. of women	% of women
Judicial experience				
None	8	26.7	0	0
1–5 years	8	26.7	1	14.3
6–10 years	4	13.3	2	28.6
11+ years	10	33.3	4	57.1
Age at appointment				
40s	4	13.3	1	14.3
50s	16	53.3	5	71.4
60s	10	33.3	1	14.3
Party				
Conservatives	12	40.0	2	28.6
Liberals	18	60.0	5	71.4
Subst. private practice	17	56.7	3	42.9
Law professor	12	40.0	2	28.6

Differences regarding law school professorships are similarly small. Finally, no law school that can lay claim particular success with female alumni who went on to the Supreme Court: the seven female justices went to seven different law schools.

Chapters 3 and 6 will explore in depth the impact of the Charter of Rights on the Supreme Court's agenda and role. At this point, it is only necessary to observe that those who have studied the Court broadly agree that the Court's policy-making role changed dramatically after the Charter was adopted. It is also apparent that the prime ministers well realized this when they were appointing justices. One might have expected them to conclude that a new type of justice was required in light of the Supreme Court's emerging role. To begin to explore that possibility, justices have been categorized not by when they *sat* on the Court but by when they were *appointed*. The ones appointed in 1982 and later are categorized for the purposes of comparison as 'post-Charter' (see table 2.6). This divides the thirty-seven justices into nearly equal groups: seventeen pre-Charter and twenty post-Charter.

Table 2.6
Differences in characteristics of justices appointed to the Supreme Court of Canada, before and after Charter of Rights and Freedoms, 1970–2006

	Before Charter (N = 17)		After Charter (N = 20)	
	No. before	% before	No. after	% after
Judicial experience				
None	6	35.3	2	10.0
1–5 years	4	23.5	5	25.0
6–10 years	3	17.6	3	15.0
11+ years	4	23.5	10	50.0
Age at appointment				
40s	4	23.5	1	05.0
50s	10	58.8	11	55.0
60s	3	17.6	8	40.0
Gender				
Male	17	100	13	65.0
Female	0	0	7	35.0
Religion				
Catholic	8	47.1	9*	47.4
Protestant	8	47.1	7	36.8
Jewish	1	05.9	3	15.8
Subst. private practice	10	58.8	10	50.0
Law professor	6	35.3	8	40.0

* The religion of one judge in the post-Charter era could not be determined

In two categories, there appear to be no differences between those appointed before and after the Charter. Similar numbers of justices had substantial private practice experience. The differences in religion also seem minor, except that three of the four Jewish judges were appointed during the post-Charter period.

In other ways, the post-Charter justices appear different from those appointed before 1982. First, prior judicial experience seems to have become the norm since the Charter was adopted. Only two justices have come to the Court without any prior judicial experience since the Charter was adopted, whereas more than one-third of the pre-Charter justices had no such experience. Perhaps because of a new expectation that justices have prior judicial experience, there has been an increase in the average age of the justices. Only one justice under fifty has been appointed since the adoption of the Charter, and the appointment of justices over sixty has become more common.

Parenthetically, this trend is precisely the opposite of what one would expect if prime ministers were growing more concerned about shaping the Court's policy output at a time when the policy stakes seem much greater. A prime minister who was concerned mainly about influencing policy would presumably want justices who could apply his or her preferences on the Court for a longer period of time and would thus look for younger candidates to appoint. This has not happened – a sign, albeit indirect, that the selection process has not become more ideological since the adoption of the Charter.

The biggest change in patterns of appointment relates to gender. All seven female justices were appointed after 1982, constituting over 35 per cent of post-Charter appointments. As noted earlier, since 1982, women have been appointed by prime ministers of both parties. In contrast, no woman had ever been appointed before 1982. It is not clear, however, whether the appointment of women has had anything to do with the Charter. The appointment of the only women to the U.S. Supreme Court occurred at approximately the same time even though there had not been an important change in the constitutional status of rights for more than a hundred years prior to that first appointment. Moreover, beginning in the 1980s in both Canada and the United States, there has been a strong increase in the number of women selected for intermediate appellate courts. Thus it seems likely that the post-Charter appointment of seven women to the Supreme Court of Canada has had as much to do with rapid increases in the 'pool' of female lawyers, who from the 1980s on began to accumulate the legal experiences that would make them attractive as appellate judges in a gender-neutral selection system, and with changes in cultural and political attitudes towards the role of women, as with the Charter per se.

Whatever the cause, the Court's composition in the Charter period has become substantially different from what it was in the 1970s and earlier. Woman are now close to becoming a majority on the Court, the Court has become older, and the justices have come to the Court with substantial judicial experience, especially in the provinces' Courts of Appeal.

Perceptions of the New Justices

A central interest of political scientists who study the courts has been how the political attitudes and values of judges influence the decisions they make. This question is explored in some depth in chapter 7 and cannot be answered simply from examining who is appointed to the courts. What *can* be explored are the political perceptions of the justices at the time of their appointment. Do other political actors and the media perceive the new justices in political terms before they actually take their place on the Court? And if so, how are they perceived? To answer a similar question in the United States, two scholars devised an innovative way of assessing the perceived ideology of nominees. All of the editorials and columns written about the nominees in four leading national newspapers were subjected to content analysis to see how the nominees were characterized. From this analysis the scholars developed an index reflecting the proportion of times the newspaper writers characterized the nominee as either a 'liberal' or a 'conservative.' The average from the four papers was then used as a measure of the perceived ideology of the nominee (see Segal and Cover 1989).

An analogous measure was developed for Canadian Supreme Court justices at the time of their appointment. This measure was then used to help explain the subsequent search-and-seizure decisions of those justices. Ostberg and Wetstein (1998) relied on articles in the *Globe and Mail*, the leading national newspaper in Canada, for their content analysis. From these analyses they developed a five-point scale to measure the perceived ideology of the new justices, the scale going from +1 (most liberal) to -1 (most conservative). The author of this book replicated the earlier scale scores developed by Ostberg and Wetstein using an independent analysis[16] and extended the time period covered in the earlier analysis. The results of this scale are presented in table 2.7.

The first thing to note in connection with the data is that since the mid-1960s, correspondents covering the Supreme Court have seemed quite comfortable describing the new judges in political terms. However, for justices appointed before 1967, it is usually impossible to derive an ideology score: back then, there tended to be very brief coverage of most new appointments; in addition, what coverage there was often contained no more than what was in the press release issued by the justice ministry, which was typically devoid of any political evaluations.

The first two rows in table 2.7 display the differences how the appointees of the Liberal and Conservative parties were perceived. There

Table 2.7
Perceptions at time of appointment of the ideology of justices who were appointed
to the Supreme Court of Canada

N	Conservative (n)	Moderate conservative (n)	Moderate (n)	Moderate liberal (n)	Liberal (n)
Cons. Party	16.7%	25.0%	41.7%	16.7%	0%
12	(2)	(3)	(5)	(2)	(0)
Lib. Party	0	11.1	33.3	33.3	22.2
18	(0)	(2)	(6)	(6)	(4)
Men	08.7	17.4	43.5	17.4	13.0
23	(2)	(4)	(10)	(4)	(3)
Women	0	14.3	14.3	57.1	14.3
7	(0)	(1)	(1)	(4)	(1)
Bef. Charter	10.0	10.0	50.0	10.0	20.0
10	(1)	(1)	(5)	(1)	(2)
Aft. Charter	05.0	20.0	30.0	35.0	10.0
20	(1)	(4)	(6)	(7)	(2)

is considerable overlap regarding the perceptions of justices appointed
by different parties. On average, though, Liberal Party appointees were
perceived to be more liberal ideologically (a mean ideology of +.33 versus a mean of –.12 for Conservatives). The only two judges perceived
as unambiguously conservative were appointed by the Conservatives,
and the only four perceived as unambiguously liberal were appointed
by the Liberals. Most of the justices appointed by prime ministers of
both parties were moderates, though there were small differences in
terms of which side of centre the appointees of each party lay.

Table 2.7 presents the same type of comparison for perceptions of
male versus female justices. The small number of female justices makes
firm conclusions difficult, but it appears that the female justices were
perceived to be marginally more liberal than their male colleagues.

The final comparison in table 2.7 examines whether there has been
a change over time in perceptions of justices appointed to the Supreme Court. Overall, there does not appear to be any clear trend.
Both before and after the Charter, the median justice was perceived to
be a moderate.

Court observers' perceptions of new justices provide no direct evidence of the motives of the prime ministers doing the appointing. That said, most new justices have been perceived as moderates, whichever party has appointed them, and there has been no increase in the appointment of more sharply ideological justices since the adoption of the Charter. All of these findings provide at least some additional indirect evidence that prime ministers have generally not pursued overtly ideological agendas when naming new justices to the Supreme Court.

When one steps back from the specifics of the justices' backgrounds, the overall picture is one of considerable diversity, especially when compared to the backgrounds of American and British justices. The Canadian justices are certainly part of the national elite in terms of education and class background, yet there is a sense in which they may be characterized as quite representative of the nation. In broad terms, the justices appear to represent Canada's diversity in terms of party, gender, religion, and geographic origins. And while they are of course all university educated, they obtained that education from a broad cross-section of undergrad schools and law schools. Given this diversity, the Canadian court can be categorized as one of the more 'democratic' courts in the common law world.

In the chapters that follow, the Supreme Court of Canada will be described as a court whose role has become much more political over the past third of a century. For the moment it is significant to note that despite all the controversy generated by that increasingly political role, the justices appointed to the Court – even in the Charter era – are still perceived at least by journalists covering the Court and its rulings as politically moderate. And despite the controversy over the selection system and concerns that the process for selecting justices is too political, there seem to be only moderate differences between the Liberal and Conservative parties in terms of the political orientation of the justices they choose.

3 Setting the Agenda

The impact of the procedures that set a court's agenda can be far reaching. Which cases do the courts hear? The answer to that question tells us a lot about how the law evolves. It also explains much about how society creates winners and losers (Flemming 2000, 40). By its nature, agenda control 'focuses attention on particular issues or concerns to the exclusion of others. At a minimum, the decision to place issues before decision makers means that other issues go unattended' (Flemming 2004, 6). So it is significant that for most of its history, the justices on the Supreme Court of Canada had little control over their agenda. Their docket was controlled by the decisions of litigants.

The Supreme Court was not established by the BNA Act of 1867 (Canada's original constitution); rather, it came into being in 1875 through the Supreme Court Act, an ordinary act of Parliament. Under the terms of that act, the Supreme Court had appellate jurisdiction over matters of both provincial and national law, but little control over which lower court decisions it actually reviewed. The Court was initially required to hear all appeals brought to it. Also, litigants who lost in the provincial courts could bypass the Supreme Court by appealing directly to the Judicial Committee of the Privy Council in Britain. In the words of one of its future chief justices, Bora Laskin, it would be a 'captive court' until well into the twentieth century (McCormick 1994).

In 1931 the Statute of Westminster granted the Canadian government control over the nation's external affairs and other matters that had always been under British control (Snell and Vaughn 1985). Having obtained this authority, the Canadian Parliament moved quickly to prohibit the continuation of criminal appeals to the Privy Council. In 1935, in *British Coal Corporation v. The King*, the Judicial Committee of the Privy Council upheld the validity of this action, making the Supreme Court of Canada finally 'supreme' in practice in the resolution of criminal cases.

With the end of criminal appeals to the Privy Council in 1933, the push for the complete abolition of such appeals continued into the 1940s (Snell and Vaughn 1985; Bushnell 1992). A backlog of cases during the Second World War from Canada to the Privy Council had generated concerns about the practicality of the appeal system; also by then, a series of Privy Council decisions on the validity of Canadian New Deal legislation had greatly eroded public support for the Privy Council (Snell and Vaughn 1985). In early 1947 the Privy Council ruled that Canada did have the power to end all appeals to it (Bushnell 1992). Shortly thereafter, a bill was introduced in the Canadian Parliament to end all such appeals. There was little debate by this point, and the measure passed easily (Snell and Vaughn 1985). When the bill became law in December 1949, the Supreme Court became 'supreme' in fact as the final arbiter of Canadian legal disputes (Bushnell 1992; Snell and Vaughn 1985).

Yet even after appeals to the Privy Council were abolished, the Supreme Court lacked control of its own docket; losing litigants in the intermediate appellate courts could still bring an appeal 'as of right.' The Supreme Court was thus required to hear all cases appealed to it except for civil appeals involving disputes over less than $10,000. These civil suits involving small sums could only come before the Court through the grant of a petition for 'leave to appeal.' The inevitable result as the country grew in size and complexity was that the Court's caseload continued to increase.

By the 1970s, both government officials and members of the bar were growing concerned over the Court's ever expanding workload (Bushnell 1992). To address that concern, Parliament in 1975 granted the Supreme Court nearly complete discretionary control of its docket. When the bill came to the floor in Parliament, there was virtually no debate; all agreed that steps had to be taken to bring the Court's workload under control (Bushnell 1982). The 1975 law gave the Court discretion in deciding which civil cases of 'public importance' it would accept for review (*Statutes of Canada 1974-75-76*). Some criminal cases would still have to be heard if dissent existed in the court below; but the 1975 Act ended the automatic right to appeal in writs of mandamus or habeas corpus when dissent was not present in the decision below (*Statutes of Canada 1974-75-76*). Since 1975, then, most cases must be granted leave to appeal before the Supreme Court will hear them.

The effect of the 1975 law was immediate and dramatic. In 1974–5, about seventy cases came before the Court as of right; the following year, only thirty-two; and after 1978, an average of twenty per year (Bushnell 1982, 497). The number of appeals as of right remained relatively static early in the Charter period but then began to track upwards again, reaching thirty-six in 1987 and remaining at that level or higher for all but one year over the next decade. In 1997, however, the Criminal Code was amended so as to substantially narrow the circumstances in which an appeal as of right would be permitted, and this has reduced appeals to the Court to 'just a handful' each year (Monahan 2000, 4).[1]

Review of some criminal cases remains mandatory, however. Also, every year the Court decides a small number of 'reference questions,' which are brought to it by the federal government. Reference cases are essentially requests by the government for an advisory opinion, usually on the constitutionality of some course of action it is contemplating.[2] The Court has usually felt itself obligated to answer reference questions, though there is some question as to whether this is a legal obligation (McCormick and Greene 1990) In any event, reference questions are a negligible part of the Court's docket, averaging less than one case per year during the Charter period. Until 1997, criminal appeals to the Supreme Court as of right included cases in which an acquittal had been overturned by a provincial appellate court and those in which there had been a dissent on a point of law by the appeal court. Similarly, the Crown has a right of appeal when an appellate court overturns a conviction. Finally, leave to appeal in civil cases may be granted by the appeal courts; however, the most detailed study of this practice concluded that such grants were rare (Bushnell 1982, 499).

There has been a steady increase in the number of leave-to-appeal petitions coming to the Court. Between 1970 and 1990 the Supreme Court typically received fewer than 300 leave petitions per year and granted leave to 25 to 35 per cent of them. Between 1990 and 2000 the number of petitions rose steadily, from 424 in 1990 to 642 in 2000. However, the Court did not decide to increase the number of cases it decides on the merits each year; as a result, the success rate of petitions (i.e., the percentage granted the right of a hearing) dropped from 22 per cent at the beginning of the decade to only 13 per cent by 2000 (Flemming 2004, 30). In contrast, by the year 2000 the U.S. Supreme Court was receiving upwards of 6,000 petitions asking for review.

The Criteria for Granting Leave to Appeal

As the result of the Supreme Court Act of 1975 and the 1997 amendments, the Supreme Court now largely controls its own agenda. With the exceptions noted earlier, no case is heard by the Supreme Court unless the appellant is granted leave to appeal. The power granted to the Court to determine which cases it will hear is both broad and vague. Section 40(1) of the act states that leave is to be granted if

> The Supreme Court is of the opinion that any question involved therein is, by reason of its public importance or the importance of any issue of law or any issue of mixed law and fact involved in such question, one that ought to be decided by the Supreme Court or is, for any other reason, of such a nature or significance as to warrant decision by it.

The statute does not define 'public importance,' and the court has not published any clarifying guidelines. Most commentators have interpreted this criterion to mean *national* importance, but there has been widespread agreement that the Court has left the standard deliberately vague (Flemming 2000, 2004; Greene et al. 1998; Baar 1988). One former clerk for the Supreme Court confirms that the justices focus on issues of national importance – that is, those on which the provincial appeal courts have split and in which the law itself is uncertain (Sossin 1996, 289). More recently, several other clerks have offered a similar perspective. They note that when clerks are asked to write memoranda on leave petitions to help the justices reach decisions, they are specifically asked to indicate whether the case involves a question of national importance, whether the rule of law is subject to any current uncertainty, and whether the central legal issues in the case have been decided differently by different provincial appeal courts. The clerks note that they are not asked to offer an opinion or analysis as to whether the case was decided correctly in the lower court (McInnes et al. 1994). Similarly, Bushnell (1982) reports that leave is most likely to be granted when there is either a question of national scope, a conflict among provincial appeal courts regarding the interpretation of some point of law, or a question about the proper interpretation of some new provision of a federal statute. Leave is unlikely to be granted simply because the petitioner asserts that the decision was decided incorrectly in the lower court (1982, 515–16).

Interviews with several of the justices on the Lamer Court provided only minor additions to our understanding of what the justices are looking for in leave petitions. These justices confirmed that it was only questions of general importance to the whole country that were granted leave; also, they preferred that the issue not go to the Supreme Court until several appeal courts had had a chance to rule on it. They also suggested that leave is most likely to be granted when the lawyers filing the petition are able to describe the central issue clearly and succinctly (Greene et al. 1998, 109–12).

As noted earlier, the leave-to-appeal amendment was introduced in 1975 solely as a caseload control procedure and was uncontroversial for that reason. There was clear evidence of a growing need for the Court to get its docket under control. Some, however, including Justice Wilson, were more concerned about the amendment's substantive effects. From the beginning of her tenure, Justice Wilson was certain that it would transform the role of the Court so that it focused on the law's development rather than on the correction of errors (Anderson 2001, 240–1). She maintained that the decision to grant leave in a private law case should indicate that the Court recognized that the law required modification; whereas denial of leave should indicate that the Court was not prepared to open up or reconsider a given area of the law.

There have been few empirical analyses of the reasons why leave petitions are granted or denied. Only one study has tried to unearth the reasons why leave to appeal has been granted by examining the actual cases accepted and denied leave. Flemming (2004) concludes that neither the nature of the litigants nor of the lawyers preparing leave petitions has had a major impact on decisions to accept a petition. There is a small community of lawyers whose expertise is drafting leave petitions to the Court, but they do not dominate the process; indeed, they have not been any more successful than lawyers with little or no experience in filing such petitions. Nor have lawyers from large, prestigious law firms been more successful than other petitioners. In this respect, the Canadian process is substantially different from the certiorari process in the United States, where a 'litigant-centred' account largely explains variance in the success of petitions for review. As in the United States, petitions by the federal government have had significantly better chances to be granted leave. Business litigants do not fare better than individuals in the leave process.

Instead, the chances that leave will be granted seem to depend more on a 'jurisprudential model.' In this respect, the results of the analysis of Canadian leave petitions look very similar to those for the United States (see Perry 1991). In the latter country, the likelihood that leave will be granted increases when the appeal is from a divided appeal court or when the circuit courts are divided regarding their answers to the issues raised in the appeal. Also, petitions that raise issues never before litigated by the Supreme Court or that may have a strong impact on federal interests are more likely to be accepted for review. Petitions that are mainly seeking correction of errors in the lower courts are less likely to be reviewed, as are fact-intensive issues.

The Process for Reviewing Leave Petitions

Leave applications are sent to the Law Branch (called Registrar's Legal Services before 1999), where they are read first by staff lawyers. Those lawyers prepare objective summaries of the applications that outline the facts of the case, describe the legal history, and describe the legal issues raised by the case. These summaries are then sent to all nine justices.

Each leave petition is sent to one of three panels. Each panel has three justices and is appointed by the chief justice. Membership on these panels rotates each year. It is these panels that make the formal decision whether to grant leave. Majority vote is sufficient; in practice, though, the votes are almost always unanimous. Of almost 1,200 petitions, only 30 resulted in a divided vote by the leave panel (Flemming 2004, 15).

Before the justices vote on leave petitions, the petition is assigned to a law clerk. For the purpose of considering leave petitions, the clerks of all the justices are assigned to a single pool and each petition is assigned to only one clerk. That clerk then writes a memorandum of law, which is sent to all the justices on the Court, including the three-judge panel charged with making the formal decision on the leave. The clerk's memorandum typically runs about fifteen pages; it summarizes the case's facts and procedural history as well as all related lower-court decisions. The clerk is then expected to describe the essential issues in the case and to make and justify a decision as to whether leave should be granted.

From a political perspective, one of the most interesting questions is the extent to which the Court's docket is influenced by political interest groups. Since the adoption of the Charter of Rights, there has been a substantial increase in the number of interest groups seeking to participate during the merits stage of Supreme Court cases, as well as in the Court's willingness to allow their participation as interveners (see chapter 5). However, the justices discourage participation by interveners at the leave-petition stage; as a result, such participation is quite rare. The result is a major difference in the agenda-setting process between the Supreme Court of Canada and the U.S. Supreme Court. In the latter, interest groups often file petitions in support of or in opposition to petitions for certiorari (which are very similar to a Canadian petitions for leave to appeal). Several studies have found that in the United States, the support of an interest group greatly increases the probability that a cert petition will be granted.

Granting Leave to Appeal: The Perspective of the Justices

Justices on the McLachlin Court were asked what they looked for when evaluating petitions for review.[3] Though no specific mention was made of 'official' criteria, every single justice agreed with the succinct summary of Justice G: 'National importance is the key.' Justice E admitted the truth of the widespread complaint about the absence of specific guidance on leave criteria: 'Essentially there are no formal guidelines – it is just a matter of what is a major issue.' He added: 'It is a lot like what your justices [i.e., on the U.S. Supreme Court] say about obscenity – we know it when we see it.' Justice E argued that despite the absence of specific guidelines, in 'the vast majority of the cases' the decision to deny leave is easy. All the justices agreed that in most petitions, the Court's decision is unanimous. When asked what constituted an important versus a non-important issue, he said that all the justices were interested in law development, especially in new areas of law where there are few precedents to guide lawyers and lower-court judges. 'We won't take cases on which the law is well settled,' he said, 'and we are generally not interested in cases that are "fact driven" – "who done it" is a question for the lower courts.'[4] He said that generally the Supreme Court was not interested in error correction – that is a job for appeal courts. Put another way, the justices were not primarily concerned with whether the court below 'got it right or wrong [pause] – unless something went *really* wrong and you just have to fix it' (emphasis of the justice).

   This ambivalence about error correction was expressed in almost all the interviews. The justices first indicated that they didn't see their job as correcting the lower courts' mistakes, but they almost always qualified that initial remark by indicating that on relatively rare occasions, the errors were so egregious that they just had to step in to fix the problem. With slightly varying language, all of the justices seemed to agree with the assessment of Justice C – that 'in theory just because the case was wrongly decided below you won't necessarily hear it. Instead there must be some indication of national importance – that is, some point of law that has national significance. But sometimes the decision is so far off track that you just can't let it stand.'

These comments echo a number of others made by U.S. Supreme Court justices and their clerks. Time and again, they insisted that the U.S. Supreme Court 'was not there to ensure justice' (Perry 1991, 36). One clerk noted that all the U.S. justices insisted that they do not engage in 'error correction'; but then that same clerk added that nevertheless, there appeared to be something like 'the Zorro concept, where they strike like lightning to do justice' when the result below was so egregious that the justices could not let it pass (ibid., 100). While none of the Canadian justices explicitly referred to a 'Zorro concept,' it seems that a similar response occurs in Canada in those relatively rare instances when a lower-court decision is so clearly in error that to let it stand would be to bring the whole system of justice into disrespect.

The issue of the law's uniformity does loom large for Canadian justices. Unanimously, they thought it important for federal laws to mean the same thing throughout a highly diverse country. This strong concern about maintaining national uniformity in the law as a key role of the Court was strikingly parallel to the views of the U.S. justices as expressed to Perry, and to the views of the Law Lords as expressed in recent interviews with the present author.[5] It is interesting that the importance of national uniformity applied both to the common law and to the statutory laws of the provinces. That is, this concern was not reserved exclusively for cases raising questions of national law or constitutional interpretation. Justice A went so far as to assert that national uniformity was 'especially' important with regard to the common law. Since it is judge-made law, the judges have an obligation to speak with one voice so that there is no perception that justice depends on the 'luck of the draw,' with the rules varying from case to case depending on which judge hears it. As a consequence, conflict among the provincial appeal courts over the interpretation of some question of law is usually taken as a strong indicator of the 'national importance' of the issues a case raises. However, like their colleagues on the U.S. Supreme Court, the justices also indicated a clear preference for waiting until an issue was ripe for review. That is, when a new issue arises, if it is perceived to be an issue that is likely to arise in many contexts, the Court is likely to deny leave on the first petition raising the issue and to wait until the issue has been vetted more extensively in the lower courts.

In studies of case selection in the United States, there has been speculation that the identity of the petitioner's lawyer may affect the chances for review (either positively or negatively) as the reputation of a given lawyer in the small 'Supreme Court bar' serves as a cue for the justices. The Canadian justices agreed that a lawyer's skill at framing the issues for appeal was likely to affect the chances for review, but they also doubted whether a lawyer's reputation had any impact on decisions to grant leave. As Justice D pointed out, there is not a small, identifiable 'Supreme Court bar' in Canada that might lead the justices to become familiar with the reputations of individual justices; besides, the names of counsel are not included in summaries of leave petitions provided to the justices by staff lawyers. Consequently, most justices do not know at the leave stage who the lawyers on each side are. Similarly, the justices denied that the standing or reputation of the judge who wrote the lower-court opinion had a measurable effect on the leave decision. Several justices did indicate, though, that the presence of dissent in the appeal court was often an important signal that there was an unresolved question of law and that if the dissent was by an especially well respected judge, that would carry some weight in their minds.

Finally, in stark contrast to the practice in the United States, the justices do not perceive any pressure to deny petitions for leave to appeal. Participants in the United States often assert that when they examine cert petitions they are looking for reasons to deny a petition (see Perry 1991); justices evaluating leave petitions in Canada are looking for reasons to *grant* leave. Justice F was most emphatic, asserting that his Court had never turned away a case just because its docket was full. When asked about the cross-border difference, several Canadian justices suggested that it was probably simply a function of numbers. The Supreme Courts in the two countries hear roughly the same number of cases each year, but in the United States the number of petitions for review is around ten times as great as in Canada.

The formal process for evaluating leave petitions seems straightforward at first glance and was outlined earlier in this chapter. A petition is sent to the Law Branch,[6] where a staff lawyer prepares an objective summary, which is sent to all nine justices. Each full petition, with supporting materials,[7] is sent to a panel, which decides whether to grant or deny leave.

The formal process is thus quite decentralized. The justices maintain, though, that in practice any justice on the Court can get involved in the decision on any petition in which she or he has a particular interest. Also in practice, before a panel makes a formal decision to grant or deny leave, it circulates a memo to the rest of the Supreme Court bench stating that it will deny or grant leave unless it hears an objection from another justice. If a single justice objects to this tentative decision, the petition is placed on the agenda of the next Court conference. At the conference, all of the justices have an opportunity to discuss whether to grant leave to appeal. The justices stressed that conference consider-ations are literally 'discussions' during which no formal decisions are made, though at the end of discussion someone will sometimes ask for a show of hands as to how many favour granting leave. But there is no rule on the number of raised hands in conference that are required in order to grant leave. Justice G: 'There is no absolute rule on the number required to grant leave ... nor is it a matter of deference [to a colleague who wants to hear the case] – it is a matter of persuasion.' When asked about similarities to the 'rule of four' in the United States,[8] there seemed to be agreement with the assessment of Justice G that though a case will not automatically be granted leave to appeal if leave is fa-voured by four justices, in such a case 'there would be a much better than even chance that the panel would grant leave.' The final decision is made by the panel, but there seems to be a general expectation that the panel members will give great weight to their colleagues' senti-ments. According to Justice D, the panel 'almost always' follows the sentiment of the conference, but there will be 'possibly two or three times a year when the panel does not follow the recommendation of the conference.'

A panel's recommendations tend to carry significant weight in con-ference discussions of leave petitions because all the justices recognize that the panel members are usually the ones who have examined the petition most closely. Moreover, as noted in other aspects of the Court's work, the McLachlin Court appears to be highly collegial. While the justices do not extend automatic deference to colleagues' decisions, there is a widely held conviction that they all share a general concep-tion of what 'national importance' means and that colleagues can be trusted to make decisions according to professional standards. For ex-ample, it seems that no justice worries that some faction will use its majority status on a leave panel to advance private policy goals. Thus the unanimous initial decisions of a panel are not often challenged at a conference. Several justices admitted that they usually gave only cur-sory attention to objective summaries of the leave petitions going to other panels unless the issue raised was of particular interest to them or unless one of the other non-panel members had already asked for a conference discussion.

Before 1988, arguments were held on leave petitions before three-judge panels. Each side was usually limited to fifteen minutes for oral argument. After 1988, however, Chief Justice Dickson succeeded in having the statute changed to allow leave decisions to be made on the basis of written arguments. Before the panel met to decide the leave petition, lists of the petitions and the memorandum from a clerk were circulated to all nine justices so that every justice had a chance to comment on the petition before the panel met (Sharpe and Roach 2003, 195–6).

On the whole, the leave process seems less political or ideological than the cert process in the United States. A large majority of decisions appear to be unanimous, and though several justices noted that some of their colleagues had one or two particular issues that they were especially interested in getting on the docket, no justice perceived the existence of stable 'blocs' that consistently aligned on leave decisions. Since the justices are able to hear a much higher proportion of the petitions than is possible in the United States, it is easier to accommodate the wishes of even one or two justices who have a strong preference to hear a given case. The potential for political conflict on leave petitions is probably also lessened by the near absence of participation by anyone other than direct parties. Interest groups are not allowed to submit briefs in support of or in opposition to leave petitions, and government actors rarely attempt to intervene at the leave stage. Provincial governments often appear as interveners, especially in cases involving other provinces, but such participation is almost always confined to the merits stage; briefs filed in support of leave petitions by other provinces are rare. Finally, there is no office in the Canadian federal government directly analogous to that of the U.S. Solicitor General; thus no national official regularly monitors leave petitions. Indeed, Justice G indicated that the federal government did not appear to be very selective regarding which cases it sought leave to appeal. He speculated that there was no centralized process within the government to coordinate leave decisions.

The Agenda of the Supreme Court: The Big Picture

An initial assessment of the broad issue areas addressed by the Supreme Court at the end of the twentieth century is provided in figure 3.1. All categories reflect the percentage of total decisions issued during the years 1970 to 2003. A more detailed breakdown of the agenda is provided in table 3.1.

Looking first at the broad categories of issues, it is clear that a large portion (approximately two-fifths) of the Supreme Court's business involves criminal appeals. As one might expect, serious crimes account

Figure 3.1
Issues decided by the Supreme Court 1970–2003

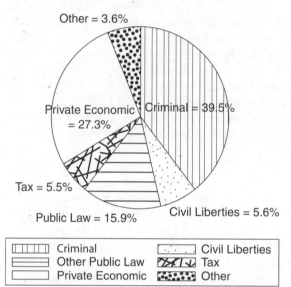

Other = 3.6%

Private Economic = 27.3%

Criminal = 39.5%

Tax = 5.5%

Public Law = 15.9%

Civil Liberties = 5.6%

⬛ Criminal		▱ Civil Liberties
≡ Other Public Law		▨ Tax
☐ Private Economic		⬤ Other

for the bulk of criminal appeals; crimes of violence by themselves account for about one-fifth of the Court's total docket. Perhaps surprisingly, considering the attention the media give to drug-related crimes, drug offences account for only one-tenth of the criminal appeals heard by the Supreme Court.

The next-biggest category of issues heard by the Court, accounting for more than one-quarter of its caseload, might be referred to as private economic disputes. Chief among these are tort actions, typically brought by private individuals against either corporations or other individuals. The remaining cases in this category are divided among conflicts over contracts, insurance disputes, debt collection actions, private employment disputes, and miscellaneous matters relating to corporate law.

Civil public law cases occupy approximately half as much of the Court's time as criminal appeals (21 per cent of cases). Disputes over government taxation are the largest single category of public law cases, followed by a host of cases dealing with agriculture, land use, labour/ management relations, health and environmental regulations, and government regulation of business.

Table 3.1
Overview of issues decided by the Supreme Court of Canada, 1970–2003

Issue	Number of cases	% of docket
Criminal	1379	39.5
Murder	320	9.2
Other violence	321	9.2
Property crimes	171	4.9
Drugs	140	4.0
Other criminal	427	12.3
Civil liberties	194	5.6
Prisoner petitions	24	0.7
Equality	49	1.4
Religion & indigenous	24	0.7
Privacy	13	0.4
Other civ. lib.	84	2.4
Public law	556	15.9
Health, environ. regs.	48	1.4
Business reg.	96	2.8
Land use, agriculture	105	3.0
Labour regulation	52	1.5
Govt. benefits	37	1.1
Public employment	68	2.0
Immigration/citizenship	43	1.2
Federalism	25	0.7
Other public law	75	2.2
Tax	191	05.5
Private economic	954	27.3
Creditor/debtor	108	3.1
Insurance	101	2.9
Corporate/contracts	182	5.2
Labor vs business	86	2.5
Motor vehicle tort	88	2.5
Other tort	252	7.2
Other private economic	182	5.2
Family	125	3.6
Other	92	2.6
	3491	100

The rest of the docket comprises less than 12 per cent of all cases. While civil liberties cases often generate both media attention and political controversy, such disputes take up less than 6 per cent of the cases on the Court's docket. Family law matters have an even less prominent place, generating fewer than 4 per cent of all cases heard by the Court.

Understanding the Court's political role requires an understanding of the hand it takes in resolving disputes that involve conflicting interpretations of statutes and the constitution. In modern democracies, political conflict over the direction of public policy often does not end in Parliament. Those who lose the parliamentary battle often look to the courts to regain all or part of what they lost in the legislative struggle. Litigation, especially in the Supreme Court, may therefore represent a continuation of a political struggle begun in the legislature. Moreover, the complexity of modern policy making sometimes makes it either technically difficult to anticipate all the problems involved in implementing policy or politically difficult to devise a clear compromise that can command the necessary legislative support. The result is often ambiguity regarding the precise terms of statutes and constitutional provisions – ambiguity that in effect leaves the details of policy making to the courts. These conflicts often are expressed in cases that demand that the justices engage in either statutory construction or constitutional interpretation. The extent of the activity of the Supreme Court in these acts of policy making is shown in figure 3.2.

Figure 3.2 indicates that over the past third of a century, the Court has often been called on to engage in both these significant types of policy making. In roughly one-fifth of the cases it hears, the Court has engaged in statutory construction; in another one-fifth, the resolution of the case has involved constitutional interpretation. These figures suggest that the Court has played a powerful role in resolving political controversies, but it is important to note that these activities do not represent the Court's primary role. Nearly two-thirds of the cases decided by the Supreme Court have *not* involved statutory construction or constitutional interpretation. That is, much of what the Court does involves resolving disputes that, while very important to the litigants involved, do not have much national political or policy-making significance.

The most significant and often the most controversial policy-making role of the Supreme Court relates to its power of judicial review.

Figure 3.2
Issues decided by the Supreme Court 1970–2003,
frequency of constitutional and statutory interpretation

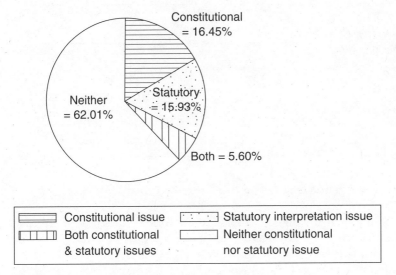

Throughout its history the Court has had the power to examine the conformity of both statutory law and the actions of executive officials with constitutional provisions and to declare null and void any law or action it finds incompatible with those provisions. While a non-trivial number of actions have been challenged under the nation's original constitution, more than three-quarters of the requests for judicial review since 1970 have arisen under the Charter of Rights and Freedoms (see table 3.2). The Court has been called on to exercise its power of judicial review in 579 cases over the past third of a century. The actions and laws of both the national government and the provinces may be challenged under either the Constitution Act of 1867 or the Charter of Rights. Table 3.2 indicates that the two levels of government have been subject to roughly the same number of constitutional challenges. The consequences of these challenges for governmental power are explored in chapter 6 in the context of the Court's role in policy making. For now it is sufficient to note that the Court has had many opportunities to delineate powers of the provincial and national governments under the constitution.

Table 3.2
The exercise of judicial review in the Supreme Court of Canada, 1970–2003

Court action	Number of cases	% of cases
Challenged action	579	17.8
Basis of constitutional challenge		
Charter of Rights	462	73.8
Constitution Act, 1867	164	26.2
Unknown	7	1.2
Level of government reviewed		
Federal	316	53.9
Provincial	270	46.1

Assessing Agenda Change on the Supreme Court

As noted above, the biggest change in the formal rules governing case selection occurred in 1975, with further, minor adjustments in 1997. In this section, attention shifts from these formal and informal processes for determining the Court's docket to an empirical examination of changes in that docket. As one might expect, the Charter of Rights has had a strong impact on the types of cases reaching the Court. Thus the focus of analysis is on four periods of time: the years before the Court gained substantial discretional control of its docket (1970 to 1975), the initial, pre-Charter period of docket (1976 to 1983),[9] the post-Charter period until the additional changes in procedure adopted in 1997 (1984 to 1996), and the current period (1998 to 2003). An overview of the changes in the agenda over time is presented in Table 3.3.

Just a glance at Table 3.3 indicates that the Supreme Court's agenda has changed profoundly over the past third of a century. In the most general terms, the Court has been transformed from a Court primarily concerned with resolving private disputes between individuals and businesses into a court of public law. Private economic disputes took up half the Court's agenda in the early 1970s. But as soon as the Court gained control of its docket in 1975, the proportion of private economic cases fell dramatically. Even fewer private economic cases have been heard by the Court since the adoption of the Charter of Rights, and the main cause of this decline has been the elimination of the right of automatic appeal. After the Charter of Rights, private economic disputes

Table 3.3
Change over time in the issues decided by Supreme Court of Canada, 1970–2003

Issue	1970–75	1976–83	1984–97	1998–2003
Criminal	16.2%	33.2%	52.5%	42.7%
	(102)	(279)	(765)	(228)
Civil liberty	02.2	02.4	07.8	08.4
	(14)	(20)	(114)	(45)
Public law	16.3	20.7	13.5	15.0
	(103)	(174)	(196)	(80)
Tax	09.2	06.1	03.5	04.9
	(58)	(51)	(51)	(26)
Priv. Econ.	50.5	31.2	16.4	22.7
	(319)	(262)	(239)	(121)
Family	04.3	03.7	03.4	03.0
	(27)	(31)	(49)	(16)
Other	01.3	02.7	02.9	03.4
	(8)	(23)	(42)	(18)
	100%	100%	100%	100%
	(584)	(680)	(1343)	(533)

continued to occupy about one-fifth of the Court's agenda – an indication that the justices continue to believe they still play an important role in defining the legal rules for resolving contract disputes, torts, property law issues, and so on. However, such issues are no longer their top priority when they consider leave-to-appeal petitions.

The proportion of tax cases heard by the Supreme Court has followed a trajectory similar to the one noted for private economic cases. After 1975, once tax cases could no longer come to the Court as appeals as of right, the number of cases actually *heard* by the Court declined substantially. The number of tax cases further declined after the Charter was adopted, and it has remained below 5 per cent of the Court's docket in the Charter period.

In sharp contrast, the proportion of the Court's docket devoted to criminal appeals has risen dramatically since the 1970s. The number of such appeals heard by the Court doubled once most automatic appeals were ended, indicating that criminal law issues were becoming an important priority for the Court even before the Charter was adopted.

Figure 3.3
Agenda change on the Supreme Court
Criminal cases vs private economic disputes 1970 to 2003

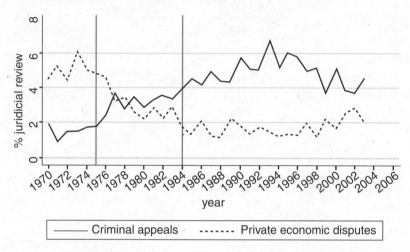

Figure 3.3 illustrates how the decline in private economic disputes closely mirrored the increase in criminal cases. After the Court gained greater docket control in 1975, the percentage of criminal cases it heard rose sharply, surpassing the number of private economic cases even before the Charter was adopted. Then, after the Charter, the proportion of criminal appeals again increased dramatically, to the point that such cases took up most of the docket during the first fourteen years of the Charter period. This increase seems directly related to the large number of Charter issues raised in criminal appeals. Since the Charter's adoption, 60 percent of all cases in which a provision of the Charter of Rights was litigated in the Supreme Court have involved a criminal appeal. Many of the Court's most controversial Charter decisions have involved abortion, child pornography, and language rights; that said, the bread and butter of the Court's work of Charter interpretation has related to the rights of criminal defendants.

As already noted, an amendment to the Criminal Code in 1997 narrowed the grounds for automatic appeals to the Supreme Court in criminal cases. Figure 3.3 indicates that, as might be expected, these jurisdictional changes have reduced the number of criminal appeals heard by the court since 1998. Yet even in this most recent time frame, criminal appeals still account for more than two-fifths of all cases heard by the Court. Thus, criminal appeals continue to account for more of the Court's docket than any of the other major categories of cases, and they continue to be heard at a rate far above the rate at which criminal appeals were heard before the adoption of the Charter.

That said, the most dramatic change in the Court's docket has involved civil liberties cases.[10] Non-criminal civil liberties claims have never been a large proportion of the Court's docket. However, that category's share of the docket has nearly quadrupled since the 1970s. After the Court gained control of its civil docket in 1975, the proportion of civil liberties cases remained low and essentially unchanged. With the adoption of the Charter, this changed instantly. In 1984, the year that Charter cases began reaching the Court, the Supreme Court decided six civil liberties cases – more than the total from the previous two years combined. This increased prominence of civil liberties cases has remained essentially the same ever since, averaging about 8 per cent of the Court's docket since 1984 compared to 2 per cent between 1970 and 1983.

Other categories of cases have remained essentially unchanged on the Court's agenda over time. The proportion of family law cases dipped slightly after 1975 and then remained static after the Charter was adopted. Other public law cases (i.e., other than criminal, tax, and civil liberties) have fluctuated slightly on the docket; for those, no clear trend is evident over the thirty-four years examined.

This broad profile is helpful in sorting out general trends. To examine more carefully changes in issue agendas, we need to profile case categories within each of these broadly defined areas and the changing proportion of the docket occupied by each of these subcategories. We begin this analysis with changing patterns of criminal appeals over time (see table 3.4).

As noted, the proportion of criminal appeals heard by the Supreme Court has increased dramatically over time. Increasing docket control (since 1975) and the Charter of Rights (since 1982) have helped raise the prominence of criminal appeals. However, this greater focus on criminal appeals varies strongly with the *type* of crime. The agenda space devoted to crimes of violence increased fourfold between the mid-1970s and the end of the century. The number of appeals involving murder and other acts of violence also increased after 1975, especially after the Charter was adopted. Similarly, more and more drug cases appeared on the Court's agenda after 1975, though the rate of increase began to taper off in 1997. In contrast, there have been only marginal increases in the number of property crime appeals heard by the

Table 3.4
Change over time in issues decided by Supreme Court of Canada, 1970–2003:
Proportion of criminal appeals on the docket

Issue	1970–75 (n)	1976–83 (n)	1984–97 (n)	1998–2003 (n)
Murder	3.97%	7.99%	10.81%	13.1%
	(25)	(67)	(157)	(70)
Other Violence	2.54	4.53	12.39	16.1
	(16)	(38)	(180)	(86)
Property crimes	3.82	5.96	5.16	4.1
	(24)	(50)	(75)	(22)
Drugs	0.95	4.17	5.57	3.4
	(6)	(35)	(81)	(18)
Other criminal	4.93	10.61	18.72	06.0
	(31)	(89)	(272)	(32)

Note: Percentages are column percentages, representing the percentage of all cases
decided by the Supreme Court in the indicated years that fell in the specific category.
The actual number of cases is displayed in parentheses beneath the percentage.

Court. It was noted earlier that the somewhat vague concept of 'public
importance' has guided the Court's decisions on petitions for leave to
appeal. These data suggest that when it comes to criminal appeals, importance is defined in part by the gravity of the offence.

As noted earlier, from the early 1970s to the end of the century there
was also a dramatic increase in the proportion of civil liberties cases on
the Supreme Court's docket. Table 3.5 indicates that for every specific
aspect of civil liberties, the Charter seems to have been responsible for
the Court's heightened attention. Cases revolving around equality, religion, indigenous people, privacy, and the rights of prisoners all began
to reach the Court in substantially greater numbers after the adoption
of the Charter. The Court's greater power to control its agenda had little effect on the number of rights claims reaching the Court until the
Charter became a reality.

Other public law issues were much less affected by the Charter and
by the Court's new agenda control powers. Moreover, it seems that
the effects of both these institutional changes varied across subcategories of this general category. There are no consistent changes over
time in the proportion of cases raising issues related to most forms of

Table 3.5
Change over time in issues decided by Supreme Court of Canada, 1970–2003: Proportion
of civil liberties cases on the docket

Issue	1970–75 (n)	1976–83 (n)	1984–97 (n)	1998–2003 (n)
Prisoner petitions	0.16%	0.60%	1.03%	0.6%
	(1)	(5)	(15)	(3)
Equality	0.32	0.24	2.27	2.2
	(2)	(2)	(33)	(12)
Religion & indigenous	0	0	1.10	1.5
	(0)	(0)	(16)	(8)
Privacy	0.17	0.24	0.48	0.6
	(1)	(2)	(7)	(3)
Other civ. lib.	1.75	1.31	2.89	3.6
	(11)	(11)	(42)	(19)

Note: Percentages are column percentages, representing the percentage of all cases
decided by the Supreme Court in the indicated years that fell in the specific category.
The actual number of cases is displayed in parentheses beneath the proportion.

government regulation, including general business regulations, relations with labour unions, and more specific regulations related to
health, safety, and the environment. Such regulatory regimes have
been generally unaffected by most of the Charter's provisions.
Table 3.6 indicates that as soon as the Court began using its new
docket control powers to reduce the number of private law disputes it
heard, it began filling to resulting docket 'holes' with criminal rights
cases and other civil liberties claims rather than with regulatory cases.

Other areas of public law were affected by these institutional changes.
After the Court gained more docket control in 1975, tax cases, land use
litigation, and immigration and citizenship disputes all declined in frequency as a proportion of the Court's caseload; after the Charter was adopted, such cases never regained their prominence on the docket. It
seems to be a hard sell to convince the Court that issues such as these
raise concerns of 'public importance' – the threshold criterion that a
leave petition must meet.

Finally, some issues gained agenda space once the Court gained more
control of its docket, only to lose those gains after the adoption of the
Charter. Claims to public benefits, disputes over public employment,

Table 3.6
Change over time in the issues decided by Supreme Court of Canada, 1970–2003:
Proportion of public law cases on the docket

Issue	1970–75 (n)	1976–83 (n)	1984–97 (n)	1998–2003 (n)
Health, environmental regulation	1.27%	1.19%	1.31%	2.1%
	(8)	(10)	(19)	(11)
Business regulation	2.38	2.62	3.23	2.2
	(15)	(22)	(47)	(12)
Land use, agriculture	5.72	4.29	1.72	1.3
	(36)	(36)	(25)	(7)
Labour regulation	1.59	2.74	0.83	1.3
	(10)	(23)	(12)	(7)
Government benefits	0.32	1.55	1.24	0.8
	(2)	(13)	(18)	(4)
Public employment	0.64	3.22	1.38	3.0
	(4)	(27)	(20)	(16)
Immigration/citizenship	1.91	1.07	1.03	1.3
	(12)	(9)	(15)	(7)
Federalism	0.48	1.43	0.48	0.6
	(3)	(12)	(7)	(3)
Tax	9.22	6.08	3.51	4.9
	(58)	(51)	(51)	(26)
Other public law	1.59	2.62	2.13	2.1
	(10)	(22)	(31)	(11)

Note: Percentages are column percentages, representing the percentage of all cases decided by the Supreme Court in the indicated years that fell in the specific category. The actual number of cases is displayed in parentheses beneath the proportion.

and federalism disputes all fall into this category. In other words, when the Court first obtained greater docket control, these issues gained in priority. There is no specific indication that the Court lost interest in these issues in later years. It does, though, seem that once the Charter was adopted, a large number of new issues began competing for the Court's attention, and older public law issues fell to a lower priority as a result.

Table 3.7
Change over time in the issues decided by the Supreme Court of Canada, 1970–2003:
Proportion of private economic cases on the docket

Issue	1970–75 (n)	1976–83 (n)	1984–97 (n)	1998–2003 (n)
Creditor/debtor	4.61%	3.93%	1.86%	3.4%
	(29)	(33)	(27)	(18)
Insurance	3.50	3.22	2.34	3.2
	(22)	(27)	(34)	(17)
Corporate/contracts	10.97	6.67	2.62	2.8
	(69)	(56)	(38)	(15)
Labour vs business	3.34	2.62	2.06	2.4
	(21)	(22)	(30)	(13)
Motor vehicle tort	7.95	2.03	0.89	1.1
	(50)	(17)	(13)	(6)
Other tort	12.72	6.91	5.02	6.9
	(80)	(58)	(73)	(37)
Other private economic	7.63	5.84	1.65	2.8
	(48)	(49)	(24)	(15)

Note: Percentages are column percentages, representing the percentage of all cases decided by the Supreme Court in the indicated years that fell in the specific category. The actual number of cases is displayed in parentheses beneath the proportion.

The docket space the Court devotes to private economic disputes has declined dramatically since the early 1970s. However, that decline has not been evenly spread across specific issue areas (see Table 3.7). The proportion of the docket devoted to creditor/debtor cases, insurance claims, and labour/management conflict was small throughout the period examined, but it was also relatively constant, with only small declines evident when one compares the post-1997 period to the early 1970s. On the other hand, the areas of contract law, torts, and remaining private economic disputes all experienced sharp declines as soon as the Court obtained a substantial degree of docket control in 1975. Their share of the docket then declined even further once Charter cases began to compete for the justices' attention. The result has been that each of these areas now commands only one-half to one-third of the docket space they were receiving before 1975.

Switching from specific issues to a more general consideration of the Court's policy-making role, one can see that its involvement in both statutory construction and constitutional adjudication has grown substantially over the past third of a century (see figure 3.4).

Figure 3.4 supports what one might expect: once the Court gained the power to fashion its own agenda through its leave-to-appeal decisions, it focused increasingly on cases involving questions of statutory construction and constitutional interpretation rather than on cases involving 'mere' disputes between private litigants of the sort that have little significance for those not directly involved. The proportion of the docket devoted to statutory interpretation increased by over 40 per cent once the Court gained control of its civil docket; the same years, the proportion devoted to constitutional adjudication increased by over 80 per cent. Clearly, then, even before the Charter the Supreme Court was beginning to perceive itself as a policy maker rather than an adjudicator of private disputes.

The data show – perhaps surprisingly – that the Court has become increasingly involved in statutory as well as constitutional interpretation since the adoption of the Charter. By the beginning of the twenty-first century, the Supreme Court was engaged in statutory construction in more than one-quarter of its cases – more than double the rate of the early 1970s. A subjective analysis of the Court's decisions suggests that the frequency of statutory construction increased during the Charter period because constitutional challenges to legislation forced the justices to take a hard look at the *language* of statutes; thus, they often searched for plausible constructions of statutes for the purpose of rendering judicial review unnecessary. Empirically, this much can be observed: in the early 1970s, less than 7 per cent of statutory cases also involved constitutional interpretation; after the adoption of the Charter, 30 per cent of statutory cases also involved a constitutional interpretation.

Less surprising is the finding (see figure 3.4) that the proportion of cases on the Court's docket involving constitutional interpretation increased dramatically after the Charter was adopted. Even with docket control, before 1984 only 7 per cent of the Court's decisions turned on constitutional interpretation. But in the twenty post-Charter years, more than one-quarter of all cases decided by the Supreme Court have involved constitutional interpretation. This increase is due almost entirely to litigation directly involving the Charter. About 84 per cent of the constitutional cases since 1984 have involved interpreting the

Figure 3.4
The changing agenda of the Supreme Court
Constitutional and statutory interpretation before
and after the Charter

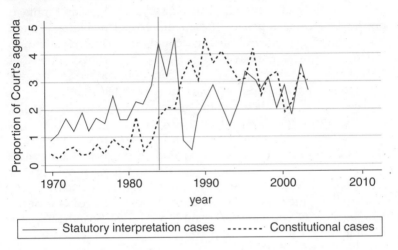

Charter rather than the Constitution Act of 1867. Since the adoption of the Charter, the Court has continued to decide roughly six cases a year involving the Constitution Act of 1867 – roughly the same number decided by the Court after it gained docket control in 1975 but before the Charter was adopted. The resolution of constitutional disputes has long been part of the Supreme Court's role. However, since the adoption of the Charter, a number of new constitutional issues have emerged. These have not displaced the earlier constitutional issues from the Court's agenda; they have simply taken their place on that agenda beside the older issues.

Agenda Change from an International Perspective

The increased policy-making role of the Supreme Court of Canada and its increasing attention to rights claims noted earlier appear to be part of a worldwide phenomenon: courts are becoming more active in the politics of both well-established and emerging democracies. Scholars in many countries have been devoting more attention to this phenomenon, which has been dubbed by some as the 'judicialization of politics.' In more and more countries across the world, 'judges are making public policies that previously had been made or that, in the opinion of most, ought to be made by legislative and executive officials' (Tate and Vallinder 1995, 2) In many countries this increased role of the courts has been part of a growing awareness of rights. In Europe, for example, the European Convention and the Court of Human Rights in Strasbourg have done much to spread the gospel of judicialization (ibid., 3). According to one prominent account, the increasing attention to rights claims in Canada has been part of a 'rights revolution' that has been sweeping much of the English common law world. It is argued that trends in Canada are part of a broader trend that has touched a number of other common law countries, including the United States, India, and England (Epp 1998).

To put the trends in the changing agenda of the Supreme Court of Canada into better perspective, the next step in the present analysis is to compute the proportion of the docket devoted to criminal appeals and civil liberties for Britain and the United States. To facilitate the comparison, the same years will be examined for all three countries.[11] The data for the U.S. Supreme Court are based on the Spaeth Supreme Court Database.[12] The data on the House of Lords are based on the Comparative Courts Database Project. The comparisons are displayed in Table 3.8.

When comparing the agenda space devoted to criminal appeals and civil liberties disputes in Canada, the United States, and Britain, it should be remembered that the dates chosen to compare change over time are based solely on a significant institutional change in Canada (i.e., the adoption of the Charter). No similar major institutional changes took place in either Britain or the United States during this period. Throughout the period examined, the high courts of both countries enjoyed essentially complete docket control. Also, the United States had constitutional protection for rights similar to the provisions of the Charter of Rights and Freedoms throughout the period studied. Britain, in contrast, still does not have constitutional rights protections that can be enforced through judicial review.

The first point worth noting is that all three high courts allotted very similar portions of their dockets to criminal appeals between 1970 and 1983. However, after the adoption of the Charter, the proportion of criminal appeals heard by the Supreme Court of Canada increased dramatically while the proportion of the docket devoted to criminal appeals in Britain and the United States remained essentially unchanged. The data do not permit a definitive conclusion as to why this is so; that

Table 3.8
Change over time in the proportion of criminal appeals and civil liberties issues decided by the U.S. Supreme Court and the Judicial Committee of the House of Lords, 1970–2003

Issue	U.S. Supreme Court		British House of Lords	
	1970–75 (n)	1976–83 (n)	1984–97 (n)	1998–2003 (n)
Criminal	20.33%	23.69%	24.06%	22.2%
	(535)	(556)	(153)	(205)
Civil lib.	30.55	27.78	03.62	07.7
	(804)	(652)	(23)	(71)
Other	49.12	48.43	72.32	70.2
	(1293)	(1139)	(460)	(649)
	100%	100%	100%	100%
	(2632)	(2347)	(636)	(925)

said, several institutional differences among the countries seem to be contributing factors. First, most criminal cases in the United States heard by the lower courts are not within the Supreme Court's jurisdiction, which means that appeals to that Court are not possible. Contrast this with Canada, which has a unified judicial system so that losing litigants in all criminal cases may petition for leave to appeal. Also, differences in the legal definition of double jeopardy mean that the Canadian government may appeal a number of adverse criminal decisions that cannot be appealed by the U.S. government. Given the very high rate of success that the U.S. government has in its petitions for review by the Supreme Court, these constitutional limitations perhaps explain certain non-trivial differences between Canada and the United States. Finally, it may simply be that Canadian and American justices define 'public importance' differently in the context of petitions for review of criminal cases. Unfortunately, this topic was not explored in the interviews with the justices and must await future research.

A different picture emerges from the comparison of civil liberties cases on the dockets of each Court. Between 1970 and 1983, in the absence of any constitutional basis for rights claims, the high courts of Canada and Britain heard very few civil rights and liberties cases. In the United States, which has constitutional protections for rights, civil liberties cases made up over 30 per cent of the Supreme Court's docket.

As might be expected, the proportion of rights cases heard by the U.S. Supreme Court did not change much after 1984, reflecting the absence of any structural, political, or cultural change that might affect civil rights litigation. At the same time, as noted earlier, the proportion of rights claims heard by the Supreme Court of Canada more than tripled after the adoption of the Charter of Rights. It is interesting that the proportion of rights cases heard by the House of Lords in England also rose dramatically without a change in the constitutional status of rights. In other words, rights cases continued to claim a similar share of high court dockets in Canada and Britain despite the constitutional change in Canada and the absence of corresponding change in England. This raises two questions: Why did the number of rights cases on the docket in Britain increase as much as it did in Canada after 1984? And why has the proportion of the Canadian Court's docket devoted to rights claims remained so much lower (less than one-third) than the docket space devoted to rights cases in the United States even now that Canada has adopted a level of constitutional protection of rights similar to what is enjoyed by Americans?

Epp (1996 and 1998) suggests that the number of rights cases gaining access to a top court's docket has very little to do with whether those rights have constitutional protection; in his view, the number is influenced more by the nature and extent of the resources available for the legal mobilization of rights claims. He suggests that in both Canada and Britain these resources grew significantly during the 1980s and 1990s, which led to the increased attention to rights claims in the respective high courts. However, Epp fails to provide any convincing evidence that the resources available for rights mobilization in the United States are so much greater than those in Canada in the late 1980s and 1990s that one should expect that there will be three or four times as many rights cases heard in the United States. Moreover, as the analysis in the following section suggests, Epp may have misjudged the importance of formal constitutional protection for the likelihood that rights cases will become part of the agenda of national top courts. But if Epp's thesis leaves much to be desired, the data in table 3.8 leave unresolved the question of why the U.S. Supreme Court devotes so much more of its docket than the Canadian Supreme Court to rights claims.

Do Constitutions Matter?

The analysis to this point leaves little doubt that since the early 1970s the agenda of the Supreme Court of Canada has been profoundly transformed. The aspect of that transformation that has received the most attention in the media and in scholarly analyses has been the increasing attention to constitutional conflicts in general and especially to civil rights and liberties. The ramifications of this increasingly political role of the Court has been noted by many observers, and the normative effects of this new involvement in critical aspects of public policy have been subject to heated debate. Virtually all scholars who have joined the debate over this new policy-making role of the Court seem to have assumed (at least implicitly) that the Charter of Rights was the critical event that enabled the Court (or in the eyes of some, *required* the Court) to adopt a more overtly political role (see, for example, Mandel 1989; Greene et al. 1998; Morton and Knopff 2000; Manfredi 2001, 2004). In stark contrast, Epp (1996, 775) argues that 'the Charter's influence is overrated.' Epp (1998, 194) admits that a 'dramatic rights revolution has occurred in Canada in the last several decades' and that the Charter served as a useful legal foundation for rights advocates. But he also contends that the Charter was not the primary event that made this 'rights revolution' possible. Instead, he argues that the agenda changes on the Court 'appear to have resulted from the combined influence of two developments, the shift to a discretionary docket in 1975 and the development of a support structure for legal mobilization' (1996, 775).

To bolster his arguments, Epp presents a series of line graphs that trace developments in the Supreme Court's agenda from 1960 to 1990. Unfortunately, several of his methodological choices raise serious questions about the validity of his conclusions. Most significantly, he examines the Court's agenda every five years (e.g., in 1960, 1965, 1970) and for that reason cannot establish precisely when agenda changes took place. Furthermore, his examination of trends includes only two data points (1985 and 1990) after the adoption of the Charter. Moreover, his definition of 'civil rights and liberties' combines all criminal appeals – whether or not the appellant raised a specific rights claim – with traditional categories of civil liberties such as religious liberty, privacy, equality rights, and freedom of expression. Finally, when focusing on constitutional decision making, Epp concerns himself solely with constitutional challenges to statutes and ignores constitutional challenges to administrative action. When one examines the changing agenda of the Court on a year-by-year basis, disaggregates criminal and other civil liberties issues, and takes a more comprehensive view of constitutional lawmaking, a picture emerges that is somewhat different from the one Epp describes. This examination is undertaken below.

Table 3.3 indicated that there were dramatic increases in the proportion of both criminal appeals and other traditional categories of civil liberties on the docket of the Supreme Court following the adoption of the Charter of Rights. But table 3.3 is inadequate as a test of Epp's argument because the data on agenda change are presented only for broad time periods rather than for individual years. To better test Epp's claim that the Charter's influence was quite modest, the earlier analysis is broken down into figures for the agenda of the Court in each calendar year between 1970 and 2003 (see figure 3.5).

As in the previous analysis, the Charter period is defined as starting in 1984, the year the first case raising a Charter issue reached the Court (represented by the vertical line in figure 3.5). Two data trends are presented. The solid line indicates the proportion of all of the cases in which a civil rights or liberties issue was raised during a non-criminal appeal. The broken line reflects Epp's definition of civil rights; this is, it combines criminal appeals with more traditional concepts of civil liberties.

Looking first at the more limited, traditional concept of civil rights, it is obvious that before 1984, civil liberties issues rarely appeared on the Court's agenda. The highest number of cases heard by the Court in any of these fourteen pre-Charter years was six, and there were only two years during which five or more civil liberties cases were on the agenda. As a proportion of the docket, those two years were the only two years during which civil liberties cases made up 5 per cent of the docket. Perhaps even more devastating to Epp's thesis is that there was no trend toward increasing attention to civil liberties as the 'support structure' for civil liberties (which Epp saw as the crucial influence on the rights agenda) gradually increased.

In sharp contrast, the number and proportion of rights cases increased dramatically after the Charter was adopted. For every one of the first eleven years of the post-Charter period, the number of rights cases on the Court's agenda equalled or exceeded the highest number of rights cases heard in any pre-Charter year. In ten of these same eleven years, the proportion of the docket devoted to rights cases exceeded the highest proportion of rights cases in all fourteen pre-Charter years examined.[13]

Turning to the combined total of criminal appeals with other rights issues, there does seem to be some support for Epp's argument that docket control had a significant impact on the Court's rights agenda. From 1970 to 1975, there were fewer than thirty rights cases on the docket every year and the proportion of the docket devoted to his

Figure 3.5
Do Constitutions matter?
Change over time on the Supreme Court:
Civil liberties cases before and after the Charter

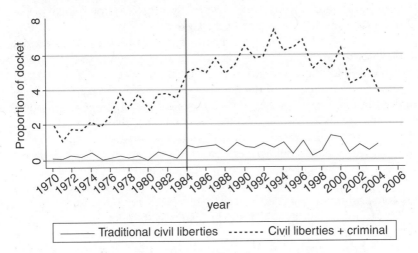

definition of rights cases stayed below 30 per cent every year. There
was no noticeable change in the first year after the Court gained
docket control; but starting in 1977, there were forty or more cases involving rights in five of the seven years. Also, the proportion of the
docket devoted to criminal appeals and other rights cases fluctuated
between 30 and 40 per cent in six of the seven years.

Nevertheless, even using Epp's own measure of 'rights' cases, the
Charter seems to have had immediate and persistent effects. Prior to
the Charter, there had not been a single year in which criminal and
other rights cases made up as much as 40 per cent of the Court's
docket. Yet in the single year between 1983 and 1984, the proportion of
rights cases jumped 15 per cent, becoming more than 50 per cent of the
docket for the first time. Moreover, the proportion of the docket
devoted to this expanded definition of rights cases did not dip below
50 per cent for seventeen consecutive years and has never dropped to
the level of the pre-Charter high point.

In summary, there seem to have been two sharp break points in the
increasing tendency of the Court to hear rights cases using Epp's expanded definition of rights cases and only one sharp break point using
a more limited, traditional understanding of what constitutes a rights

case. The Charter's adoption was a crucial turning point for both agenda changes. The trends in agenda change do not reveal the more gradual or linear increase in the attention to rights cases that would be expected if the gradual increase in 'the development of a support structure for legal mobilization' posited by Epp were the critical cause of the increasing rights agenda of the Court.

A second piece of evidence used by Epp to support the argument that the impact of the Charter is 'overrated' relates to trends in the proportion of cases on the Court's docket either seeking or receiving judicial review. An examination of the actual incidence of judicial review is reserved for chapter 6. The present analysis is limited to agenda change. Epp's analysis is limited to data points positioned five years apart and, as noted earlier, is limited to challenges to the constitutionality of statutes. In the analysis below, year-by-year data are provided both for challenges to the constitutionality of statutes and for a more inclusive category: all requests for judicial review (i.e., including challenges to the constitutionality of executive actions as well as to statutes).

Prior to 1984, statutes could only be challenged under the Constitution Act of 1867. Most challenges involved questions of federalism. The trends shown in figure 3.6 suggest that in this pre-Charter period there was considerable fluctuation in the number of such constitutional challenges, from a high of twelve cases in 1981 to a low of just one in 1970 and 1983. Significantly for Epp's thesis, there was no linear trend toward increasing use of judicial review over time as the support structure for rights litigation grew. Perhaps even more damaging to Epp's thesis, few of these cases involved civil liberties. Only 9 per cent of the pre-Charter challenges to statutes involved traditional questions of civil liberties, and another 9 per cent involved challenges to criminal statutes. In contrast, more than half the constitutional challenges were raised against the exercise of economic regulation by federal or provincial governments.

Even a casual examination of the trend data in Figure 3.6 suggests that the Charter has had a dramatic effect on the Supreme Court's exercise of judicial review. In the final two pre-Charter years, the Court considered only five cases raising constitutional challenges to statutes; that number then tripled during the first two years of Charter litigation. Pre-Charter, there had been only three years during which the Court considered six or more requests for judicial review; post-Charter, the Court has considered at least that many constitutional challenges in every year,[14] and the median number of constitutional challenges considered by the Court in a year has been twelve (i.e., the post-Charter median has equalled the pre-Charter maximum). Moreover,

Figure 3.6
Do Constitutions matter?
Change over time on the Supreme Court: Judicial review before
and after the Charter

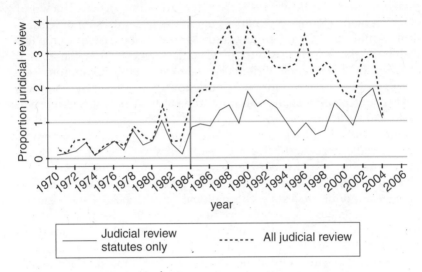

while most pre-Charter constitutional challenges involved government economic regulation, 64 per cent of post-Charter challenges have involved civil liberties issues.

The effect of the Charter on judicial review is even more dramatic when one considers *all* constitutional challenges rather than just challenges to the constitutionality of statutes. Figure 3.6 indicates that prior to the Charter, the number of constitutional challenges to either legislative or executive actions fluctuated widely over the years without any clear trend. The year 1981 was the high point for constitutional litigation, with 15 per cent of the Court's docket involving constitutional challenges. Yet in each of the next two years, constitutional challenges made up less than 5 per cent of the Court's docket.

There was a dramatic increase in constitutional litigation as soon as the first Charter cases reached the Court. In the very first year of Charter litigation, the proportion of the docket devoted to constitutional challenges was three times as great as in the previous two years, and in every year after that the docket space devoted to constitutional challenges was greater than the proportion of litigation asking for judicial review in any of the fourteen years of pre-Charter litigation examined in the current study.

In summary, the answer to the question posed at the beginning of this section is 'yes' – at least in the Canadian experience, constitutions *do* matter. This is not to suggest that constitutional protection of rights is self-executing or that the actions of well-resourced groups determined to push for the expansion of rights are unimportant. The world has seen many examples of paper guarantees of rights with little practical significance. Yet the timing of the dramatic increase in rights litigation in the Supreme Court of Canada suggests that the formal constitutional protection of rights is vital to any rights revolution.

The justices of the Supreme Court now possess nearly complete docket control; almost all cases now come to the Court through leave-to-appeal petitions, which are granted at the justices' discretion. Whether a case is heard depends largely on the justices' preferences. The official criteria in this regard do not seem to constrain the justices in any substantial way, nor do they indicate clearly which cases are likely to be selected. Interviews with the justices suggest that it is their own perceptions regarding the national importance of the issue in play, and its significance for clarifying legal rules, that makes a case worthy of review. The justices expressed little interest in attempting to correct mistakes by the lower courts. Perhaps the best way to ascertain what the justices mean by 'national importance' is to examine the patterns of the choices they have made. An analysis of agenda changes on the Court indicates that cases requiring constitutional and statutory interpretation have increasingly occupied the justices. They continue to explicate the rules governing private disputes, but those disputes now occupy a much smaller portion of the Court's docket, for the justices no longer see themselves as the final arbiters of conflicting facts. Instead, the justices have become a court of *public* law; they continue to define the limits of government policy making, but they are also increasingly concerned with procedural justice and with substantive rights claims made under the Charter.

The justices are now essentially free to pick and choose from among the more than six hundred petitions for review they receive each year. Yet their power remains limited: they can resolve only those disputes that have been brought to them by litigants who have lost in the lower courts. Who, then, are those litigants? And what resources do they possess to pursue either individual gain or broader policy concerns? The answers to those questions go a long way toward defining the Court's agenda. The next chapter discusses the role of litigants.

4 A Look at the Players: Who Participates and Who Wins?

Much of the debate surrounding the Supreme Court of Canada has focused on the political impact of the Court as an institution. This debate on what role the Court plays has often been mixed with normative debate about what role the Court *should* play. These commentaries (which are discussed more fully in chapter 6) have subjected the Court to attack from both the left and the right of Canadian politics. Often these commentaries raise the key question of politics: Who wins and who loses in the Court?

The Court's political impact has come under increasing scrutiny from the media, political interests, and scholars since the adoption of the Charter of Rights and Freedoms brought the Court's political role into the full glare of public attention. But as McCormick (1993a) reminds us, it is not that the courts suddenly came to possess political power with the adoption of the Charter, but rather that many have only become aware of that power since 1984.

Decisions of the Supreme Court can be viewed as a valuable resource for which a variety of parties compete. Those decisions resolve concrete conflicts, some of which involve millions of dollars or the basic liberties of individuals or groups; they also often involve the development of precedents – that is, they guide future applications of statutes and of the constitution itself. But like other political conflicts, the competition for the Court's resources is not waged on a level playing field: 'Some parties, some classes of litigants, enjoy substantial and continuing advantages over others, and these advantages affect the general pattern of decisions that flow from the courts' (ibid., 523).

Scholars in many countries have sought to understand the political consequences of appellate court decisions by conducting empirical, quantitative studies of who wins and who loses. The question of who wins and loses in appellate courts is perhaps the most important question confronting judicial scholars. In fact, 'Who gets what?' has long been viewed as the central question in the study of politics generally. So an understanding of who wins in the courts is essential if we are to fully appreciate the Court's potential political impact. One might even say that in a democracy, the state's legitimacy depends heavily on whether citizens believe that resources and benefits are distributed relatively equally and are not monopolized by a privileged elite. Thus the extent to which a regime may be categorized as 'democratic' is influenced by the pattern of winners and losers generated by official policies – policies that include the decisions of its courts. A long string of studies employing 'party capability theory' have examined how litigants' backgrounds and resources have affected their chances for success in the common law. Unfortunately, very little of that scholarship has focused on the Canadian judicial system.

This chapter considers who wins and who loses before the Supreme Court of Canada and whether the profiles of winners and losers have changed over time. But before proceeding to a direct examination of 'who wins?' one must first understand who participates. Pluralist perspectives on politics that focus exclusively on who wins and who loses in the context of specific decisions have been criticized for overlooking institutional structures and rules of the sort that preclude the effective participation of some groups or individuals when key decisions are being made. In other words, before one can safely interpret the patterns of winners and losers in courts, it is necessary to understand who participates.

Participation in Litigation in the Supreme Court of Canada

The next section provides a descriptive overview of the litigants in cases decided by the Supreme Court of Canada. To influence the outcome of judicial policy making, first one must secure a place on the Court's docket. Which leads to this good question: Did the 1975 changes in the Court's docket control powers affect the types of litigants appearing before the Court? Prior to 1975, there was a formal bias against small individuals and businesses. In civil cases, litigants raising claims in excess of $10,000 were guaranteed a right of appeal to the Supreme Court. Litigants in the lower courts seeking smaller sums could take their grievances to the Supreme Court only with the Court's permission (more specifically, only if the Court granted leave

Table 4.1
Who participates in the Supreme Court of Canada?

	Total (%)	70–75 (%)	76–83 (%)	84–90 (%)	91–99 (%)	00–03 (%)
Individuals	70.7	61.0	66.0	76.2	78.6	68.8
Business	31.2	50.0	36.2	24.8	21.1	27.4
Associations	06.9	06.2	05.9	06.5	06.4	11.2
Local govt.	07.3	13.7	09.0	04.4	04.0	07.1
Provincial govt.	43.5	18.8	37.6	52.0	55.2	47.7
National govt.	19.9	15.4	23.4	20.6	19.9	19.7
Total cases	3247	584	680	588	923	365

to appeal). Then in 1975, all litigants in civil cases were placed on an equal footing; all had to petition for leave to appeal, granted at the discretion of the Court, in order to gain access to the Court.

Who succeeds in getting a dispute decided by the Supreme Court? Table 4.1 indicates, rather strikingly, that in a large majority of cases that reach the Court, the participants include one or more 'natural persons' (i.e., individuals who are not appearing as officers or owners of businesses or private organizations and who do not hold any public office).[1] This pattern has persisted across time. In each of the five time periods examined, more than three-fifths of the cases involved an individual not associated with any business, organization, or government as either the appellant or the respondent or both. This is important, given the widespread concern in many modern democracies as to whether ordinary people are in effect precluded from participating in government. Table 4.1 suggests that whatever the actual access of individuals to parliaments and cabinet members, when it comes to the judiciary they *are* able to be heard at the highest level. Indeed, they are able to gain access more than twice as often as the representatives of businesses, and individuals gain access at rates comparable to those of all levels of government combined.

Table 4.1 also suggests that the Charter of Rights may have democratized access to the Court at least marginally. The proportion of cases in which individuals participated increased by 10 per cent immediately after the Charter became effective and since then has never returned to pre-Charter levels. In contrast, the proportion of cases in which business interests participated declined steeply in the post-Charter period.

The next step in the analysis was to determine whether, for each category, litigants before the Supreme Court participated as appellants or as respondents. Those trends over time are presented in tables 4.2 and 4.3. The same tables provide additional details about the litigants that could be derived from the opinions. It is usually impossible to determine the wealth or education of an individual from the facts presented in a court opinion; for this study, though, it was possible to determine how many of the cases involved children rather than adults. Similarly, precise estimates of the size of business litigants were usually not available, but the coding did permit the identification of some businesses that were obviously quite small. Businesses were classified as small businesses if it was clear that they were owned and operated by a single family or limited in scope to a single location that did not employ many people. Finally, associations were subcategorized according to the types of interests they represented.

When the two tables are considered together, it is apparent that in the Supreme Court, individuals appear much more often as appellants (i.e., as losers in the lower courts) than as respondents. Overall, by the time they arrive in the Supreme Court they are almost twice as likely to be appellants as respondents. This tendency is apparent in all five time periods examined, albeit with some evident change over time. Before 1975, when the Court gained increased docket control, individuals appeared as respondents in over 30 per cent of cases. After 1976, the proportion of cases in which individuals appeared as respondents declined while the proportion of times they appeared as the appellants increased. This suggests two things: private individuals are frequent participants in the lower courts; and they lose much more often than they win in those courts.

Expressed slightly differently, more than half the cases heard by the Supreme Court since the Charter was adopted began as appeals brought by private individuals. Thus it is private individuals, not businesses or governments or organized interest groups, that have had the biggest impact on the agenda of the Court.

In contrast, businesses are as likely to be appellants as they are respondents. However, their participation in both roles declined sharply after the Supreme Court gained control of its civil docket and declined even more after the Charter was adopted. By the Charter period, three times more individuals than businesses were heard by the Court as

Table 4.2
Change over time in the nature of appellants to the Supreme Court of Canada

	Total (%)	70–75 (%)	76–83 (%)	84–90 (%)	91–99 (%)	00–03 (%)
Individuals	51.4	42.9	47.7	59.0	57.9	44.7
Adults	50.0	42.0	46.5	57.3	56.1	44.1
Child	1.4	0.9	1.2	1.7	1.8	0.6
Business	20.9	32.9	25.9	15.8	13.7	17.8
Small	1.7	1.0	2.1	2.2	1.5	1.6
Other	19.2	31.9	23.8	13.6	12.2	16.2
Associations	4.4	3.9	3.9	4.6	4.4	5.5
Business	0.8	0.5	0.6	1.0	0.4	1.6
Union	1.9	1.9	2.6	2.2	1.6	1.4
Other	1.7	1.5	0.7	1.4	2.4	2.5
Local govt.	3.0	5.7	3.5	1.9	1.4	3.3
Provincial govt.	12.5	7.7	10.6	11.9	14.3	21.1
National govt.	6.0	5.3	7.1	5.1	6.2	6.8
Foreign govt.	0.5	0.3	0.3	0.5	0.8	0.0
Fiduciaries	1.3	2.2	1.0	1.2	1.2	0.8
Total cases	3242	583	678	588	921	365

appellants; individuals were also (marginally) more likely than businesses to participate as respondents.

Regarding specific categories of litigants, children have been only a tiny fraction of litigants appearing before the Court. For that reason, no further analysis of participation by children is included below. Similarly, less than 2 per cent of all litigants can be identified as small businesses. Thus the following analysis of litigants' success rates does not try to distinguish among categories of businesses or individuals.

Participation rates for governments before the Supreme Court have varied by level of government. Local governments appeared less often as either appellants or respondents after the Court gained control of its docket, and less often still after the Charter was adopted. In contrast, the presence of provincial governments on the Supreme Court's docket has increased dramatically over time. In the latest period examined,

Table 4.3
Change over time in the nature of respondents in the Supreme Court of Canada

	Total (%)	70–75 (%)	76–83 (%)	84–90 (%)	91–99 (%)	00–03 (%)
Individuals	26.1	30.7	24.9	23.2	25.8	27.7
Adults	25.5	30.0	24.5	23.0	25.4	26.6
Child	0.6	0.7	0.4	0.2	0.4	1.1
Business	19.1	32.6	20.8	14.4	12.6	18.4
Small	1.7	2.4	1.9	1.4	1.2	2.2
Other	17.4	30.2	18.9	13.0	11.4	16.2
Associations	3.0	2.7	2.7	2.4	2.2	6.6
Business	00.4	0.5	0.2	0.2	0.2	1.1
Union	1.4	1.2	1.8	1.2	0.8	3.6
Other	1.2	1.0	0.7	1.0	1.2	1.9
Local govt.	4.6	8.6	6.0	2.6	2.7	3.8
Provincial govt.	31.5	12.2	27.4	41.2	41.0	28.0
National govt.	14.1	10.1	16.5	15.8	14.1	13.4
Foreign govt.	0.2	0	0	0	0.2	1.4
Fiduciaries	1.5	3.1	1.6	0.5	1.3	0.8
Total cases	3237	583	678	583	921	365

provincial governments appeared three times more often as appellants and two times more often as respondents than they did in the 1970–5 period. In every time period, however, provincial governments appeared more often as respondents than as appellants. Note that in the post-Charter periods, provincial governments have brought roughly as many appeals as business litigants to the Court.

Perhaps surprisingly, the federal government has been a less frequent litigator before the Supreme Court than either provincial governments or businesses. In all periods, it appeared more often as a respondent than as an appellant. Note as well that its participation rate in both roles has increased over time. Nevertheless, the federal government has accounted for only 6 per cent of the cases successfully appealed to the Court and has appeared as respondent in less than 15 per cent of all cases, and these low percentages hold even in the

Table 4.4
Matching appellants and respondents – the opponents of appellants in civil cases in the Supreme Court of Canada

Appellant	Indiv. (%)	Bus. (%)	Assoc. (%)	Local (%)	Prov. govt. (%)	Fed. Govt. (%)	N
Individuals	30.3	21.4	3.3	7.1	12.6	25.2	705
Business	19.1	43.6	4.7	7.6	9.2	15.9	643
Associations	11.8	25.9	11.8	11.1	23.7	15.6	135
Local govt.	36.8	33.3	11.5	9.2	4.6	4.6	87
Provincial govt.	39.2	32.0	8.0	4.8	10.4	5.6	125
National govt.	48.6	34.5	4.7	2.0	6.1	4.1	148
Total cases	506	586	96	131	206	318	1843

Table 4.5
Matching appellants and respondents – the opponents of appellants in criminal cases in the Supreme Court of Canada

Appellant	Indiv. (%)	Bus. (%)	Assoc. (%)	Local (%)	Prov. govt. (%)	Fed. Govt. (%)	N
Individuals	–	–	–	1.5	85.2	13.2	937
Business	–	–	–	4.8	66.5	28.6	21
Associations	–	–	–	–	100	0	2
Local govt.	0	0	0	0	0	0	0
Provincial govt.	97.1	2.9	0	–	–	–	279
National govt.	77.7	22.2	0	–	–	–	45
Total cases	302	17	00	14	810	132	1291

post-Charter years. Thus the national government has a relatively minor direct role in setting the Supreme Court's agenda.

Examined next are the rates at which different *pairs* of litigants appear. Courts resolve disputes between adversaries. Thus one cannot appreciate the impact of any particular type of litigant without considering who the opposing litigant is. Litigation varies substantially according to the issues being disputed, so tables 4.4 and 4.5 are separated according to whether the Supreme Court case is civil or criminal.

In civil cases, individuals bring more appeals against other individuals than against any other type of litigant. However, individuals also appeal often against the federal government and businesses.

Similarly, businesses appeal most often against other businesses. All levels of government are most likely to appeal against individuals, though their appeal rates against businesses are almost as high. Few appeals by any level of government are brought against other governments.

Most criminal appeals originate as prosecutions filed by some level of government against either an individual or a business. Canada's Criminal Code, a federal statute, is often the legal provision litigated; however, most prosecutions are initiated by a provincial government; therefore it is not surprising that most criminal appeals filed by both individuals and businesses are against a provincial government. Appeals by provincial governments are overwhelmingly against individuals, whereas more than one-fifth of criminal appeals filed by the federal government are against business defendants.

The final element to be examined is the *source* of appeals. Tables 4.6 and 4.7 show the province of origin of cases heard by the Supreme Court.

Table 4.6 displays the origins of cases. Canada's provinces vary greatly in population: Ontario is home to 38 per cent of Canadians and Quebec to 24 per cent; Prince Edward Island, Yukon, and the Northwest Territories *combined* account for less than 1 per cent of the country's total population.[2] The Supreme Court's docket reflects these population differences, with some variations between relative population and relative docket share. In four of the five time periods examined, more cases came from Ontario than from any other province; yet in every period, Ontario was 'underrepresented' on the Court, in the sense that the proportion of the docket coming from Ontario was smaller than the province's population might warrant. In the most recent period (2000 to 2003) there were actually fewer cases from Ontario than from either Alberta or Quebec.

At the other extreme, British Columbia – one of the fastest-growing provinces – has generated a substantially larger number of cases than might be expected. Since 1991 more than 20 per cent of all cases on the Court's docket have come from BC even though the province has barely 13 per cent of the national population. Manitoba, too, has generated more Supreme Court cases than its population size would predict, though in absolute terms the proportion of the docket coming from that province has always been small. This 'overrepresentation' does not seem to be a consistent regional characteristic; for example, the flow of cases from Alberta does closely reflect population share.

Table 4.6
Change over time in the source of appeals to the Supreme Court of Canada:
Change in province of origin

Province	Percentage of cases from province					
	Total	70–75	76–83	84–90	91–99	00–03
British Columbia	16.9	13.5	12.0	15.1	21.2	22.6
Alberta	10.0	11.21	09.3	10.9	09.9	07.8
Saskatchewan	04.5	05.8	04.1	05.6	04.0	02.8
Manitoba	06.4	06.4	06.6	09.6	04.7	05.0
Ontario	28.3	30.4	28.8	25.3	28.8	17.9
Quebec	26.9	23.5	28.0	23.6	16.9	23.5
New Brunswick	03.5	03.5	04.3	02.9	04.0	02.2
Nova Scotia	04.3	04.0	04.6	03.4	05.7	02.2
PEI	00.8	00.6	00.4	00.4	01.6	00.6
Yukon	00.4	00.4	00.2	00.8	00.2	00.6
Nfld & Lab.	02.3	00.6	01.4	02.3	02.9	04.7
Total cases	2684	481	558	521	805	319

Table 4.7
Change over time in the source of appeals from provincial governments to the Supreme
Court of Canada

Province	Percentage of cases from province					
	Total	70–75	76–83	84–90	91–99	00–03
British Columbia	16.1	23.1	11.8	2.9	16.9	29.3
Alberta	10.8	7.7	20.6	11.6	8.5	6.7
Saskatchewan	4.7	2.6	4.4	11.6	4.6	0
Manitoba	5.8	2.6	5.9	10.1	3.8	6.7
Ontario	22.6	33.3	20.6	23.2	22.3	18.7
Quebec	23.7	20.5	19.1	33.3	20.0	26.7
New Brunswick	4.5	2.6	5.9	2.9	6.2	2.7
Nova Scotia	4.2	7.7	7.4	0	4.6	2.7
PEI	1.8	0	0	0	4.6	1.3
Yukon	0.3	0	0	0	0.8	0
Nfld & Lab.	5.0	0	2.9	4.4	7.7	5.3
Total cases	380	39	68	69	130	75

These disparities among the provinces are interesting, but there is no obvious explanation for them. BC and Manitoba were overrepresented and Ontario was underrepresented both before and after the 1975 docket control reforms – and, for that matter, before and after the Charter was adopted. None of the justices interviewed could suggest any reasons for the provincial disparities.

Table 4.7 focuses on cases in which a provincial government was a litigant in the Supreme Court. The results are again roughly in line with provincial population figures, and the disparities generally parallel the ones just described: the Ontario government is underrepresented, while the BC and Manitoba governments are overrepresented. Among the other large provinces, Alberta and Quebec appear about as often as would be expected based on population.

Who Wins in Cases Decided by the Supreme Court?

The next section considers who wins and who loses in Supreme Court litigation. More than thirty years ago, Galanter (1974) made a compelling case that the 'haves' tend to come out ahead in litigation. Since then, a host of studies have examined the advantages of being a 'repeat player' (RP) in various courts. Most scholarly studies have found that the classes of litigants with the greatest resources and the lowest relative stakes in litigation have the highest rates of success in trial courts; that governments have been more successful in litigation than have businesses and other organizations; and that organizations have been more successful than individual litigants (Atkins 1991; McCormick 1993a; Songer, Sheehan, and Haire 1999; Wheeler et al. 1987).

Galanter (1974) also suggests that these 'haves' win more often because they are likely to have favourable law on their side, superior material resources, and better lawyers, and because a number of advantages accrue to them as a result of their RP status. Superior resources allow the 'haves' to hire the best available legal representation and to incur legal expenses, such as those associated with extensive discovery and expert witnesses; this may increase the chances of success at trial. In addition, as RPs, they reap the benefits of greater litigation experience, including the ability to develop and implement a comprehensive litigation strategy, which may involve forum shopping and making informed judgments regarding the prospects of winning at trial or on appeal.

At the appellate level, there is some support for Galanter's proposition that the 'haves' come out ahead in a wide variety of venues. Wheeler and his colleagues (1987) studied the decisions of sixteen state

Supreme Courts in the United States from 1870 to 1970, applying the general framework of Galanter's analysis in order to examine the relative success on appeal of five general classes of litigants. Overall, their findings were quite consistent with Galanter's proposition (though the relative advantage of RPs was modest). In match-ups between stronger and weaker parties, the stronger, RP party was consistently more successful, with its advantage averaging 5 per cent. Most notable was the consistent success of governments compared to that of litigants without organizational resources (ibid., 438).

Why do stronger parties enjoy greater success? The Wheeler study's explanation is consistent with the one offered by Galanter. According to Wheeler and colleagues, 'the greater resources of the stronger parties presumably confer advantages beyond hiring better lawyers on appeal. Larger organizations may be more experienced and thus better able to conform their behaviour to the letter of the law or to build a better trial court record, matters on which we have no evidence. Experience and wealth also imply the capacity to be more selective in deciding which cases to appeal or defend when the lower court loser appeals' (ibid., 441).

In 1999, Farole updated the Wheeler study by examining the decisions of five state Supreme Courts between 1975 and 1990. He found general confirmation that the 'haves' still come out ahead. Specifically, he found that the advantage of the stronger party was greatest when it was the appellant, which suggests that the ability of RPs to exercise greater selectivity in deciding which cases to appeal was an important contributor to success. However, what Farole found most striking was the substantial increase since the Wheeler study in the magnitude of the net advantage enjoyed by governments (on success of government, see also Kritzer 2003).

Further confirmation of Galanter's insights came in an analysis of decisions by U.S. appeals courts. An analysis of published and unpublished decisions concluded that the success rates of governments were roughly four times as high as the success rates of individuals and one-and-a-half times the success rates of businesses. Similarly, businesses consistently won a substantial majority of the cases in which they were pitted against individuals without organizational support (Songer and Sheehan 1992). Applying the measure of 'net advantage' developed by the Wheeler study, businesses enjoyed an advantage of nearly 20 percentage points over individuals but were disadvantaged compared to the federal government by over 40 percentage points. In a multivariate analysis with controls for the type of issue and judicial ideology, litigant status continued to be strongly related to case outcome. Moreover, these patterns in the appeals courts have persisted for at least three-quarters of a century (Songer, Sheehan, and Haire 1999).

Several analyses applying Galanter's theoretical perspectives to court decisions in other countries have generated comparable findings. Atkins (1991) found that in the British Court of Appeals, governments enjoyed a 25 per cent advantage over corporate litigants and that corporations enjoyed a 14 per cent advantage over individuals (1991, 895). Preliminary studies of the South African and Indian high courts have noted a similar pattern, with the 'haves' enjoying higher success rates than the 'have nots' (Haynie, Sheehan, and Songer 1994). Thus the general thesis that RP 'haves' tend to fare well and that one-shotter litigants often lose seems to have considerable cross-national validity, at least among countries in the English common law tradition.

The major exceptions to the general pattern of success in appellate courts have been observed in the Supreme Courts of the United States and the Philippines. Sheehan, Mishler, and Songer (1992) examined the success of ten categories of parties in the U.S. Supreme Court over a thirty-six-year period and found little evidence that RP status or litigants' resources had a major impact on success in that forum. The federal government was the most successful litigant, and poor individuals had the lowest overall rates of success; however, other patterns of success were not consistent with predictions derived from Galanter's theory. A similar failure to find a consistent pattern of success for the most advantaged litigants was observed in an analysis of the decisions of the Philippines' Supreme Court. In fact, Haynie (1994 and 1995) found that individuals tended to have higher rates of success than either governments or business litigants. Haynie suggests that in developing societies, courts may encounter pressure to support redistributive policies as a means of enhancing their political legitimacy. This concern for legitimacy may tend to outweigh the advantage that the 'haves' would otherwise tend to enjoy as a result of superior experience and resources. Haynie's (2003) subsequent analysis of the decisions of the South African Appellate Division from 1950 to 1990 (approximately the rise and fall of apartheid) found that the government had the highest average success rate as both appellant and respondent, 'but only barely' (2003, 110).

To date, only one study has applied party capability theory to Canadian courts. McCormick (1993a) investigated Supreme Court decisions between 1949 and 1992. He found that the combined success rate of big businesses was slightly lower than that of the federal government and slightly higher than that of provincial governments. Other businesses and 'natural persons' had substantially lower levels of overall success. A similar finding emerged using the measure of 'net advantage' developed in the earlier studies of U.S. appellate courts (Wheeler et al. 1987; Songer and Sheehan 1992). The federal government enjoyed a net advantage approximately 5 percentage points higher than that of big businesses, 15 points higher than that of other businesses, and approximately 30 points higher than that of individuals (1993, 532).

The McCormick study provides a useful beginning point for the following analysis of winners and losers in the Supreme Court of Canada. It does, though, have several limitations. First, as with any study, it is possible that the results are time bound. The analysis below extends the examination begun by McCormick more than a decade, to the end of 2003. This longer period permits an analysis of whether there has been any substantial change over time and especially whether the Charter has affected the success of high-resource RPs relative to 'have nots.' Several studies have suggested that 'the worldwide growth of democracy and the spread of constitutionalism and multinational judicial structures outside the United States seem to be leading to a greater emphasis on rights and their protection by courts' (Grossman, Kritzer, and Macaulay 1999, 808). In spite of earlier work suggesting that formal constitutional protections by themselves are insufficient to advance rights and thus protect 'have nots' (Rosenberg 1991; Epp 1998; see also Camp Keith 2002a, 2002b), it may be time to re-evaluate this conventional wisdom by comparing the overall success of 'have nots' in Canadian courts before and after the Charter.

In addition, the success of different categories of litigants may be conditioned by the nature of the legal issues involved. McCormick (1993) provides only an overall assessment of who wins and who loses. While such an assessment is useful (especially in a path-breaking analysis like McCormick's), it would be even more useful for later investigations to explore whether the relative success of different categories of litigants depends on the differences in the rules applicable in different issue areas.

Data and Measurement

The data are derived from the universe of published decisions of the Supreme Court of Canada for the years 1970 to 2003. A total of 3,057 cases are included in the analysis. To make the findings as comparable as possible to existing party capability studies from other countries, the operational definitions of litigant classifications, outcomes, and issues have been designed to be congruent with earlier analyses of the Philippines (Haynie 1994), U.S. appeals courts (Songer and Sheehan 1992), and the U.S. Supreme Court (Sheehan, Mishler, and Songer 1992).

First, the rates of success of different categories of litigants were examined, using very broad classes of litigants similar to those applied in many other party capability studies. For each litigant a separate computation was made of the proportion of time the litigant won as the appellant and as the respondent; also computed was an overall success rate combining all appearances before the Supreme Court.[3] The index of 'net advantage used in many previous studies was also computed (see below). This index of net advantage was computed for all cases involving each general category of litigants and was also computed for specific match-ups between specified pairs of litigants (e.g., all those cases involving a business pitted against a provincial government).

As Wheeler and his colleagues pointed out in their analysis of state Supreme Courts, specific information about the wealth or other resources of particular parties in a given case is not often available in court decisions. This absence of information about litigant resources is characteristic of the decisions in the Supreme Court of Canada as well. Since the data were derived from court decisions, often it was not possible unambiguously to classify one litigant as having greater litigation resources than its opponent. Thus we adopted the strategy utilized in most previous party capability studies (e.g., Wheeler et al. 1987; Songer and Sheehan 1992; McCormick 1993a) of assigning litigants to general categories and then making assumptions about which class usually has greater litigation resources. For this analysis, litigants have been classified into seven categories: federal government (including its agencies and officials), provincial government agencies and officials, local government agencies and officials, private and not-for-profit associations, businesses (including corporations), small businesses (included in some analyses), and individuals or natural persons. It has been assumed that on average, the federal government would have the greatest litigation resources, that provinces would have the second-greatest average resources, and that local governments would be third, businesses fourth, associations fifth, and individuals last. Like Wheeler and colleagues (1987) and Songer and Sheehan (1992), the present study assumes that when business and government contend, the government is usually stronger because even when the government's financial resources are no greater than those of business, the government agency is more likely to be an RP (or at least a more frequent RP in the particular issue area at hand).

In an attempt to be consistent with McCormick (1993) and Songer and Sheehan (1992), all 'boards and agencies established by and operating under the authority of the respective levels of government, as well as ministers and agency heads acting in their official capacity' have been included in each government category (McCormick 1993a, 527). Litigants have been classified as natural persons only if it seems that they were neither government officials nor officers or owners of a business. For example, when a litigant was listed only by name in the title of the case, but it was apparent from the opinion that this litigant was the manager of an auto repair shop who was being sued for defective repair work, the litigant has been coded as a business.

Following the Wheeler study's approach (later adopted by Songer and Sheehan [1992] and by McCormick [1993]), winners and losers have been defined by looking at 'who won the appeal in its most immediate sense, without attempting to view the appeal in some larger context' (Wheeler et al. 1987, 415). Thus, for example, if the decision of a provincial appellate court to award damages to an individual allegedly injured by his employer was appealed by the employer and the appeal was allowed by the Supreme Court, the appellant (i.e., the business employer) has been coded as winning, regardless of whether the doctrine announced in the decision might be supposed in general to more often benefit workers or their employers. If in this hypothetical same case, the Supreme Court affirmed the decision of the provincial court, dismissed the appeal, or concluded that the appeal could not be allowed, the respondent individual has been coded as winning. Cases in which the winner could not be determined unambiguously (e.g., most of the decisions in which the decision of the lower court was affirmed in part and reversed in part) have been excluded from analysis.

As with earlier studies of party capability, the focus is on whether any relative advantage accrues to those classes of litigants who enjoy superior litigation resources. Appeals are brought by litigants who have already lost at least once in the lower courts. Therefore, even if appellate justice is blind and even if litigation resources are irrelevant, one would expect respondents to prevail in most appeals (Songer and Sheehan 1992, 240). Indeed, a cursory examination of the data indicates that respondents win more often than appellants. So in order to assess whether the hypothesized relative advantage of litigants with superior resources in fact exists, it is not enough to know which class of litigants won more often in an absolute sense. It is to be expected that the over-all success rate of a given class of litigants will be influenced by how often those litigants have appeared in the national high court as appel-lants rather than as respondents. We also need to know whether a given class of litigants was 'better able than other parties to buck the basic tendency of appellate courts to affirm' (Wheeler et al. 1987, 407).

To measure this aspect of relative advantage, a number of studies (ibid.; Songer and Sheehan 1992; McCormick 1993a; Haynie 2003) have computed an 'index of net advantage.' This index is computed for each class of litigants by taking their success rate as appellants and from that figure subtracting the reversal rate when they appear as respon-dents (i.e., by subtracting the success rate of their opponents). This in-dex of advantage is independent of the relative frequency with which different classes of litigants appear as appellants rather than as respon-dents. This is important because, as indicated by the results displayed earlier in this chapter (e.g., see tables 4.2 and 4.3), some litigants appear primarily as appellants and others appear primarily as respondents (e.g., individual natural persons are twice as likely to be appellants, and the federal government is more than twice as likely to be the re-spondent). In addition, it is also independent of the relative propensity of different courts to affirm and is therefore a better measure to use in cross-court comparisons than a simple measure of the proportion of decisions won by a given class of litigants would be (Songer and Shee-han 1992, 241).

Results: Who Wins in Canada?

The first step in the analysis was to compute the overall rates of suc-cess for all litigants over the thirty-four years under study. Table 4.8 presents the success rate for each category of litigant in those cases when they were the appellant, their opponents' success rate when they appeared before the Court as the respondent, and the combined suc-cess rate, which is of course influenced by the relative frequency that the litigant class appeared as the respondent rather than the appellant.[4] Since 1970, the overall pattern of who wins in Canada has been similar to the findings in other advanced democracies around the world. The federal and the provincial governments enjoy substantial higher rates of success than all of the other litigants whether success is measured by the raw ratio of wins in the Supreme Court or by the more nuanced 'net advantage' rate (see table 4.8).

Table 4.8
Combined success rates and net advantage for six general categories of litigants, 1970–2003

Litigant	Success rate as appellant		When respondent opponents' success rate		Net advantage	Combined success rate	N
Individuals	39.0	–	54.0	=	–15.0	41.4%	2500
Business	45.5	–	50.5	=	–5.0	47.4	1293
Associations	41.1	–	49.5	=	–8.4	55.5	238
Local govt.	48.4	–	47.3	=	+01.1	51.0	243
Prov govt.	56.6	–	35.2	=	+21.1	62.5	1418
Federal govt.	56.5	–	35.3	=	+21.2	62.3	644

Private individuals have the lowest rates of success by both measures, while businesses and associations have slightly higher rates of success. The success rates for each category of litigant are quite similar to those found in a recent analysis of the success of litigants in U.S. appellate courts. In Canada, the net advantage of the federal government was only slightly lower than in the United States (21 per cent compared to 25 per cent); the success of individuals was also slightly lower in Canada (–15 per cent compared to –12.6 per cent). In both countries, businesses had slightly negative rates of net advantage (–8.4 versus – 2.8 per cent).[5] These litigant success rates are also quite similar to those found by McCormick in an earlier analysis of the Supreme Court of Canada and to those discovered by Atkins (1991) in a parallel analysis of English appellate courts. Thus it appears that in Canada, as in other industrially advanced nations in the common law world, the 'haves' continue to come out ahead in litigation in appellate courts.

While these results for overall success rates are consistent with past studies, to gain a more complete understanding of the advantages and disadvantages enjoyed by different categories of litigants it is necessary to disaggregate the data to examine how each type of litigant fares against other specific categories of litigants. For that, the analysis turns to specific match-ups. How did different types of litigants fare against other specific categories of litigants? For this, see table 4.9.

Specifically, the data in table 4.9 indicate how the probability that the appellant would win was affected by different combinations of

Table 4.9
Net advantage of repeat player 'haves' for different combinations
of opposing parties

Repeat player 'Have' litigant	'Have-not'	Net advantage
Business	Individual	−11.8
Business	Association	+08.6
Association	Individual	00
Provincial govt.	Individual	+23.0
Provincial govt.	Business	+14.1
Provincial govt.	Association	+07.6
National govt.	Individual	+21.7
National govt.	Business	+15.2
National govt.	Association	+71.4
National govt.	Provincial govt.	+06.5

litigants. In the first column, each category of litigant assumed to have superior litigation resources compared to some of the other categories of litigants is listed. Those litigants are then paired with litigants in the second column who are presumed to be 'have nots' relative to the litigant in the first column. The third column then presents the net advantage of the litigant in column one when the two litigants oppose each other. A positive sign for the net advantage indicates that the litigant assumed by Galanter's party capability theory to be advantaged did in fact win more often (after controlling for who was the appellant and who was the respondent). For example, the net advantage score of +23.0 for the pair Provincial Government/Individual indicates that if one isolates only those cases in which a provincial government is opposed by an individual, the government has a net advantage of 23 percentage points.

All of the match-ups involving either the federal government or a provincial government have the expected result. In each case, the government wins more often. Both governments have a large margin of victory over individuals and a fairly large margin of victory over businesses. And when the federal government is pitted against a provincial government, the former is slightly more likely to win.

Given the previous findings of studies applying party capability theory, the results involving private parties produce more surprising results. Individuals and associations do equally well against each other (though the number of times such a match-up occurs is small). Also contrary to expectations derived from party capability theory, when individuals oppose business interests, the individuals are more likely to prevail by a fairly large margin (almost 12 per cent). These results suggest that the findings related to overall rates of success described above, and the earlier similar findings of McCormick (1993), may have been due to the difference in the frequency with which each litigant faced other types of litigants. Specifically, it suggests that the overall success rates for individuals were lower than the overall rates for businesses because all other litigants usually lost when pitted against the government (federal or provincial) and that individuals were more likely than businesses to face governments when appearing in the Supreme Court. In particular, the low overall success rates of individuals are produced to a considerable degree by the high number of criminal cases decided by the Supreme Court. Since almost all criminal cases pit an individual against government, and since individuals lose most of these cases, the low rate of success of individuals is due more to their lack of success in criminal appeals than to a more generalized lack of success in all litigation.

These findings raise a significant challenge to Galanter's party capability theory. In both Canada and the United States, individuals can certainly be expected to be less likely than businesses or associations to be repeat players and can be expected to usually have fewer resources to spend on quality lawyers, investigators, and so on. Thus, when individuals oppose businesses or associations, the prediction of party capability theory is that the individuals should usually lose. Studies in the United States of such specific match-ups (see Wheeler et al. 1987; Songer, Sheehan, and Haire 1999) have found that they do. Yet table 4.9 suggests that individuals have higher than expected success in Canada.

The next step in the analysis was to determine whether there have been any substantial changes over time in the relative success of different categories of litigants (see table 4.10).

Table 4.10 indicates that there have been no consistent linear trends over time in the tendency of the 'haves' to come out ahead. While the categories are not precisely the same as those used in McCormick's (1993) earlier study of the Supreme Court of Canada, the basic picture remains the same. Governments remain the most successful litigants according to all of the measures used in each time period in the present

Table 4.10
Change over time in the net advantage and combined success rate of appellant and
respondent for six general categories of litigants, 1970–2003

| A Net advantage | | | | | |
Litigant	70–75	76–83	84–90	91–99	00–03
Individual	−15.2	−11.1	−16.8	−20.4	−02.3
Business	−11.2	+03.5	−00.5	−07.3	−07.7
Associations	−12.8	−05.5	−02.7	−03.5	−09.2
Local govt.	+28.2	−18.5	+10.3	−10.2	−23.8
Prov govt.	+26.6	+16.8	+21.8	+24.9	+14.4
Federal govt.	+47.3	+10.7	+13.0	+30.8	+06.4

| B Combined success rates: percentage and number | | | | | |
Litigant	70–75	76–83	84–90	91–99	00–03
Individual	42.7	42.0	39.1	39.6	47.7
	(429)	(490)	(481)	(766)	(262)
Business	44.4	50.9	49.7	46.7	46.2
	(381)	(316)	(177)	(242)	(132)
Associations	43.6	48.9	41.5	46.7	45.5
	(39)	(45)	(41)	(60)	(44)
Local govt.	65.8	41.5	53.8	42.1	38.5
	(82)	(65)	(26)	(38)	(26)
Prov govt.	64.5	61.4	63.8	62.6	57.9
	(110)	(257)	(309)	(508)	(178)
Federal govt.	74.4	59.1	61.5	64.8	53.5
	(90)	(159)	(122)	(182)	(71)

study as well as for the period examined in the earlier McCormick study. The federal government, with a consistently positive net advantage, in every period has been more successful than local governments and than each of the three categories of private litigants. Similarly, provincial governments have maintained a positive net advantage in every period that is higher than the success rates of individuals, businesses, or associations. Businesses have tended to enjoy more success in court than either natural persons or associations throughout the periods examined, though they have been less successful than governments. Nevertheless, table 4.10 reveals a considerable degree of variation in success rates for some categories of litigants. For example, the net advantage of the federal government has varied from a high of +47.3 per cent to a low of +6.4 per cent, while its raw success rates have ranged from 53.5 to 74.4 per cent. Moreover, by both measures of success, the relative success of the federal government compared to that of provincial governments has varied over time. The federal government has been more successful in two periods; provincial governments have been more successful in three. Overall, however, both governments have enjoyed roughly similar levels of success, and there does not appear to be any consistent trend over time that favours one level of government over the other.

While no clear linear trends are apparent in the changes in the success rates of the different types of litigants analysed above, there is some hint that the Charter has modified the relative odds of success for some types of litigants. Theoretically, since most of the Charter's provisions restrain governments' actions in order to protect individual rights, one might expect that the overall success rates of governments would have declined and the success rates of individuals would have increased after the Charter was adopted. To examine this specific matter, the data on litigant success have been collapsed from the previous five periods into two periods representing pre- and post-Charter litigation in the Supreme Court.[6] These pre- versus post-Charter comparisons are presented in table 4.11.

The most apparent finding from this analysis is that there has been virtually no change in litigants' success rates since the Charter was adopted. Local governments seem to have had lower rates of success in the post-Charter period, but almost all the Charter litigation decided by the Supreme Court has involved either the federal government or a provincial government. This change, then, does not appear to be directly attributable to the Charter. The success rates of both the federal government and provincial governments are essentially unchanged.[7] The success rates for individuals have changed slightly, but contrary to the theoretical expectations about the Charter's impact, individuals have had marginally lower success rates since the Charter was adopted. So the data suggest that the Charter has not had any measurable effect on litigants' overall chances of success in the Supreme Court.

Table 4.11
Change over time in net advantage and combined success rate as appellant
and respondent for six general categories of litigants, 1970–2003

	Pre-Charter			Post-Charter		
Litigant	Net Advantage	Combined success rate %	(n)	Net Advantage	Combined success rate%	(n)
Individuals	−13.7	42.2	991	−16.0	40.8	1509
Business	−04.8	47.3	742	−05.1	47.5	551
Associations	−10.1	45.2	93	−06.9	44.8	145
Local govt.	+07.1	54.9	153	−09.3	44.4	90
Prov govt.	+21.0	63.4	423	+21.6	62.1	995
Federal govt.	+21.8	63.2	269	+21.0	61.6	375
			2671			3665

All of the analyses thus far indicate that for all time periods, provincial governments have been consistently successful in the Supreme Court. This raises an obvious supplemental question: Have provincial governments been successful across the board, or have some provinces been more successful than others? Table 4.12 is designed to answer that question.

The data reflect the same two measures of litigant success used in the earlier analyses: the overall success rates of the provinces, and their net advantage scores. These scores are based on the appearances of each province against all types of litigants. Most of these appearances have been against individuals or businesses. There have been too few cases in which one province opposed another province in the Supreme Court for a meaningful analysis to be conducted of such direct match-ups. All the provinces appearing before the Supreme Court in a non-trivial number of cases have combined success rates above 50 per cent and positive net advantage scores; that said, considerable variation exists. Most notable is the very low success rate for Quebec relative to all the other provinces that appear often in the Supreme Court. Ontario, BC, Manitoba, New Brunswick, and Saskatchewan all have net advantage rates more than twice as high as Quebec's. Ontario has had the greatest success among the six provinces that appear before the Supreme Court most often, but the success rates of Manitoba and BC are not far behind. When this finding is combined with the data in table 4.7, it appears that frequency of participation has no relation to a province's degree of success. The provinces with

Table 4.12
Combined success rates and net advantage for provincial governments in the Supreme Court of Canada, 1970–2003

Litigant	Success rate as appellant (%)		When respondent opponents' success rate (%)		Net advantage	Combined success rate	N
British Columbia	59.1	–	37.2	=	+21.9	61.7	230
Alberta	52.4	–	35.3	=	+17.1	61.4	158
Saskatchewan	72.2	–	35.9	=	+36.3	66.7	57
Manitoba	60.9	–	35.6	=	+25.3	63.5	96
Ontario	51.1	–	24.8	=	+26.3	69.7	393
Quebec	52.8	–	42.9	=	+09.9	55.5	254
New Brunswick	88.2	–	47.5	=	+40.7	63.2	57
Nova Scotia	57.9	–	44.6	=	+13.3	56.0	75
PEI	50.0	–	30.0	=	+20.0	62.5	16
Yukon	00	–	25.0	=	–25.0	60.0	5
Nfld & Lab.	63.2	–	42.9	=	+20.3	59.6	47

the highest success rates are drawn from provinces with low relative rates of participation (Ontario) as well as those with high rates of participation (BC and Manitoba).

There do not seem to be any obvious explanations for the provincial variations just described. Based on party capability theory, one might predict that the most frequent RPs win most often; but that prediction is not supported by the data. Alternatively, one might surmise that the quality of legal representation varies among the provinces; but none of the justices interviewed suggested that the quality of legal representation varies by province or that some provinces' courts are more closely attuned to trends on the Supreme Court. Finally, one might speculate that the provinces that are best 'represented' with their own justices on the Supreme Court fare the best; but that prediction is also not supported. Indeed, throughout almost the entire period studied, the two provinces with three justices included both the province with the highest success rate (Ontario) and the one with the lowest (Quebec).

The final step in the analysis of litigant success was to examine the effect of litigant characteristics within the framework of a multivariate model. The basic question to be answered by the model in table 4.13 is

Table 4.13
Logistic regression models of the likelihood of a decision for the appellant in decisions by
the Supreme Court of Canada, 1970–2003

Variable	MLE	SE	Change estimated probability
Business appellant	−0.111	0.109	−.027
Association appellant	−0.213	0.190	−.051
Local govt. appellant	−0.039	0.225	−.009
Provincial govt. appellant	0.552***	0.142	+.137
National govt. appellant	0.398**	0.166	+.099
Business respondent	−0.057	0.117	−.013
Association respondent	−0.135	0.226	−.033
Local govt. respondent	−0.134	0.191	−.032
Provincial govt. respondent	−0.331**	0.129	−.080
National govt. respondent	−0.562***	0.136	−.131
Criminal case	−0.406***	0.108	−.098
Intercept	−0.004	0.104	

N = 3057
−2Log L = 4076.92
Chi sq. = 109.61***

* P < .05
** P < .01
*** P < .001

how the presence of each type of appellant and each type of respondent affects the probability that the appellant will win. Besides the variables representing the basic concern with party capability theory, a control has been added for the broad issue category in the case (i.e., whether or not the case involved a criminal appeal) to ensure that the success or absence of success of a particular type of litigant is not dependent on the particular issue involved.[8] For example, it is known that in some courts a substantial number of appeals by criminal defendants are legally frivolous; thus the appellants in such cases, who are almost exclusively natural persons, will have very low rates of success, which might not be a good indicator of their probability of success in other types of cases. Since the dependent variable is dichotomous, we employ logistic regression. The excluded categories among the litigant categories are natural person appellants and natural person respondents. For each independent variable, we have calculated the maximum likelihood estimate (MLE) along with its standard error. The MLEs represent the change in the logistic function that occurs from one unit change in each independent variable. Since these coefficients are difficult to interpret intuitively, in the last column of the table we provide a measure of the change in the estimated probability of a vote supporting the appellant caused by a one unit change in the independent variable while all other variables are held at their median value.

The results provide partial support for party capability theory. As expected from that theory, the appellant is substantially more likely to win if it is a government (federal *or* provincial) than if it is a natural person. In fact, the last column in table 4.13 indicates that the likelihood the appellant will win increases by 10 percentage points when the federal government rather than an individual is the appellant. The results are substantively strong and are significant at the .001 level. Similarly, appellants are significantly *less* likely to win if the respondent is a government instead of a natural person. The appellant's chances of victory drop by over 13 percentage points when the federal government is the respondent and by 8 points when a provincial government is the respondent. But contrary to the expectations derived from party capability theory, the likelihood of appellant success is not affected significantly by whether the respondent is a local government, business or private group, or association rather than an individual. Perhaps even more surprising, having a business or an association as the appellant instead of an individual decreases the odds of appellant success, though the coefficients fail to reach statistical significance. That is to say, the evidence suggests that when one controls for issue, individuals and natural persons tend to have greater success as appellants than do businesses.

The issue control variable is significantly related to the probability of appellant success, which justifies the decision to include such a control in the model. Specifically, the data for the change in the estimated probability of success in the last column indicate that appellants have a 10 per cent lower rate of success in criminal appeals than in other types of cases.

The next step was to follow up the preliminary analysis (above) in order to examine the possibility of change over time in the effect that particular types of litigants have had on the chance of appellant

Table 4.14
Logistic regression models of the likelihood of a decision for the appellant in decisions by the Supreme Court of Canada, pre- vs post-Charter periods

Variable	Pre-Charter MLE	SE	Post-Charter MLE	SE
Business appellant	−0.1562	0.151	−0.021	0.162
Association appellant	0.086	0.298	−0.478*	0.253
Local govt. appellant	−0.006	0.291	0.050	0.362
Provincial govt. appellant	0.464*	0.235	0.603***	0.185
National govt. appellant	0.416*	0.246	0.407*	0.230
Business respondent	−0.201	0.162	0.129	0.174
Association respondent	0.180	0.355	−0.388	0.302
Local govt. respondent	−0.409	0.252	0.323	0.312
Provincial govt. respondent	−0.460*	0.204	−0.256	0.174
National govt. respondent	0.649**	−0.203	−0.484**	0.186
Criminal case	−0.418**	0.179	−0.431***	0.138
Intercept	−0.014	0.142	−0.001	0.154
N =	1294		1781	
−2Log L =	1707.17		2352.42	
Chi sq. =	44.50***		80.14***	

* P < .05
** P < .01
*** P < .001

success. To explore this topic further, the basic model in table 4.13 above has been repeated on separate samples of cases from the pre- and post-Charter periods.

The separate analyses for each period result in very similar patterns of results. Both before and after the Charter, appellants were most likely to win if they represented a government (federal or provincial) and least likely to win if they were opposed by a government. The only surprising finding was that associations and interest group appellants were significantly less likely to win in the post-Charter period than in the pre-Charter period. These results seem inconsistent with the claims of Morton and Knopff (2000) that the Charter has been the catalyst for a number of interest groups (described by Morton and Knopff as the 'Court Party') to succeed in the courts with regard to shaping public policy.

The previous two tables indicate that appellants have significantly less success in criminal appeals than in other cases heard before the Supreme Court. To further explore the effect that issues have on litigant success, the models of the previous two tables have been run again for all non-criminal appeals. To make the interpretations more intuitively easier, the excluded categories of litigants are business appellants and business respondents. We again provide a measure in the table's last column of the change in the estimated probability of a vote supporting the appellant caused by a one unit change in the independent variable while all other variables are held at their median value. The results are displayed in table 4.15.

Once again, the success of provincial and federal government litigants is apparent. Appellants are more likely to win if a government is the appellant and more likely to lose if a government is the respondent. For example, with all other variables at their median value, the likelihood that the appellant will win rises from 46 per cent when the appellant is a business to 58 per cent when the appellant is a provincial government. Similarly, changing the respondent from a business to the federal government reduces the chances of a win by the appellant by over 8 points, from 46 to 38 per cent. The only substantial change from the earlier results is that when analysis is limited to non-criminal cases, appellants are significantly more likely to win when the appellant is an individual than when it is a business. Though the last column in table 4.15 shows that chances of a win by the appellant are only 5 percentage points higher when the appellant is an individual rather than a business, the results still stand in contrast to earlier studies in both the United States (Wheeler et al. 1987; Songer, Sheehan, and Haire 1999) and in Canada (McCormick 1993), which found that business litigants were substantially more likely than individual natural persons to win in appellate courts. However, those earlier studies combined civil with criminal appeals and thus missed the fact that the success of individuals is much greater in non-criminal than in criminal appeals. These findings raise substantial questions about the applicability of Galanter's party capability theory to the Supreme Court of Canada. Even in non-criminal cases, private persons are typically one-shotters rather than RPs, and presumably they have fewer resources than businesses to invest in litigation. But the results in table 4.15 suggest that in spite of these presumed disadvantages, individuals are more successful than either businesses or associations.

To gain insight into the magnitude of the difference in success rates of litigants in non-criminal cases, previous calculations for the com-

Table 4.15
Logistic regression models of the likelihood of a decision for the appellant in decisions
in non-criminal cases by the Supreme Court of Canada, 1970–2003

Variable	MLE	SE	Change estimated probability
Individual appellant	0.214*	0.114	+.052
Association appellant	−0.124	0.197	−.031
Local govt. appellant	−0.048	0.236	−.014
Provincial govt. appellant	0.505**	0.202	+.123
National govt. appellant	0.413*	0.188	+.101
Individual respondent	−0.133	0.125	+.020
Association respondent	−0.114	0.228	−.003
Local govt. respondent	−0.022	0.199	+.019
Provincial govt. respondent	−0.222#	0.168	−.030
National govt. respondent	−0.456***	0.147	−.087
Intercept	−0.149	0.098	

N = 1794
−2Log L = 2452.29
Chi sq. = 23.64**

* P < .05
** P < .01
*** P < .001
# .05 < P < .10

bined success rates and net advantage of each litigant type have been
repeated for non-criminal cases only. Following this examination of the
overall rates, success rates for selected match-ups between litigants
presumed to have greater litigation resources and those presumed to
be relative 'have nots' have been repeated for non-criminal cases alone.
The results appear in tables 4.16 and 4.17.

Turning first to the overall rates of success for each litigant type, it
appears that the success rates for individuals are only marginally
higher than the success rates for businesses and associations. The
combined success rates for individuals are only 2 and 4 percentage
points higher respectively than the rates for businesses and associations. Similarly, the net advantage scores are just 3 and 6 points higher.
But these overall rates are affected by the proportion of times each

Table 4.16
Combined success rates and net advantage for six general categories of litigants,
1970–2003, non-criminal cases only

Litigant	Success rate as appellant		When respondent opponents' success rate		Net advantage	Combined success rate	N
Individuals	49.7	–	51.2	=	–01.5	49.4	1242
Business	45.9	–	50.7	=	–04.8	47.5	1252
Associations	41.3	–	49.0	=	–07.7	45.3	234
Local govt.	45.4	–	50.8	=	–05.4	47.7	220
Prov govt.	57.9	–	46.8	=	+11.1	55.0	331
Federal govt.	55.1	–	40.8	=	+14.3	58.2	469

Table 4.17
Net advantage of repeat player 'haves' for different combinations of opposing parties,
non-criminal cases only

Repeat player 'Have' litigant	'Have-not'	Net advantage
Business	Individual	–13.0
Business	Association	+08.6
Association	Individual	+02.7
Provincial govt.	Individual	+16.5
Provincial govt.	Business	+09.3
Provincial govt.	Association	+04.8
National govt.	Individual	+06.9
National govt.	Business	+17.7
National govt.	Association	+73.4
National govt.	Provincial govt.	+20.7

litigant faces either the federal or a provincial government. As noted earlier, both levels of government continue to have high success rates in non-criminal as well as criminal cases, so the more often another litigant type faces one of these governments, the lower their overall success rates become.

To get around this potential skewing of the results, the data in table 4.17 allow a focus on those cases in which an individual directly confronted a business litigant in the Supreme Court. Surprisingly, in these match-ups, the natural person was more often successful, and by a substantial margin (reflected in a net advantage score of 13.0 for individuals). This success of individuals did not hold up, however, when individuals faced associations; in those match-ups, associations were more successful by a small margin.

Table 4.17 provides one more confirmation of the success of governments. Both provincial governments and the federal government were successful in match-ups against every one of the categories of private litigants in non-criminal cases.

The analysis of litigant success ends with a further exploration of the Charter's impact. Table 4.14 showed that, overall, the Charter has had little impact on the success of different categories of litigants. However, an implication of the results immediately above is that the success of litigants may be different in criminal and non-criminal cases. Thus, to gain a greater understanding of the Charter's effects on rates of litigant success, further analysis was run on the sample of cases limited to those in the Charter period that pitted an individual against some level of government. Analyses were run separately for criminal and non-criminal cases. Since the dependent variable was again dichotomous (i.e., Did the individual win or lose?), logistic regression was again used.

The independent variables in the model are whether the individual is the appellant or the respondent, whether the government opponent is the federal government (i.e., not provincial or local government), and whether the case involves a Charter issue. In criminal cases, individuals were less likely to win if they were the appellant and if they were opposed by the federal government. However, the presence of a Charter issue raised by the individual increased his or her chances of success to a statistically significant degree. In contrast, for non-criminal issues, the presence of a Charter issue decreased the likelihood that the individual would win. These results help explain why analyses of the Charter's overall effect have suggested no effect. Since those earlier analyses combined criminal and non-criminal issues, the effects of the Charter in the different types of cases in effect cancelled each other out. In contrast, table 4.18 suggests that the Charter has significantly improved the chances of victory of criminal defendants in litigation that reaches the Supreme Court.

Table 4.18
Logistic regression models of the effect of a Charter issue on the likelihood of support
for an individual litigant facing a government opponent in decisions by the Supreme Court
of Canada, 1984–2003

Variable	Criminal case MLE	SE	Civil case MLE	SE
Individual is appellant	−0.504*	0.143	0.098	0.283
Charter issue	0.273*	0.164	−0.577*	0.289
National govt. opponent	−0.764**	0.247	0.506	0.274
Intercept	−0.266	0.143	−0.360	0.278
N =	889		232	
−2Log L =	1121.36		312.07	
Chi sq. =	19.53***		7.17*	

* $P < .05$
** $P < .01$
*** $P < .001$

Discussion and Conclusion

The Supreme Court of Canada is increasingly understood as playing a major role in shaping national policy. Given its importance in policy making, many scholars and politicians have jumped into a debate over whether the Court's role is 'democratic.' In one sense, it obviously is not a 'democratic' institution. Its members are not elected and are essentially immune from removal from office; certainly they have no fear of removal motivated by a disagreement with the policy positions they support on the bench. So at least in a formal sense, they are not accountable to public majorities.

As noted in previous chapters, the justices are also far from the democratic ideal of being 'representative' in terms of reflecting the characteristics of the public at large. A portrait of the Supreme Court does not look like a portrait of Canada. Nevertheless, one might argue that elected officials in nearly all modern democracies have much more elite backgrounds than the population of the nation and that compared to other political elites, the justices seem about as representative as elected officials. And compared to the judiciaries in similar democracies, the Supreme Court of Canada *is* quite representative. For instance, there is greater geographic representation on that Court than on the top courts of either the United States or Britain. In terms of gender diversity, the Canadian Court far surpasses the courts in the United States and Britain, each of which has only one female justice out of nine and twelve respectively.

Beyond electoral accountability and representation, there is another crucial component of democracy: the ability of a broad spectrum of people and interests to gain access to decision makers and to effectively raise their concerns for deliberation and decision. In this respect, the Supreme Court of Canada appears to be more representative than that country's elected officials, though direct comparison is difficult. Nevertheless, this chapter's findings make it clear that ordinary people seem to have substantial access to the Court. In particular, the Court's agenda is heavily influenced by the concerns brought by private individuals who are not connected to businesses or organized interests.

After examining the success of different categories of litigants in bringing their concerns to the Court, the analysis turned to who actually won in those contests. This analysis was guided largely by the extensive literature on party capability theory. This theory, which has been tested in a number of courts outside Canada, and in one earlier analysis by McCormick (1993) *in* Canada, provides plenty of evidence that in many judicial contexts the repeat player 'haves' tend to come out ahead in litigation.

The findings of the above analysis provide partial support for party capability theory but also raise questions regarding the stability of Galanter's classic argument that those presumed to have greater resources are most likely to succeed. Galanter's thesis has been a mainstay of the public law literature since its introduction to the discipline in 1974. The most notable finding consistent with Galanter's thesis is that Canada's governments, especially its federal and provincial ones, were quite successful over the entire thirty-four years studied. Indeed, both levels of government tended to succeed consistently against all other categories of litigants. Overall, though, the magnitude of that support has been rather modest. In contrast, the expectation derived from party capability theory that businesses should be more successful than individual natural persons does not hold. Especially notable is that in direct match-ups between businesses and individuals, private individuals win more often. The evidence on match-ups between individuals and RP associations and groups is more mixed (owing at least in part to the relatively small number of cases to examine); overall, however, it appears that associations at best enjoy a slim advantage over individuals. Thus, instead of providing general support for Galanter's thesis that the 'haves' in general tend to 'come out ahead' in litigation, these results may be more supportive of Kritzer's (2003) argument that governments enjoy some litigation advantages – of the type shared by all RPs – and that the 'government gorilla' has proved to be an especially effective litigator in modern democracies.

Finally, a recurring question in recent Canadian debates about the judiciary is the impact of the Charter of Rights and Freedoms. The evidence here is mixed as well. In criminal cases a litigant's ability to raise a Charter claim seems to increase the likelihood of winning against the government. But in non-criminal cases, the availability of Charter claims does not seem to benefit individuals overall.

Clearly, more analysis is necessary in order to understand what is driving the variation in the relative rates of success of different types of litigants uncovered in this chapter's analysis. Litigants' resources may not be the best explanation for the variation; rather, the government/Court relationship could be the determining factor. This relationship may be partially predicated on the resources available to the government; but, as in the U.S. Supreme Court, it may also be related to the perception (a priori) the Court has of the quality of governments' cases and to the role played by governments in alleviating docket overloads. Moreover, it may reflect the ability of governmental litigants to choose cases they have a greater likelihood of winning. Clearly, governmental litigants have resource advantages in terms of being RPs, but other institutional factors contribute to this advantage. The finding indicating that businesses do not consistently have decisive advantages in non-criminal cases casts doubt on the impact of resource inequalities. Also, decisions are the collective consensus of a group of individual decision makers, whose personal ideologies clearly play a role in litigants' success rates. The ideologies of the individual decision makers and of the effects of these preferences should also be examined empirically. These concerns are addressed more directly in chapters 7 and 8.

5 Understanding the Decision-Making Process

Judging can be tough. Justice Dickson is quoted as saying that he 'sweated blood' to make his judgments as clear as possible. He often worked through ten drafts of an opinion before circulating it to his colleagues (Sharpe and Roach 2003, 201). Our interviews suggest that the job of a Supreme Court justice typically involves a substantially longer work week than the traditional forty hours. Especially since the Supreme Court gained control of its agenda in 1975, the Court has tended to focus on the tough, complex cases; for the easier cases there is usually no need to disturb the decision of a lower court. Many phrases in the Constitution are written in broad general language so that the constitution can endure for the ages to come. Statutes are often complex and are sometimes written in deliberately vague language either because Parliament knows it lacks the expertise to write precise guidelines to cover all possible future problems with application or because it is easier to reach political compromise on an ambiguous phrase than on a precise statement of the law. Given the complexity of their task, how do the justices organize themselves to handle their workload? And how do they reach and announce decisions? That is the question addressed in the present chapter. To gain a perspective on the decision-making process, a primary source of data for this chapter is interviews with the justices themselves, supplemented by other scholarly accounts that may suggest how consistent the Court has been over the thirty-four years that are the focus of this work.

There has been plenty of literature on the impact of the Court; less is known about how it operates. Indeed, one prominent scholar maintains that the 'internal decision making process of the Supreme Court of Canada has been shrouded in secrecy' (Baar 1988, 70). This chapter attempts to lift that shroud and cast some light on the main features of the decision-making process of the Supreme Court over the past third of a century. To explore these processes we rely on a set of in-depth interviews with the justices of the Court in addition to an analysis of some of the trends in recent decisions as well as other recent commentary.

The Supreme Court of Canada has nine justices, all appointed by the prime minister without the need for formal confirmation by Parliament. Judges serve during good behaviour until they reach the mandatory retirement age of seventy-five. In theory, a justice can be removed by a simple majority vote in Parliament; in practice, no justice has ever been removed from office. When asked about the possibility of removal from office, the justices were unanimously of the opinion that as a practical matter, there was no threat to their independence. The consensus was that it would be 'unheard of' for any government to attempt to remove a justice for political reasons. As Justice H put it, while the government is sometimes upset at Supreme Court decisions, 'they have no access to us' and it would be political suicide for them to be too heavy-handed. Or as Justice C put it, 'sometimes you just have to put your head down and take the abuse [from government officials or the public] ... but no one is worried about their job.'

In Chapter 3 we saw that leave petitions are formally made by panels of three justices appointed by the Chief Justice, though informally the entire Court is able to influence the decisions of those panels. Membership on the leave panels seems to be random, and there was no indication that either seniority or specialization affects which justices heard which petitions. In contrast, decisions on a case's merits can be made by panels of different sizes.

Who Decides?

Once a case has been placed on the Court's agenda (either as an appeal as of right or after a leave petition has been granted), the first decision is who will hear the appeal. Cases are heard either by panels of five or seven justices or by all nine justices sitting *en banc*.[1] The decision on the size of the panel to hear a case and the members of that panel if it is to be less than the whole Court is at the discretion of the Chief Justice.

No formal rules constrain the choice of the Chief Justice regarding panel size, and other justices are typically not consulted in advance (except as to whether a schedule conflict prevents their participation). Nevertheless, there does not appear to be any dissatisfaction among the puisne justices regarding the pattern of choices made by the Chief Justice. Most important for a political analysis of the Court's role, there have been no complaints from within the Court that the Chief Justice has ever 'stacked' a panel to advance her own or any other policy agenda. Notwithstanding these consistent disclaimers, one empirical examination of panel assignments found several interesting patterns. First, in both the Dickson Court and the Lamer Court, justices who often voted with the Chief Justice were significantly more likely than justices who disagreed with the Chief Justice to be appointed to panels. In addition, in both courts, female justices were appointed to panels proportionately more often than male justices (Hausegger 2000).

Panels of five justices are typically used for two quite different purposes. First, in cases coming from the Court of Appeal of Quebec that involve the interpretation of civil law, traditionally a five-justice panel is constituted with all three of the justices from Quebec sitting on the panel.[2] This arrangement appears to reflect the shared view of most justices and their view of the expectations of the broader legal community that civil law questions should not be decided by common law judges. However, the mere fact that a case originated in Quebec does not guarantee a five-justice panel. Appeals from Quebec involving the interpretation of federal law or the Charter of Rights and Freedoms are as likely to be decided by seven or nine justices as cases raising similar issues from other provinces.

According to the justices interviewed for this project, five-justice panels also tend to be used as a labour-saving device in appeals coming to the Court 'as of right' when it appears to the Chief Justice that the appeal does not raise a substantial, or potentially controversial, issue of national importance. In other words, we would expect the full Court to sit most often on the 'important' cases. Figure 5.1 provides some support for this expectation.[3]

The desire for all nine justices to hear a case appears to be especially strong for the most important issues. In the only previous empirical study of the relationship between panel size and case importance, Hausegger (2000) found some support for this norm – that is, that panels should be restricted to the less important cases. She found that in the 1990s, two concrete indicators of case importance – whether there was a Charter issue, and whether interveners participated in the case – were positively related to the probability that the case would be decided by the full Court. As noted earlier (see figure 5.1), our data provide a similar picture.

When the justices were asked how they defined 'importance,' most of them stressed that cases that had potential significance to a wider public rather than just the specific litigants in the case were the ones they most often considered 'important.' To test the idea that 'important' cases are decided by larger panels, two indicators of the potential impact of a case were used: whether the case involved the interpretation of some provision of the constitution, and whether it involved the construction of a federal statute.

Figure 5.1 shows that cases with either a constitutional issue or an issue of statutory interpretation are much more likely to be decided by the whole Court than cases without such issues. Most notably, cases without a constitutional issue are more than three times as likely as constitutional cases to be decided by a five-justice panel. Similarly, those without a statutory issue are more than twice as likely to be decided by a five-justice panel.

It might also be expected that the substance of the dispute would be related to justices' perceptions that an issue is important and therefore worthy of consideration by a larger than minimal panel. To investigate this possibility, most of the cases coming before the Court can be divided into six major categories of issues, all of which appear on the agenda with some frequency. That is, cases can be classified as criminal appeals, civil rights and liberties cases, tax appeals (including both individual and corporate taxes), other public law (primarily involving some type of government regulation of the economy or economic and social conflict), torts, and other private economic cases (including contract disputes). Panel sizes for each of these issue types are presented in table 5.1.

If a case does not fall into a category that tends to trigger a five-justice panel, there is usually a presumption that it will be heard by all nine justices *if possible*. That qualifier is important. It seems relatively common for at least one justice to recuse himself because of a conflict of interest or for one to be unavailable owing to illness or other official obligations. When one justice is unavailable for such a reason, the practice, according to the justices interviewed, has been to strike a panel of seven rather than eight justices in order to avoid a tie vote. In recent years' practice, the number of cases decided by a seven-justice panel has exceeded the number decided by the court *en banc*.

The data indicate that in every issue area except civil liberties, this pattern of having more seven- than nine-justice panels has held. And in civil liberties, the proportion of nine-justice panels has been only

Figure 5.1
Constitutional and statutory cases on the Supreme Court,
by panel size

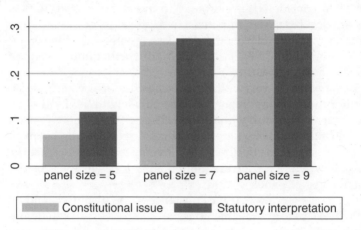

slightly higher than the proportion of seven-justice panels. It is also apparent that there are striking differences in panel size depending on the issue. In tax disputes, torts, and other private economic cases, more than half the appeals are handled by five-justice panels and only about one in six by the full Court. In contrast, more than 90 per cent of civil liberties cases are decided by larger than five-justice panels and more than two-thirds of criminal and other public law cases are decided by more than the minimal panel size.

Our interviews indicated that the justices also expect the chief justice to avoid a five- or seven-justice panel for issues that are likely to divide the Court. This norm apparently has characterized much of the Charter period. Chief Justice Lamer explained his approach, which continues to have at least the tacit support of most of the justices on the current court: 'If there is the possibility that the outcome of a case might be different with fewer than nine judges, I'll do my best to strike a panel of nine judges. How do I know if there will be a division? First, my executive legal officer helps me flag these cases. Also, I know my colleagues and I have a fairly good idea about what they are thinking on particular issues' (in Greene et al. 1998, 115).

Since the size of the panel to hear a case is a prerogative of the chief justice, one might ask whether the various incumbents of the office have taken different approaches to striking panels. Surprisingly, there

Table 5.1
Variations in panel size by issue for selected issues

Issue	Panel size			Total
	5	7	9	
Criminal	27.2%	39.4%	33.4%	
	(353)	(512)	(434)	(1299)
Civil liberties	7.8	45.8	46.4	
	(14)	(82)	(83)	(179)
Tax	51.9	33.7	14.4	
	(94)	(61)	(26)	(181)
Other public law	30.8	37.9	31.4	
	(156)	(192)	(159)	(507)
Torts	57.4	28.1	14.5	
	(178)	(87)	(45)	(310)
Other private economic	54.4	29.2	16.3	
	(300)	(161)	(90)	(551)
Total	(1095)	(1095)	(837)	(3027)

Chi sq. = 294.19; P < .001

has been little research on this question. Consequently, to provide a first descriptive overview, the rates of the use of different-size panels have been constructed for the five chief justices who have presided over the Court for the period of this study (see table 5.2).

Clearly, there have been substantial differences in the practices of the five chief justices. With regard to the use of five-justice panels, there has been a steady decline over time. The biggest decline occurred between the tenures of Chief Justice Fauteux and Chief Justice Laskin. The most likely explanation for this change is the increased docket control the Court received shortly after Laskin became chief justice. When Laskin's creation of panels is divided into cases decided before 1975 and cases decided after 1975,[4] a sharp difference becomes evident, with 62 per cent of the cases Laskin assigned before 1975 having a five-justice panel compared to only 36 per cent of those assigned after 1975. This latter rate is very close to the assignment practices of Dickson, who followed Laskin as chief justice.

Table 5.2
Variations in panel size by chief justice

| Chief justice | Panel size | | | |
	5	7	9	Total
Fauteux	77.5%	08.7%	13.8%	
	(275)	(31)	(49)	(355)
Laskin	39.9	26.9	33.2	
	(353)	(238)	(294)	(885)
Dickson	33.3	56.9	9.8	
	(191)	(326)	(56)	(573)
Lamer	25.7	43.9	30.4	
	(260)	(444)	(307)	(1011)
McLachlin	11.6	36.8	51.7	
	(38)	(121)	(170)	(329)
Total	(1117)	(1160)	(876)	(3153)

Chi sq. = 610.33; P < .001

Chief Justice Dickson assigned cases to five-justice panels at approximately the rate as his immediate predecessor (Laskin), but differed markedly in his propensity to use seven- rather than nine-justice panels. In fact, Dickson was the only chief justice who assigned fewer than 10 per cent of all cases to the full Court. This reduction in the proportion of times that the full Court sat seems to be due to a considerable degree to the high turnover in Court membership that occurred while Dickson was chief justice: six justices left the Court within six years, meaning that quite often it was physically impossible to have a full nine-justice Court sit (and Chief Justice Dickson followed the normal convention that when only eight justices were available, a seven-justice panel would be used in order to prevent a tie vote). Additionally, some of the justices left only after periods of illness that also made them unavailable to sit with a full Court.

One might have expected there to be more 'important' cases after the Charter was adopted and thus that the average panel size would increase again after 1984 before levelling off. However, that is not what happened. Instead, the tendency to use larger panels increased from Dickson to Lamer and then increased again under McLachlin. With

Table 5.3
Variations in panel size by chief justice, controlled by effect of constitutional issue
(No constitutional issue present)

Chief justice	Panel size			Total
	5	7	9	
Fauteux	80.6%	7.6%	11.7%	
	(275)	(26)	(40)	(341)
Laskin	42.4	25.6	32.0	
	(351)	(212)	(265)	(828)
Dickson	40.2	52.3	7.5	
	(155)	(202)	(29)	(386)
Lamer	30.8	44.8	24.4	
	(209)	(304)	(166)	(679)
McLachlin	18.5	41.3	40.2	
	(34)	(76)	(74)	(184)
Total	(1024)	(820)	(574)	(2418)

Chi sq. = 424.82; P < .001

the change from Dickson to Lamer and then from Lamer to McLachlin as chief justice, the proportion of five-justice panels went *down* substantially while the proportion of cases heard by the full Court went *up* substantially.

To further investigate whether the differences among justices are due to case importance or whether they reflect more idiosyncratic differences, table 5.2 is run again for each chief justice using only cases in which there was no constitutional issue present. While the numbers change slightly (see table 5.3), the basic differences among the justices remain more or less the same. Chief Justice Fauteux remains the only one to assign most cases to five-justice panels, and Laskin and Dickson continue to assign a similar number of cases to five-justice panels, but Laskin remains much more likely to assign cases to the full Court. The subsequent tenures of Lamer and McLachlin continue to show an increased tendency to use larger panels even for non-constitutional cases.

The justices interviewed for this project (all of whom were serving on the McLachlin Court at the time of the interviews) all indicated that Chief Justice McLachlin had a strong preference for having the full

Court sit whenever possible unless the issue was clearly of minimal importance.[5] The justices who had also served during the Lamer Court noted that this preference of McLachlin to use the full Court to hear cases represented a departure to some degree from the practices of the Lamer Court. In particular, the justices noted that McLachlin was more likely than Lamer to employ the full court to hear Civil Code cases from Quebec. In contrast, Chief Justice Lamer would use panels of five in some of those cases. In addition, after 1997 the number of as-of-right appeals that were likely to be viewed as candidates for five-justice panels by all of the chief justices declined as a proportion of the Court's docket. Thus, the relatively small proportion of cases using five-justice panels and the large percentage of cases heard by the whole Court under McLachlin seems to be due to a combination of the increased preference of the chief to have the whole Court decide and a decrease in the number of cases raising less important issues.

Preparation for Argument: Policy Makers Who Do Their Own Work

Once a case has been accepted for review and a panel has been struck, detailed consideration of the case begins. The Court holds three sessions a year: from January until an Easter recess; from the end of that break until sometime in June; and from October until Christmas. During those sessions, the Court typically holds hearings for two weeks, usually with two hearings a day, and then has two weeks without hearings to write decisions and prepare for the next set of hearings. Every case granted leave to appeal or appealed as of right is scheduled for oral argument. Most often, the justices designated to decide a case receive their case materials about a month in advance of the hearing date. The materials include the factums (i.e., the written legal arguments from the lawyers) from each side, the 'book of authorities' (copies of all precedent decisions and academic articles counsel wish to cite), and the trial transcripts (Greene et al. 1998). Increasingly, the case materials going to the justices also include factums from one or more interest groups or non-party government officials who have requested to participate as 'interveners' in the case.[6]

In 1981, Justice Dickson explained his approach to preparation. A judgment should reflect the 'intense thought' that ought to precede its writing. Judgment writing is a discipline that 'minimizes snap judgments and casual theorizing' and that 'compels thinking at its hardest.' An opinion must demonstrate that there has been 'intensive and thoughtful study of the record, the briefs, and the law' (Sharpe and Roach 2003, 204).

During the sitting weeks, the justices typically hear one case in the morning and one in the afternoon. The workload from such a schedule is heavy, and the justices do not enjoy the luxury of a nine-to-five day. As an illustration of the justices' workload, Anderson (2001) comments on the typical 'Friday Procession' of Justice Wilson out of her office. Leading off is her 'court messenger' carrying two enormous legal briefcases, 'one on each side for balance.' Next comes her husband John carrying additional briefcases stuffed with more of her weekend reading, and finally the justice herself comes out, often carrying an additional stack of material for the next case (2001, 159).

Each justice develops his or her own style and pace in preparation for oral argument. That said, several common features stand out. First, the norm is that the chamber of each justice prepares for oral argument independently. There is almost no contact between chambers before oral argument. Memos and research findings are not shared, and there is practically no discussion about the case among the justices. During the interviews, all the justices commented that they often approach oral argument without having a very good idea about where the other members of the Court stand on the issues. However, there is some indication that since the clerks work in close proximity to one another in a large collective office, clerks assigned the same task by different justices share their views among themselves (Sharpe and Roach 2003, 211).

To those who are more acquainted with the work habits of top officials in the other branches of government (e.g., committee chairs in Parliament and ministers in the executive), perhaps most surprising is that all justices of the Supreme Court, including the chief justice, personally do a surprisingly large proportion of the actual work required to make effective decisions. Compared to most officials in government and the private sector who hold positions of comparable authority, the justices have surprisingly small staffs. Each justice is limited to three law clerks and a few administrative assistants. Generally, the law clerks serve for a single year and are chosen from among the very top recent graduates of Canada's law schools. Because the prestige of serving as a law clerk on the Supreme Court is so great, the twenty-seven clerks represent the 'cream of the crop' of annual law school graduates (Greene et al. 1998, 114). But however high the quality of their clerks, it still works out that the justices must analyse a large volume of dense legal argumentation each week assisted only by three inexperienced staff. Thus each justice spends a substantial amount of time examining the original case materials.

Each justice relies heavily on the three clerks, though the actual division of labour varies from office to office. Typically, the justice divides the cases more or less equally among the three clerks. Justice H tells his clerks to read the case summaries and then divide responsibilities among themselves; other justices prefer to simply assign cases, either randomly or taking into account what they know about the special interests of each clerk. The clerk assigned to a given case is usually asked to prepare a 'bench memo,' that is, a ten- to fifty-page essay that provides an overview of the facts and issues with particular attention to whatever recent case law the clerk considers relevant to possible dispositions. A typical bench memo synthesizes and summarizes the arguments of both sides and analyses the strengths and weaknesses of those arguments. Some justices reported that they ask their clerks to include a suggested disposition of the case in each memo; other justices prefer that the memos stick to an objective analysis of each issue. The justices often ask their clerks to conduct additional original research, beyond that presented in the factums, on points the justice considers key to the resolution of a particular case.

While the clerks are preparing their bench memos, the justices are reading extensively from the case materials. However, most judges indicated that unless the case is especially straightforward, they are unable to read all of the case materials before oral argument. Justice E says that he typically first reads the objective summary of the case provided by the staff lawyers in the court's Law Branch and then instructs his clerks about the legal points on which to focus their research. He then reads the decision of the lower court, including concurring and dissenting opinions. After finishing with those, he usually turns to the jury instructions at trial and then carefully reads the factums of each litigant. Finally, a day or two before the hearing, he reads his clerk's bench memo and (usually) sits down with the clerk for an informal give-and-take session about tentative ideas for a disposition of the case and remaining questions that need further clarification at oral argument.

In contrast, Justice F waits until he gets his clerk's bench memo, which he expects at least a week before the hearing. Only then does he begin his serious preparation. After digesting the memo, he reads the lower court's decision and then the factums. If possible, he then turns to all of the cited precedents that seem central to the key issues and rereads them thoroughly. However, he admitted that most of the time, he doesn't have time to read all of these precedents in their original form; for that, he relies on his clerks.

Justice D follows a modified version of Justice F's approach. He assigns cases to his clerks without at all suggesting what he considers the key issues. Nor does he suggest what his leanings are. He then analyses each factum, referring back to the lower court's opinions and to cited portions of the record only as they are relevant to evaluating the argument in the factum. He approaches each factum as if he were cross-examining it, looking for ways to tear down the crucial elements of the argument. Once he has completed his own analysis, he reads the bench memo and schedules a face-to-face meeting with the clerk who wrote it. These sessions with his clerk are usually held one or two days before the hearing. Justice D likes his clerks to engage him in a vigorous debate on all of the key issues – to act as a sounding board for his tentative ideas about resolving the case and to vigorously defend their own alternative solutions.

A pattern stands out in all of this: during preparations for oral arguments, the justices prefer that their clerks write their bench memos from a fresh perspective. Some justices point their clerks toward what they consider key issues; none of them, however, suggest early on how those issues ought to be resolved.

Argument before the Court

At the hearing for a case before the Supreme Court, each side's attorneys of record are typically granted one hour to present their arguments to the justices. In front of the large elevated dais at which the justices sit, there is a lectern for counsel. On the lectern are three small lights controlled by the clerk. The green light indicates that counsel may continue to speak; the yellow light comes on when counsel has five minutes to finish the argument; the red light means that counsel's time is up and that he or she must stop and sit down (McCormick and Greene 1990, 200). Counsel may petition the Court for additional time, but such requests are not often granted. Typically, counsel for interveners are given less time to present oral arguments. As in most common law countries, oral argument is a highly interactive process. The justices often interrupt counsel with questions – sometimes before counsel are more than a few minutes into their presentation. Both the justices' questions and counsel's answers count towards the one-hour time limit. Prior to the Lamer Court, the English practice of allowing counsel unlimited time to present their case was generally followed. But with some gentle arm twisting, Chief Justice Lamer obtained fairly widespread acceptance of the new limits (McConnell 2000). Supreme Court hearings are now recorded and broadcast on the Canadian Parliamentary Channel (in both audio and video).

The justices disagree on how much impact hearings have on the Court's ultimate decisions. All of them indicated that the questions and answers can be very useful in exposing the strengths and weaknesses of counsels' positions. Several justices said that hearings allow them to test ideas before committing themselves. In other words, a justice may take a tentative position on a key issue and pose it as a hypothetical to counsel for one or both sides. If the answers received or the reactions from other justices indicate that the position is not viable, they are able to avoid going 'on record' with their colleagues as supporting the position.

Besides clarifying positions and gathering information, hearings can serve other functions. At one time or another, all of the justices have used their questions formally addressed to counsel to make a point to the other justices. The justices all insist that it is inappropriate to make 'speeches' or 'arguments' during the hearing; whatever the justices say, it should be in the form of a question.[7] Yet Justice F noted that in practice, questions can be framed to point out (to the rest of the justices or perhaps to a single justice perceived to be undecided) weaknesses either in the position of one counsel or in the position of another justice. For example, when counsel is struggling with a question just asked by one of the justices, another may step in to suggest his or her own answer to that question by saying something like, 'But isn't it also true that our decision in XYZ case could be interpreted to mean ...' and then providing a plausible answer to the earlier question. Such a strategy, Justice F said, is especially attractive for more senior justices who by Court tradition are the last to speak at the conference. Justices B and D suggested that asking questions in order to 'feel out' the positions of other justices or to influence other justices can serve a useful purpose, because the near absence of communication among the justices about a case before oral argument means that a justice often enters a hearing without a very good idea of where the other justices stand. According to Justice A, this informal exchange among the justices at the hearing can be instrumental in getting the Court to coalesce around a given position.

There is no clear consensus among the justices as to how often minds are changed by oral argument. Justice C said that in 70 to 80 per cent of cases, his mind is pretty well made up before the hearing begins. In contrast, Justice F said that his mind is made up no more than half the time before oral argument, and Justice D indicated that he forces himself to not make a decision before he hears oral argument. Other justices had a somewhat different view on the effects of oral argument. Justice E indicated that the effects are less about changing sides than about changing how one thinks about a given issue. Similarly, Justice H indicated that one doesn't often change sides as a result of hearing the argument but may develop a more nuanced position and begin to flesh out reasons to support a position or rethink an initial view about what the scope of the solution should be.

A Word about Interveners

One cannot fully understand the process of decision making without paying some attention to the environment in which it occurs. Part of the decision-making environment is that the Court is attracting more and more actors who are not formal litigants. 'Interest groups pay attention to the Supreme Court because interest groups pay attention to any institution that wields political power and the Supreme Court certainly wields political power' (Brodie 2000, 195). Canadian courts have been allowing interveners to participate since the 1880s (Swinton 1990, 69). However, while interest groups have always attempted to influence the Supreme Court, those efforts have become more common and more focused since 1970. Since 1982 the number of applications to intervene in a case before the Supreme Court has varied dramatically from year to year without any clear pattern. The total number of applications ranges from a high of 139 in 1996 to a low of 11 in 1985 (Brodie 2002, 37). Since the Court changed its rules in 1987, the success rate of applicants (i.e., whether they are permitted by the Court to participate) has increased substantially. Since 1991 the success rate of applications to intervene has usually been over 90 per cent. The most frequent intervener has been the Attorney General of Canada, followed closely by the Attorney General of Ontario. Other frequent interveners include the Women's Legal Education and Action Fund (LEAF), the Canadian Civil Liberties Union, bar associations, and other provincial attorneys general. In more general terms, there have been roughly equal numbers of interveners from three broad categories:

governments, economic interests, and citizens' groups. Among citizens' groups, rights groups have been most common, followed by representatives of indigenous peoples. Among economic groups, professional societies have appeared more often than either business associations or individual corporations (ibid., 38–9).

It is fairly obvious why interest groups want to try to influence the Court; it may be less apparent why the Court permits their participation. One scholar has suggested that the Court gains two valuable commodities. First, it often gains information – not only information about the narrow legal issues in a case but also information that may help it gauge the policy impact and consequences of its actions. This is especially important the more the Court is engaged in policy making, because the outcomes of disputes between specific litigants increasingly have the potential to affect many groups, individuals, and governments that are not formal parties to the suit (Swinton 1990). Justice Wilson, writing early in the Charter period, when the Court followed a fairly restrictive policy towards interveners, put it this way: 'If constitutional decisions have ramifications for a broad range of interests and involve distinct choices between conflicting social policies, then we must devise some way of bringing these interests before the Court' (1986, 242). In addition, 'by listening to interest groups, the Court also adds to its legitimacy as a political institution' by creating a more open and accessible court process (Brodie 2000, 195).

It is Charter cases that most often have attracted interveners, be they governments or rights-oriented groups. Participation by interveners in Charter cases has become the norm in recent years. During the 1990s there was only one year in which interveners participated in fewer than half the Charter cases;[8] one or more interveners have participated in 61 per cent of all Charter cases (Brodie 2002, 43). The actual impact that interveners have on decisions is very much in dispute. In Charter cases there is a clear pattern in terms of support, but less agreement on whether support translates into victory. Overwhelmingly, when attorneys general intervene they do so in opposition to rights claims. In contrast, non-governmental interveners in Charter cases have supported the rights claim by a margin of more than two to one (Brodie 2002, 46).

Brodie suggests that before 1970 the Court was reluctant to hear from interveners; since then it has opened up the process. At first the Court experimented with allowing interveners to appear sporadically; then, immediately after the Charter was adopted, it embraced a more restrictive policy. From 1983 to 1986 the Court accepted fewer than half the intervener requests of interest groups. For example, it denied a petition by the Canadian Civil Liberties Association to intervene in the first significant case to interpret the meaning of the 'reasonable limits' clause of Section 1 of the Charter; it denied the Seventh-day Adventist Church the right to be heard on a challenge to Sunday closing laws; and it refused to allow unions to intervene in critical Charter cases involving labour law (ibid., 296). Then the Court appeared to reverse course, accepting petitions to intervene from over 85 per cent of the interest groups that applied between 1987 and 1990. Since then it has allowed 'virtually all' interest groups to intervene who request such participation (Brodie 2000, 201). To examine these trends more systematically, figure 5.2 shows how interveners' participation rates have changed since 1970.

Clearly, participation by interveners has increased dramatically over time. Before 1975, such participation was relatively rare – less than one case in fifteen. That rate almost doubled after the Court gained control if its docket and then more than doubled in the first seven years of the Charter period. Thus the accounts just mentioned that suggest that the Court restricted interveners in the early years of the Charter are only partially correct. It is clear that the early Charter years were characterized by much smaller rates of participation by interveners than the most recent terms of the Court, but even in the early Charter years interveners were more common than they had been in the past.

When one looks at the trends by year, several break points in the data become obvious. The first significant increase in intervener participation occurred in 1975. Then there was a small increase between 1983 and 1984 corresponding to the beginning of Charter litigation. There was a substantial increase, from 23 to 33 per cent, in the rate of participation from 1987 to 1988, presumably reflecting a more lenient attitude towards interveners. Finally, it seems that the participation rate increased again at the beginning of the McLachlin Court for reasons that appear to have escaped notice by scholars studying the Court.

Unfortunately, our interviews with the justices shed little light on the impact of interveners. Only three of the justices mentioned interveners when they described the Court's decision making. Justice D dismissed the role of interveners, saying that they usually are not at all useful because they tend to be 'too political.' In contrast, Justice A said their contribution is 'often valuable' because they tend to bring perspectives that are different from those of the formal litigants. Justice F took the

Figure 5.2
Participation of interveners on the Supreme Court:
Civil liberties cases before and after the Charter of Rights

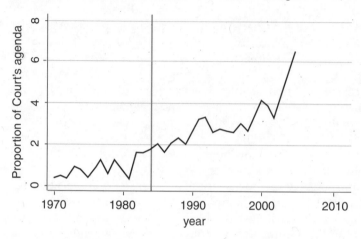

middle ground, saying that the use of interveners 'varies enormously.' He contended that some interveners just want to make a political statement to get in the papers, and he quoted an unnamed counsel for one group who actually described his role this way: 'If you can't make law you can at least make headlines.' But then he added that some interveners make valuable contributions because they have considerably more expertise in a particular area than is often found among the counsel for the formal litigants.

On the other hand, several studies have indicated that some groups have been highly successful as interveners before the Court. Perhaps the most successful has been LEAF. In forty-seven appearances between 1982 and 1996, LEAF won 72 per cent of the cases in which it appeared and made substantial changes in public policy in seventeen instances (Morton and Allen 2001). In a subsequent study, Manfredi (2004) reinforced this view, concluding that LEAF has transformed Canada's jurisprudence pertaining to equality claims under the Charter.

The Conference and Assignment of the Opinion of the Court

Immediately after the end of (most) hearings, the justices all enter the conference room. Conferences last anywhere from a few minutes to several hours. One justice said that under Chief Justice Laskin the conferences were typically only six to eight minutes. When Dickson became chief justice the conferences became longer and tended to become more like discussions than straightforward votes (McCormick 1990, 203) At the conference, the justices sit around a large round table in order of seniority. With the chief justice presiding, the justices express their views of the case. They speak in order of reverse seniority, the most junior speaking first and the chief justice last. The point of this is to prevent the more junior justices from feeling inhibited by the opinions of the more experienced ones (Anderson 2001). However, Justice Wilson observed that she doubted that was really a problem; she concluded soon enough that all of her colleagues were highly independent and strong minded (Wilson 1986). The practice of going around the table in reverse order of seniority and having each justice state his or her views follows the practice of the English Law Lords but is opposite the practice in the United States, where the chief justice speaks first.

Each justice briefly summarizes his or her view of the case and its major issues. In this process, the chief justice is 'first among equals,' providing some structure and leadership but ultimately having no greater power than any of the other justices. By the end of these comments by each justice, even without a formal vote, it is usually obvious by the time the chief justice speaks how the case will be decided (see Greene et al. 1998, 119–20).

The first thing decided at conference is whether the case will be disposed of with an oral opinion announced shortly after the Court reconvenes in the courtroom. An oral disposition generally indicates that the justices have discovered quickly that they are all in agreement about the disposition of the case and that resolving it will not require any significant change in precedent. A large majority of these oral dispositions arise in as-of-right cases – most typically, in criminal appeals that probably would not have been granted leave to appeal. This view is consistent with the finding in our data that as the proportion of as-of-right cases on the docket has declined in recent years, so has the proportion of cases disposed of orally.

The conference discussion among the justices rarely resembles a debate. Often the justices simply go around the table, summarizing their views without responding to one another. Justice H remarked that there is often only a clarification of positions, with little or no give and take. Justice D, however, noted that after the first three or four justices have indicated that the Court is divided on the resolution, subsequent justices tend to focus their remarks on *why* they agree or disagree with the earlier statements. Such remarks often lead to responses from the more junior justices who spoke earlier. Justice E concurred that most of the time, the justices simply 'go around the table,' but that in the more complex cases there is often more free-flowing discussion. Justices B and C said that at conferences there is 'a fair degree of actual discussion' and noted that the discussion usually got going after one of the more senior justices responded directly to something said earlier by one of the more junior justices instead of simply stating his or her own position. Justice A observed that while the justices are always polite to one another, quite often one of the justices will break into someone's statement with an observation or question, which then sets off more responses from other justices and may require the chief justice to serve as a referee.

At the end of the discussion, the chief justice often attempts to summarize how the Court is aligned as to outcome and what the main issues are that still need resolution. While the formal power to assign the writing of the Court's decision ultimately resides with the chief justice, the actual practice of assignment is more informal. Determining who will write a decision seems to involve interplay between comments volunteered by the chief justice about who might be an appropriate person to try to pull the Court together and offers from members to volunteer to write the first draft. If no one volunteers, of course, the chief justice will ask one of the justices to write it. Justice Wilson recalled a time during her first term on the Court when the justices convened after arguments in a particularly complex patent case. The conference discussion had been brief, with no one evidencing much enthusiasm one way or the other. After the discussion, Chief Justice Laskin asked who would like to write the opinion and was greeted with complete silence. After a moment, he continued: 'Well Bertha, you have come out of a great big corporate commercial law firm, you must know all about ... the law of patents ... Why don't you write it?' And Wilson remembered thinking, 'And of course, I was so new that I couldn't possibly say "I know nothing about patents either" so I said "fine" and I remember how hard I had to work on that, because it was my first case and it was a subject with which I was quite unfamiliar' (Anderson 2001, 151).

Several of the justices interviewed suggested that under some past chief justices, seniority seemed to be the main determinant of who was assigned the Court's opinion. For instance, Justice Dickson once recounted that as a 'rookie justice' from 1973 to 1975, he ended up writing for the Court in many as-of-right disputes that involved no important legal issue (Sharpe and Roach 2003, 144). But the justices interviewed also said that in the McLachlin Court, while seniority still counts when two or more justices volunteer to write the opinion, the most senior justice does not automatically end up with the opinion.

The empirical evidence on the effect of seniority on the choice of who writes the opinion of the Court is mixed. One scholar has provided data on opinion assignments for a forty-five-year period that 'confirms the notion of a Supreme Court apprenticeship period.' Justices were found to have a lower rate of opinion delivery during their first four years on the Court than in later years (McCormick 1994b, 506–7). A similar study has concluded that opinion leadership on the Court has tended to be dominated by the chief justice on most recent courts, and the chief justice has always been one of the most senior members on the Court (McCormick 1993b). However, a recent analysis of opinion assignment and panel participation has found that though first-year justices tend to sit on fewer panels than their more senior colleagues, there is no evidence that they are less likely to author the opinion of the Court (Ostberg, Wetstein, and Ducat 2003).

Most of the justices interviewed seemed to feel that there are no clear rules for determining who will write the opinion of the Court. Instead, a number of factors are in play, including these: seniority, special expertise, the intense interest of a particular justice, who is behind and who is on schedule with other writing assignments, and the chief justice's vague sense of who might succeed best at uniting the Court. Several of the justices interviewed indicated that the chief justice often simply asks for a volunteer, in which case usually there is just a single volunteer. Justice Wilson wrote that a similar practice was followed on the Dickson Court, with the chief justice becoming involved only when there were no volunteers or when there were multiple volunteers (Wilson 1986). Unfortunately, there have been no empirical studies of differences among the chief justices in their opinion assignment practices. Several indicators of the differences among chief justices are provided in table 5.4.

The first column in table 5.4 presents a straightforward measure of the seniority of the person chosen to write the opinion of the Court by each chief justice. The measure used is simply the average (mean)

Table 5.4
Variations in seniority of justice writing the opinion of the Court, by chief justice

Chief justice	A. Mean seniority, justice writing opinion	B. Mean seniority, most senior justice	Col. A as % col. B	Per cent opinions by	
				most senior justice	least senior justice
Fauteux	12.3 yr	20.8 yr	59.1	18.3	21.1
Laskin	9.3	21.3	43.7	14.8	15.5
Dickson	6.5	13.5	48.1	18.3	20.6
Lamer	6.4	12.7	50.4	20.6	17.5
McLachlin	7.8	13.8	56.5	9.1	13.6

number of years served on the Court by the justice writing the Court's opinion. By this measure, opinion writers tended to be more senior under Chief Justices Fauteux and Laskin than under more recent chiefs. However, that may be due at least in part to the greater number of quite senior justices during those early courts. To gain a perspective on this possibility, the second column presents the mean number of years on the Court for the most senior justice on each panel. The third column in the table presents the ratio of these two numbers, to give a rough estimate of how senior the average opinion writer was compared to the maximum possible seniority for each panel. The higher the ratio in this third column, the greater the weight one might say was given to seniority in opinion assignments (e.g., the ratio would be 100 per cent if the most senior member on the panel was always assigned to write the opinion). Using this measure in the third column, there has been no trend towards a decreasing importance of seniority in opinion assignment. The ratio is still highest for Fauteux, but it is only marginally higher than the ratio for McLachlin, who is credited in interviews with her colleagues with being more willing to depart from the 'traditional' reliance on seniority. And contrary to the expectation created by the interviews, both Dickson and Laskin have substantially lower ratios than McLachlin.

The final two columns provide some additional perspective on who wrote the opinion of the Court under each chief justice. The columns indicate the percentage of the opinions that went to the most senior member on each panel and the percentage going to the most junior member on the panel. The most surprising feature of the comparison of these two columns is that under all five chief justices, the most junior member on the panel wrote the opinion of the Court almost as often as the opinion was written by the most senior member. Lamer seems to have been the chief justice least supportive of junior justices, but there is no clear trend over time in the data.

Of course, all of these measures in table 5.4 provide only a rough indication of the opinion assignment practices of the chief justices. Perhaps most important, they are based only on total number of opinions and do not reflect any possible differences in the quality or the desirability of the opinions given to junior versus senior justices on the panels.

One pattern of opinion writing is especially noticeable: justices from Quebec write most of the opinions involving Quebec civil law. According to McCormick (1994a, 93), 'on appeals from Quebec, the Quebec members of the Court play such a dominant role that one would think they constituted two-thirds or more of the Court's membership rather than one-third; on appeals from the appeal courts of other provinces, they play such a muted role that one would think that they had only a single judge rather than three.' This finding of regional specialization in opinion writing might lead one to question whether justices specialize in other ways as well in their writing. A system that seems to be based in part on justices volunteering for the opinions they want to write may encourage many types of specialization. A first look at such specialization is the summary provided in table 5.5 of issue specialization in writing.

The cases were divided into the same six major issue categories used in the analysis of panel size in table 5.1 above (i.e., cases were classified as criminal appeals, civil rights and liberties cases, tax appeals, other public law, torts, and other private economic cases). Admittedly these are fairly gross categories, and it is likely that some justices specialize in much more specific types of cases than the categories in this table. A justice was considered to specialize in one of these six areas if the proportion of the opinions he or she wrote was more than 10 per cent above the proportion of cases on the docket falling into the category. By this definition, most of the justices had some specialization. Table 5.5 simply lists the justices who had such a specialization and what that specialization was.

Table 5.5
Specialization in the writing of the opinion of the Court

Justice	Specialization
McIntyre	Criminal
Le Dain	Public law
Lamer	Criminal
Sopinka	Criminal
Gonthier	Private economic
Cory	Criminal
Major	Torts
Bastarache	Civil liberties
Binnie	Private economic
Arbour	Criminal
Ritchie	Torts
Laskin	Public law
Lebel	Torts
Pigeon	Private economic
Pratte	Torts
Cartwright	Private economic
Abbott	Torts
Judson	Tax
Hall	Torts

The Negotiation and Writing of the Opinion of the Court

There is often little give and take among the justices before or during the conference; that is decidedly *not* the case when opinions are being written. All of the justices viewed the opinion-writing stage as key to decision making. With slight variations in phrasing, they all contended that lawyers, journalists, and academics place too much emphasis on the outcome of the case – often conceived too narrowly as simply who won and who lost – and pay far too little attention to the nuances of the opinion. The justices all seemed to view their opinion-writing chores as their most time-consuming *and* most important activity. As one simply listens to the justices, it is easy to conclude that it is also the most satisfying part of their work.

Writing an opinion of the Court is a time-consuming, intensive task that takes anywhere from several weeks to several months. While there is considerable variation in the individual styles of the justices, all are heavily invested personally in the details of the actual writing. One thing that characterizes opinion writing in important cases is that the justices do a great deal of research about the issues presented. Most justices feel no reluctance to go beyond the materials presented by counsel; indeed, they often conduct extensive supplementary investigations of precedent and scholarly writing. Justice Dickson recalled that in a case involving alleged prisoner abuse, he tried to influence his colleagues by circulating a *Globe and Mail* editorial calling for Canadian courts to follow the recent rulings of the U.S. Supreme Court that extended procedural rights to parolees (Sharpe and Roach 2003, 164). The justices sometimes also investigate how other common law courts (especially those in Britain, Australia, and the United States) have resolved similar legal issues, though of course, other countries' precedents are not binding on Canadian courts.[9] The justices typically make heavy use of their clerks for this supplemental research, but they also do some of it themselves.

An earlier study found that two of the justices typically had their clerks write a first draft of the judgment after a detailed post-conference discussion with the justice. The other justices reported that they produced the first draft and then asked their clerks to critique their work (Greene et al. 1998, 120). Our interviews suggest that a similar pattern remains the norm. Whether a clerk will be asked to write all or a portion of a first draft of an opinion varies among the justices (and varies *for* justices depending on the nature of the issue), but four generalizations seem appropriate. First, the clerks are heavily involved in meaningful work on the opinions authored by their justice. Second, the justices are always intensely involved in the detailed crafting of the opinion, and the final product always reflects the position and priorities of the justice rather than those of the clerks. Third, the final product is always the product of considerable collegial interaction unless the case is so simple and straightforward that the conference revealed that there was a clear consensus among the justices from the beginning. And finally, after the lawyers have had their say at the hearing, there is no influence and virtually no input on the opinion from anyone outside the small community of the Court and its staff.

Justice Wilson typically began by going through the notes she had taken in her 'bench book' during the oral argument and the conference.

She then took some time to produce a rough outline in her head of where the opinion needed to go. Then she dictated a very rough first draft into her Dictaphone, which was later typed up by her secretary. This draft provided her with a 'provisional map' of the steps in the legal argument that would be required for the final opinion. Using this map, she divided each of the main issues into their specific components and assigned her clerks the task of delving into the case law, statutes, and academic writing on each of the issues that she needed to address when fleshing out her argument. After receiving the memos back from her clerks, she often invited them into her office to discuss the lines of argument they had developed. Having digested the initial research and the discussions with the clerks, she then began revising the original draft in earnest (Anderson 2001, 160–1).

Justice B suggests that after conference, the outcome is usually settled in terms of which litigant is going to win. However, the writer of the Court's opinion does 'not necessarily have a roadmap of how to reach that result.' That comes only after further research and attempts to write a coherent set of reasons for the decision. And he notes that there is always a chance that the writing process and the discipline of working through the precedents will expose a problem that had not been considered at conference. On occasion, a writer actually switches sides after trying to write and returns to his or her colleagues with a memo laying out the reasons why they reached the wrong outcome at conference.

Justice Wilson provides one anecdote of such a switch from her first experience writing an opinion for the Court. The case involved a woman accused of murdering her abusive lover.[10] The case turned on the understanding of the reasonableness of the threat perceived for a plea of self-defence by the accused. The conference ended without a formal vote but with an apparent consensus that the appeal should be dismissed. Wilson volunteered to write the opinion. As she remembers, she had been doing extensive reading in preparation to give her (later famous) speech, 'Will Women Judges Really Make a Difference?' She recalls, 'It was when I was writing that [speech] and thinking about it that I realized that there were quite a number of aspects of the law that needed to be re-thought from a gender perspective and that was one.' She then had her clerks do additional research on expert psychological evidence on the effect of battering and how that would affect the mental state of the victim. She ended up arguing that the standard for a self-defence claim should be what a reasonable battered woman would think about the degree of threat rather than what the 'reasonable man' of precedent would think. So she wrote the opinion that way, justifying a reversal of the conviction. In the end, she succeeded in obtaining a unanimous Court for an outcome opposite to what had been agreed on in conference (Anderson 2001, 219–21).

The justices interviewed were in remarkable agreement on how the process of opinion writing works in practice. The ten interviews produced only minor variations on a set of common themes. When the assignment of the opinion writer is made, the chief justice lays out a time line for the process to be completed, one that depends on the perceived difficulty of the case, but that time line is flexible. When the opinion is officially announced depends on how quickly the author works and how much negotiation is needed before agreement is finally reached.

After the criticisms and revisions and polishing within the office of the justice assigned to write, a draft is completed for simultaneous circulation to all the other justices on the panel that heard the case. All of those justices feel free to comment on what everyone understands is only a first draft. The first thing most justices do on receiving this draft is assign a clerk to write a 'comment memo' analysing its strengths and weaknesses. Typically, this memo is for the eyes only of the justice who assigned the memo. The clerk is admonished to be completely frank in the analysis. Most of the time, this is a rush job. When a justice decides to respond to a draft of an opinion, the comments are typically in writing and go simultaneously to all of the justices on the panel. Sometimes, though, a justice will pick up the phone to call the author or informally drop by his or her office.

There is an informal rule that after receiving the first draft, the justices wait at least two weeks before formally 'signing on' to it. The point of this is to allow other justices a chance (a) to raise objections to some aspect of the opinion and (b) to offer suggestions for revisions. Similarly, even when it was clear during conference that one or more justices disagreed with the majority, a dissenting opinion is never circulated among the justices until two weeks after the draft of the majority opinion has been received. However, a dissenter will usually circulate a brief memo during those first two weeks indicating that there will be a dissent and usually presenting an outline of the basis for it. Justice Wilson has said that this process – which the current justices discussed during the interviews – was well established by the time she joined the Court more than twenty years ago. She adds that once a memo indicating an intention to dissent is distributed, 'it grinds the

process of concurring to a halt since it is viewed as bad form to concur
… until you have seen the dissent' (1986, 237). However, it is unclear
whether there has been a consensus over time on this point. Justice
L'Heureux-Dubé is said to agree with Wilson's view, and Justice Cory
is on record expressing a similar position; however, Justice McIntyre
has said that he does not believe there has ever been an unspoken
agreement to wait and see what the dissenting reasons might be before
signing on with the majority opinion or crafting a concurrence (Anderson 2001, 163).

Extensive comment on the draft opinion, with a good bit of give and
take among all concerned, seems to be the norm rather than the exception. For example, in one case involving the distribution of marital
property in a divorce, Justice Dickson was persuaded to change his
original draft to a 50/50 split (instead of 40/60) after objections from
Justices Laskin and Estey (Sharpe and Roach 2003, 188). Many opinions, then, go through multiple drafts before finally being released. According to the justices, perhaps two or three times a year the original
draft is rewritten from scratch; about as often, the Court holds a second
conference after comments on several drafts in an attempt to reach
agreement on points of contention. Most of the time, the basic positions that the justices announced at conference remain constant
throughout the negotiations over the opinion; sometimes, however,
those positions change during later discussions. Justice E estimated
that perhaps 10 per cent of the time, at least one justice switches sides,
and that two or three times a year the actual majority of the Court
changes so that the published opinion provides a ruling opposite to the
tentative judgment arrived at in conference.

Reaching Accommodation

Several justices indicated that the current chief justice prefers to have
the Court speak with one voice and that she encourages justices who
have expressed differences to try to work them out. Justices E, F, and H
indicated that there is more 'pressure' from the chief to eliminate
concurrences[11] than there is to eliminate dissents, because when the
majority is divided it tends to confuse the legal community in its attempts to understand the meaning of the new precedent. Other justices
(especially Justices A, B, C, and D) do not like the term 'pressure' and
instead refer to the general willingness of their colleagues to 'compromise' or to 'accommodate' the views of others if this can be done without violence to deeply held principles. Though no one else used the

exact same metaphor, there seemed to be widespread agreement with the view of Justice B: 'I think that it is important for us to get a blend of individuality and collegiality. I try to remind myself that we are not just soloists, but instead are members of a choir.' Consequently, he said that he looks first for consensus but feels free to dissent.

Some recent chief justices have applied at least 'gentle' pressure to reach a unanimous outcome. Dickson was especially concerned that 5–4 judgments tend to produce weak law and felt that the more unanimous decisions there were, the stronger the jurisprudence of the Court would be. 'Quite often I, and other members of the Court would make modifications – maybe not major ones – in a draft in order to get somebody else's concurrence, and to get as few dissents as possible. The authority of the judgment is not formidable where the Court divides three or four ways' (in McConnell 2000, 77).

Often the attempt to avoid concurrences comes in the form of a suggestion that discussion of some of the issues initially included be dropped from the opinion as not essential to the resolution of the dispute between the litigants. The result has been that the final judgment rests on narrower grounds than the opinion writer would have preferred. Chief Justice Lamer was quite willing to resort to a narrower opinion in order to avoid dissent. He is reported to have said, 'If I feel that a case can be decided on one issue rather than two issues, and one of the issues is irking one or two judges, I prefer to have a 9 to 0 decision rather than a 7 to 2 decision ... I'll horse trade. I'll leave the other one to another day' (in McConnell 2000, 77). According to most of the justices, it is also common to search for possible changes in wording that do not change the basic substance of the opinion but that do allow all to 'live with' the final opinion. This may involve switching to a deliberately more ambiguous statement of the precedent. Justice G: 'Opinions are sometimes "fudgier" ... or more limited than the opinion writer initially preferred in order to obtain a unanimous decision.'

Justice C maintained that the justices often make implicit bargains about the wording or content of the opinion, but that one always tries to approach a colleague tactfully. Justices rarely use the word 'bargain' when proposing changes in a draft opinion. Instead, one might say something like, 'I think it would strengthen the opinion if the approach to the second issue was such and such.' Or a justice might write, 'Subject to the following reservations, I agree with your excellent analysis' (followed by details on the 'reservations').[12] Two justices, though, said that bargains are sometimes fairly explicit. For example, according to Justice D, a justice might write a memo in response to a draft of the opinion that said something like, 'If you could see your way to change section III of the opinion in the following way – and sometimes then several alternative paragraphs would be included – then I would be comfortable joining the opinion of the Court; otherwise I am inclined to write separately.'

Some of the justices seemed comfortable characterizing interactions during opinion writing as 'bargaining'; however, all three of the justices who used that term immediately clarified (without any prompting) that such bargaining was a means to reach compromise *only* in the context of a given case. They were emphatic that there was absolutely no 'logrolling' – that is, there was no trading of votes on one case for consideration on another case. Nor were there any 'side payments' of any kind – in other words, no justice expects any future benefits from the chief justice or anyone else as a reward for support on a given case.

The tension between the clarity of unanimity and the flexibility of multiple opinions seems to have created differences of perspective that the justices have never resolved. It is known that Justice Laskin concluded that unanimous decisions carry more weight and increase public confidence in the Court. Justice McIntyre has said that 'the ideal is a unanimous judgment; next best is a strong judgment going one way and, say, one dissent going the other way; but concurring judgments are not particularly useful' (Anderson 2001, 154). Nonetheless, it seems that on the present court (as reflected in the interviews), as on several past Courts (as reflected in earlier published accounts), before an opinion is released to the public there is often a substantial amount of negotiation and give and take among the justices.

Law Clerks: Invaluable Assistants or Usurpers of the Judicial Role

All of the justices interviewed seemed to view their clerks as valuable resources; some scholars, though, are highly critical of their role. Morton and Knopff (2000) contend that clerks have been an important factor in the success of the 'Court Party' before the Supreme Court. According to them, courts should decide disputes between litigants based solely on the arguments presented by the litigants themselves. What happens instead is that the clerks open the gates for advocacy scholarship that should not properly be before the justices. When they do, arguments enter through 'the back door' in such a way that litigants are unable to respond. This gives some litigants an unfair advantage, especially since the clerks may be bringing to the justices' attention law review articles and other academic advocacy written by professors with whom the clerks studied in the recent past – this, even though those same activist professors may be interveners in the case before the Court.

That said, it is obvious to most observers that the job of a Supreme Court justice requires both research and clerical assistance. As noted earlier, while the justices are provided with some help, they still work long hours doing much of the basis research and analysis on their own. Anderson has observed that the amount of assistance the justices are provided is 'remarkably little compared with other government or private business executives at a comparable level, given both the quantity and the importance of the workload they are expected to process' (2001, 155). Clerks were first provided to the justices in 1968, with each justice initially getting one clerk. In 1984 a second clerk was added for each justice; within three years, Justice Dickson's conference notes indicated that there was a consensus on the Court that 'most of the clerks worked many hours of overtime every week, including Saturdays and Sundays' (Sharpe and Roach 2003, 207). The justices subsequently lobbied for more clerks, and in 1989 the number of clerks was increased to three for each justice.

How clerks are actually used varies considerably among the justices. Justice H said that he does not involve his clerks at all in the writing of opinions in French because he is quite comfortable with his own style. But he does ask for extensive critiques from his clerks when he is drafting an opinion or a memo in English, and he will sometimes ask a clerk to write a first draft of an opinion in English. Justice F, on the other hand, always writes the first draft himself; usually, though, he inserts a number of questions in boldface throughout the draft and asks his clerk to make specific responses or to do additional research addressing those questions. He also asks his clerks to critique the overall thrust of the opinion. He often gets responses such as, 'I don't agree with your conclusions in paragraph 36 because it ignores X precedent.'

Justice Dickson would have his clerks, for each case, prepare a bench memorandum of twenty to fifty pages. He expected them to go beyond a summary of the arguments of each side. Indeed, he explicitly told them to go beyond the authorities provided by the parties and to check Canadian, American, and European authorities as well as the law reviews (Sharpe and Roach 2003, 209). To help prepare them for their research assignments, clerks were invited to attend the oral arguments and to listen to the orally dictated notes that Dickson made immediately after conference.

Justice G often divides the initial writing into segments dealing with different issues that need to be addressed in the opinion. He then writes some segments himself and assigns others to one of his clerks. Each then critiques the initial draft of the other. Justice B usually asks a clerk to write up the 'preliminary stuff' that has to go into the opinion (e.g., a summary of the facts, the history of the case in the courts, and an explanation of the issues raised by the appellant) while he writes a draft of the reasoning section. He then asks his clerk to write a 'comment memo' on his first draft and discusses that memo with the clerk before starting revisions and polishing.

Justice Wilson discussed what was expected of clerks when she addressed one of their September orientation sessions: 'We want your views. You have reviewed the facts, read the judgments below, studied the factums and researched the law. What would you do with this case if you were in our shoes? This is what we want to know. Don't be shy. Don't be modest. If you disagree with us, say so. If you think we've missed the point, say so. This is one of your most important functions – be a critic and a sounding board for your judge. Through argument and discussion and debate our thinking is refined and our insights are sharpened.'

For Justice Dickson, clerks could help justices keep up with new trends in judicial scholarship. For instance, he related that his positions on Aboriginal rights were influenced by the expanding literature in the law reviews and by his reflections on how those issues were being taught in law schools in the late 1970s – reflections based on what his clerks were telling him (Sharpe and Roach 2003, 177). He often asked his clerks to search for cases from jurisdictions throughout the world; as a consequence his case files were filled with clippings and articles that his clerks had unearthed and that might not have been cited by the contending lawyers. The 'final product' of all this research indicates that Dickson was often more influenced by his clerks' research than by the arguments of counsel (Sharpe and Roach 2003, 202).

The picture that emerges from all of these accounts is of an intensely hard-working Court in which the justices do much of the work themselves, with valuable but limited help from a handful of staff. The transformation of the Court's role – from a body mainly concerned with resolving private economic disputes to one heavily involved in constitutional and statutory interpretation on issues raising substantial political controversy – has been accompanied by some changes in the process. As the Court has become more involved in complex and controversial issues of public law, its workload has increased, and the use of five-justice panels has decreased. To deal with the increased complexity and the higher political stakes, the Court has come to rely more heavily on its clerks. Nevertheless, the justices remain personally invested in the details of research, writing, and negotiation to far greater extent than other public officials with comparable responsibilities.

Another theme that emerges from all this is the extent to which the justices – both personally and through their clerks – have immersed themselves in the law. Scholars continue to debate the extent to which the decisions of appellate judges throughout the common law world are influenced by their own political preferences. The interviews with the justices do not help much to resolve this question. We *can* say that the individual life experiences of the justices and their personal political ideologies do perhaps matter; yet it is also clear that all the justices spend an enormous amount of time and energy figuring out what the relevant law is on each case being considered. The next chapter discusses the trends in the outcomes of their deliberations.

6 Policy-Making Trends
on the Supreme Court

The previous chapter focused on process and the central question was how do the justices go about making their decisions? In the next three chapters we turn to the decisions they actually make. This chapter focuses on the Court as an institution and its political impact. After exploring recent accounts of the actual legal policies that have been supported by the Court as well as the debate over the Court's proper role in the political system, we present a new analysis of the decisional trends of the Court for the period 1970 to 2003. In chapter 7 the focus will shift to the decision-making patterns of individual justices. A key concern will be the cleavages within the Court on those occasions when the Court is divided. Then in chapter 8 we will turn to the Court's unanimous decisions and reasons for the high rate of unanimity.

The Political Impact of the Supreme Court in Canada

According to traditional Canadian legal and political thought, 'judges do not, and should not, "make law" ... "The Law" has been portrayed as something that already exists "out there," and the role of the judge is merely to find or "discover" its meaning and to declare it' (Morton 2002b, 31) However, writing four decades ago, Weiler suggested two possible models of judicial behaviour, an 'adjudication model' and a 'policy-maker model,' and concluded that at that time, neither model fit Canada perfectly. He then speculated that the policy-making model might become dominant with the passage of some form of a bill of rights (1968). Yet even before the Charter, the Court was being forced to deal with constitutional issues of federalism that inevitably thrust it into the middle of some of the hottest political issues of the day. Thus there has been a growing recognition that the Court has been moving away from solely adjudicating disputes towards a greater policy-making role. The adoption of the Charter of Rights and Freedoms accelerated this shift towards a policy-making role, and one consequence has been to stimulate greater scholarly concern about the nature and consequences of that new role. Some scholars maintain that besides directly affecting how politically divisive issues are resolved, the courts may have a long-term impact on policy by the very manner in which they shape the public's perceptions of political values (Russell 1995).

A substantial literature now exists that has established beyond doubt that the Court's decisions have sometime had powerful political consequences. A few examples will serve to illustrate. Some would say that the most important and overtly political decision ever made by the Court was the Patriation Reference,[1] which helped pave the way for the Charter of Rights. Regarding the significance of that case, Chief Justice Lamer was quoted as saying, 'I think we saved the ruddy country' (McConnell 2000, 70). In *Vriend v. Alberta* (1998)[2] the Court ruled that the omission of sexual orientation from Alberta's human rights act violated Section 15(1) of the Charter. As Manfredi (2001) notes, reading sexual orientation into the protected categories of the act was important because it imposed a specific policy choice on the legislature. Moreover, it was a policy choice that the legislature had explicitly rejected and one that was clearly opposed by the province's majority. Considerable controversy also surrounded the Court's two *Morgentaler* decisions.[3] Henry Morgentaler, a Montreal physician, was charged with the crime (at that time) of performing an abortion on a seventeen-year-old girl. Even though the doctor admitted performing the abortion, the jury acquitted him. Unfortunately for Dr Morgentaler, the Quebec Court of Appeal set aside the jury verdict and, instead of ordering a new trial, entered a conviction. On appeal, the 1976 Supreme Court by a 6–3 vote upheld the conviction imposed by the appellate court (see Snell and Vaughan 1985, 242–43). While the Court's decision was based on quite technical grounds of statutory interpretation, for most Canadians it was a highly charged political decision on a 'hot button' issue. Twelve years later, in 1988, with several of the same justices still on the Court, Dr Morgentaler was back before the Supreme Court appealing a second conviction for performing an illegal abortion. In the interim, however, the Charter of Rights had taken effect. This time, the Court by a 5–2 vote ruled that the prohibition on abortion violated Section 7 of the Charter. Moreover, (now) Chief Justice

Dickson had switched sides from his 1976 vote for conviction; indeed, this time he wrote the majority opinion to overturn it. The two *Morgentaler* decisions demonstrate that Charter or not, the Court has long been willing to hear legal challenges in highly controversial matters and to make policy with strong political overtones. The Charter has not in itself created a political role for the Court but, as this example shows, it has had the potential to change political outcomes when the Court made policy.

Perhaps less controversial but certainly as powerful was *Askov* (1990).[4] At first glance, many would have seen this case as revolving around an arcane question of criminal procedure – namely, whether Section 11(b) of the Charter, which guarantees accused persons 'trial within a reasonable time,' meant that unreasonable delay, even if not attributable to the Crown, should result in a dismissal of charges against the accused. The Court interpreted the Charter to mean that it should; it then announced a standard of reasonableness that had the practical effect of releasing about 40,000 prisoners (Baar 2002).

A number of scholarly works trace the evolution of doctrine in the Court. Many of these works focus on the development of legal doctrine per se, but a number include at least some commentary on the political or social significance of the decisions. In perhaps the most comprehensive such effort, Bushnell (1992) traces the succession of what he considers the most consequential of these decisions from the very beginning of the Court until the date of his writing. The account is replete with cases in which the justices involved themselves in important political controversies of their time. In 1950, in *Canadian Wheat Board v. Hallet & Carey Ltd. and Nolan*,[5] the Court ruled on the federal government's controversial application of the National Emergency Transitional Powers Act (NETP). Bushnell describes the context of the decision: 'Battle lines were forming; critics were appearing and speaking out. There was a very clear message that times were changing both socially and in the legal system' (1992, 287). The Court's decision to strike down the government regulations (later overturned by the Privy Council) helped energize a heated political debate over the exercise of government price controls in the postwar years. Perhaps more surprising to those who have come of age in the Charter period, the Court showed a willingness to grapple with controversial civil rights issues three decades before the Charter provided an express constitutional basis for such activism. Similarly, in a series of cases involving attempts by Quebec to impose sanctions on Jehovah's Witnesses in the province, the Court indicated that it 'was prepared to stake a claim for the judicial protection of civil liberties despite inadequate statutory provisions' (Snell and Vaughan 1985, 207).

Bushnell (1992) catalogues the ongoing political impact of the Court over the following decade, noting that 'with the arrival of the 1960s it did not take long for the non-creative, conservative nature of the bench to display its continuing domination of the institution' (1992, 331). This conservative impact was spelled out in Bushnell's analysis of the failure of judicial interpretation of the 1960 Canadian Bill of Rights to live up to the hopes of civil rights groups. In the following decade, Justice Laskin's dissent in *Murdoch v. Murdoch*[6] (1973), which addressed the proper standards for distributing matrimonial property, generated so much support among Canadians that 'Laskin was to become a "folk hero" in the eyes of many Canadians' (1992, 385). Within a few years, 'pressure on the provincial governments ... had created radical new reform legislation' (ibid., 391). Such examples could easily be multiplied; taken together, they make it clear that even before the Charter, Canadians were aware that the Court often involved itself in important political controversies (see also Snell and Vaughan 1985; Balcome et al. 1990; Bevilacqua 1990).

There is little doubt that the Court has played an important role in the politics of federalism. Manfredi (2001) notes that the perceived distortion of federal power by the Privy Council led directly to the abolition of appeals to the Privy Council in 1949. As well, advocates of stronger federal powers (i.e., relative to the provinces) were not disappointed when in 1952 the Supreme Court adopted the 'inherent national importance test,' which expanded Ottawa's power when disputes over federalism arose (2001, 14). Monahan contends that by the mid-1980s the 'Canadian judiciary had assumed centre stage in the politics of Canadian federalism' (1984, 142). That the Court plays a role in the politics of federalism is perhaps inevitable, given that a constitutional division of power between competing levels of government needs an umpire. The point is that this role has thrust the Court into the heart of many highly controversial conflicts, with its decisions almost certain to generate heated responses from the losing litigants. In the 1970s the Court often found itself accused of bias against the provinces (Swinton 1990). Tremblay (1986) maintains that if the Court was more favourable towards the federal government, it was not because of such bias but rather 'because of its conception of what Canadian sovereignty requires at the international level' (1986, 182). The Court was determined to give the federal government the legal capacity to fulfil all of its obligations under international law. Monahan (1986) stresses that the Court's decisions have been crucial to balancing competition in the domestic economy and to preventing predatory behaviour by corporations – behaviour that in practical terms the provinces would not be able to police. Swinton (1990) notes that many of the cases that came before the Court in the 1970s and 1980s raised issues with important implications for the scope of government power, and that this affected the dynamics of federal–provincial relations as well as the policy instruments resorted to by governments. She cautions that while the Court's role is important, it does not unilaterally set policy; it is best viewed, rather, as one of several major players in this critical area of politics (1990, 19–20). Monahan (2002) agrees, noting that the outcomes of constitutional cases are 'much less determinative of public policy than is often supposed' (2002, 476). The Court's decisions are more likely to affect the bargaining strategies of future participants when policy is being made, advantaging some and limiting the options of others.

Observers agree that Supreme Court decisions have become more ideological since the Charter. The more obviously ideological nature of the issues decided under the Charter has led to increased debate and commentary on what the Court has done and what it should do. Much of this commentary has strong normative overtones. As one scholar put it, 'the study of law and politics in Canadian political science is dominated by normative claims about the Charter's impact ... at the expense of empirical explorations' (Smith 2002, 8). The Court's role in the Charter era has been attacked from both the right and the left. Mandell (1989) argues that there has been a profound shift in the role of the Court and that the Charter has led to the 'legalization' of politics, with the consequence that judicial policy making has been biased towards the rich. Yet Knopff and Morton (1992) assert that the Charter has contributed to the transfer of political power to left-wing social activists.

Morton and Knopff (2000) are the best-known critics of the Charter from what might be characterized as the political 'centre right' (Greene et al. 1998). They argue that since the 'charter revolution ... a long tradition of parliamentary supremacy has been replaced by a regime of constitutional supremacy verging on judicial supremacy' (Morton and Knopff 2000, 13). As a result, the courtroom has become a political arena in ways it never used to be. In brief, the Charter has led to the 'legalization or judicialization of politics' (Knopff and Morton 1992, 34).

Their concern is that in the Charter era, justices, who are neither elected nor required to undergo the intense scrutiny of something like the U.S. confirmation process, have abandoned the canons of self-restraint that properly guided the judiciary in Canada for its entire pre-Charter history. They consider this increase in judicial power unfortunate because the power to influence the Court has become concentrated in a 'Court Party' of left-wing social activists. Interest groups have received a new point of access to decision making, one that has advantaged – among others – environmentalists, feminists, minority-language rights groups, and social liberals, all of whom aim to overcome majority preferences on lifestyle issues such as abortion and gay rights. As a consequence, policy making has taken on a somewhat insidious character because it is now 'covered by a legalistic veil' (ibid., ix). They decry the capacity of justices to engage in the social engineering advocated by members of the Court Party, arguing that elitist groups should not be allowed to use the courts to impose their policy preferences on the rest of society without the normal give and take of electoral and legislative processes. They fear that an activist Court will use the Charter to in effect rewrite the constitution without democratic restraint.

Mandell (1989) is also concerned that the Charter has resulted in the 'legalization' of politics. However, he does not seem to share Morton and Knopff's perspective on who the winners have been in the new politics. In his view, the Charter has increased the power of privileged social elites, which have used their power to advance their own class interests. The result is that society's 'have nots' are worse off than before. The Charter, he asserts, has not transferred 'power to the people'; rather, it has transferred it to 'the people in the legal profession,' who disproportionately come from the wealthier segments of society and whose livelihood depends on satisfying wealthy clients (1989, 3). The elites gain from Charter politics because the judicial process is inherently biased towards the rich and powerful. The best lawyers are expensive, so there is a sense in which people get only as much justice as they can afford. Other forms of politics, including legislative lobbying and protest activities, have few rules for filtering out which points can be articulated and which evidence can be argued; in contrast, the elaborate and complicated rules of court procedure filter out many potentially relevant considerations, and this filtering process often works to the disadvantage of the poor and the oppressed. As a result, the more politics becomes 'legalized,' the greater the advantages to the rich and well connected. Mandell opposes the 'legalization' of politics, asserting that it is fundamentally dishonest in that its political nature is deliberately hidden within a maze of complicated legal rules.

An Empirical Account of Outcomes of the Supreme Court

It would perhaps be inappropriate for an outsider to join the normative battle that continues to rage in both popular and scholarly outlets over the proper role of the Supreme Court in the Charter era. Thus the analysis below confines itself to an empirical exploration of outcomes in the Court between 1970 and 2003. For most of the analysis, trends in outcomes are examined across the same five periods as were used for the analysis of agenda change in chapter 3. The pre-Charter era is divided into two time periods: between 1970 and 1975, the Court lacked substantial control over its docket; then in 1976, it gained docket control though it still had no constitutional basis for resolving rights controversies. The Charter period is then divided into three periods that roughly correspond to the terms of the three chief justices who have served since the Charter was adopted.

We begin the analysis by examining the most basic question in politics: 'Who wins?' There are a number of ways to think about winning and losing in court. One of those ways was the focus of chapter 4, which described trends in the success of different categories of litigants. Several alternative ways to think about winning and losing are explored in this chapter.

We focus first on the most basic decision that an appellate court must make: whether to allow an appeal and overturn the decision of a lower court.[7] Outcomes for the litigants are presented in two graphs, divided first by time period (figure 6.1) and then by the primary nature of the dispute before the Court (figure 6.2).

Overall, slightly less than half of all appeals are successful: petitioners have won just over 44 per cent of the time in the past thirty-four years. There is extensive year-to-year fluctuation but no clear trend in the proportion of appeals allowed. This is in marked contrast to the pattern in the U.S. Supreme Court, where petitioners have won two-thirds of the time in many recent terms. When the justices were asked how leave-to-appeal decisions were decided, several said that they do not see their job primarily as correcting errors in the lower courts. They are more concerned about making judicial policy on new and important questions and about resolving conflicts in the interpretation of the law when courts in different provinces have decided the same question

Figure 6.1
Changing decisions on the Supreme Court:
Appeals allowed before and after the Charter

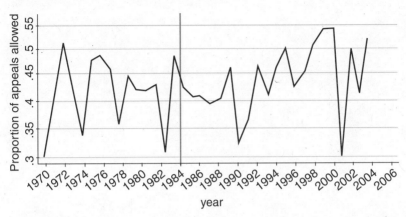

year

differently (see chapter 3 for an elaboration of the justices' views on accepting leave petitions). The relatively low rate of disturbing lower-court decisions is consistent with how the justices view their role. If they were principally concerned with correcting all possible lower-court errors, one would expect them to grant leave to decisions that initially seemed wrongly decided, and as a result a large percentage of appeals would be allowed.

One might have expected the percentage of successful appeals to increase after 1975, when the Court gained greater control of its docket. After all, during the time when many appeals came to the Court 'as of right,' losing litigants would have tended to appeal regardless of the merits of their position. This in turn would have led to a substantial number of appeals without merit, which the Court would then summarily dismiss. Yet there is no indication in the data that this is what happened. Indeed, it seems that the proportion of successful appeals actually declined after 1975. These results must be interpreted with some caution, however, since they are based only on the decisions published with opinion in the *Supreme Court Reporter*. Before 1975 a number of appeals were disposed of without a published opinion, whereas the recent practice has been to publish at least a very brief opinion in all cases (including those with a disposition announced from the bench). A reasonable guess is that most of the pre-1975 decisions without a published opinion were those in which the appeal was

Figure 6.2
Appeals allowed, by issue

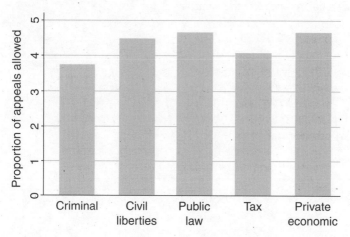

dismissed. If that is true, the proportion of appeals allowed must be lower than indicated by the data in figure 6.1.

When we shift attention to who wins by the types of cases coming to the Court, we find that differences across issues are modest (see figure 6.2). Appellants in criminal cases have the lowest success rate, but only marginally lower than the success of appellants in tax cases. However, when one examines changes in the success rates over time, the extent of variation across issues is more substantial.

Criminal appeals are least likely to succeed, and as table 6.1 shows, the rate of success in criminal appeals is low in all five of the time periods examined. Most criminal appeals are brought by the defendant, and appeals to the Supreme Court are especially likely in more serious cases of the sort that presumably draw lengthy sentences (see chapter 4). Conversely, when the stakes are economic, it can be presumed that litigants often make rational calculations about the expected utility of the appeal, factoring in both the cost of the appeal and the potential economic gain if successful. Clearly, it is irrational to appeal such cases when the probability of success is low. Someone who is facing many years in prison may calculate utilities very differently and decide that even an appeal with a very low probability of success is rational if the alternative is spending, say, twenty years in prison. Adding to the possibility that cases with little objective merit will come

Table 6.1
Who wins? Changes over time in proportion of appellants who win in the Supreme Court of Canada, by issue area

Time period	Issue area	Appeal allowed (appellant wins) (%)	N
1970–75	Criminal	37.4	91
	Civil liberties	41.7	12
	Government regulation	49.5	95
	Tax	28.6	56
	Torts	58.5	118
	Other private econ.	48.3	176

Time period	Issue area	Appeal allowed (appellant wins) (%)	N
1976–83	Criminal	34.3%	233
	Civil liberties	15.3	13
	Government regulation	45.3	139
	Tax	35.6	45
	Torts	44.1	59
	Other private econ.	50.7	144

Time period	Issue area	Appeal allowed (appellant wins) (%)	N
1984–90	Criminal	33.7%	293
	Civil liberties	44.8	49
	Government regulation	48.4	84
	Tax	56.2	16
	Torts	58.3	36
	Other private econ.	43.7	71

Time period	Issue area	Appeal allowed (appellant wins) (%)	N
1991–99	Criminal	41.1	492
	Civil liberties	52.9	70
	Government regulation	51.4	109
	Tax	59.1	44
	Torts	54.5	55
	Other private econ.	56.3	87

Table 6.1 (*continued*)
Who wins? Changes over time in proportion of appellants who win in the Supreme Court of Canada, by issue area

Time period	Issue area	Appeal allowed (appellant wins) (%)	N
2000–2003	Criminal	44.9	118
	Civil liberties	50.0	24
	Government regulation	46.5	43
	Tax	40.0	10
	Torts	52.0	25
	Other private econ.	31.0	42

before the Court is the fact that even after 1975, some criminal appeals continued to reach the Court as of right. Some justices indicated during the interviews that they were particularly sensitive to the seriousness of a person losing his or her liberty. When the stakes were more than 'only money,' they were more willing to entertain the possibility that an appeal had merit.

At the other end of the distribution, petitioners in tort cases have the highest rate of success; indeed, they are the only appellants who win more than half the time. Their success has not varied much over time; tort petitioners won more than half the time in all but one of the time periods examined. There is no obvious explanation for this; perhaps it is because tort law is the area most dominated by purely financial calculations about the expected gain from an appeal.

Civil liberties is the area in which there has been the greatest change in success rates over time. The most obvious explanation is that the Charter 'changed the rules' in the middle of the time frame being examined. The significance of these changes is explored later in the chapter, when the specific impact of the Charter is examined.

Given the justices' interest in deciding new and important questions of law in order to give guidance to the lower courts, the nature of the opinion that explains the reasons for judgment and that interprets the law is arguably more important than who won and who lost (except, of course, to the litigants themselves). The elements of opinions that are important tend to be idiosyncratic and are not easily summarized empirically. One characteristic of opinions does, however, lend itself to

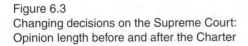

Figure 6.3
Changing decisions on the Supreme Court:
Opinion length before and after the Charter

empirical description: the length. Figure 6.3 presents the average length of the Court's total output, including dissenting and concurring opinions. Page lengths were determined from the *Supreme Court Reports*, which provide parallel English and French translations of the opinions.

The most obvious finding is that the Court has been writing a lot more in recent years than it did in the 1970s. The significant break point appears to be the adoption of the Charter. The total length of opinions in all six categories of issues increased beginning in 1984 (when the first Charter cases were decided by the Court). The greatest increases in opinion length have been in civil liberties cases, most of which have involved resolving a Charter issue. But even issues such as torts, which have been relatively little affected by the Charter, have become characterized by longer opinions. One speculates that the increasing volume of writing put out by the Court may be related to the increase in the number of law clerks available to assist the justices, to a greater volume of material coming into the Court as the proportion of cases with interveners has increased (see Chapter 4), and perhaps to a feeling among the justices that they must justify their decisions in greater detail now that the Charter has heightened media and public attention to Court decisions.

It is a maxim among the media that conflict sells papers (or garners higher TV ratings). The interviews with the justices indicated that they are aware that the Court tends to receive the most scrutiny when it is publicly divided, and that the more sharply worded the dissenting opinions, the stronger the media's stare is likely to be. While most scholarly writing on the Court has focused on its substantive decisions, patterns of agreement and dissent have not gone unnoticed. Probably the most comprehensive accounts of these patterns have been provided by McCormick (2000), who detailed individual justices' tendencies to side with the majority or to write a separate concurring or dissenting opinion. He found that since 1963, the justices have varied greatly in their tendency to dissent, ranging from Justice Pigeon of the Laskin Court, who never wrote a dissent, to Justice Laskin, whose dissent rate was 50 per cent between 1963 and 1973. In second place to Laskin (if one can put it that way) was Justice L'Heureux-Dubé of the Dickson Court (39.2 per cent), followed by Justice Wilson of the Laskin Court (37.9 per cent). Given that McCormick has already provided extensive detail about justices' individual behaviour, the present analysis concentrates on providing a 'big picture' account of overall rates of dissent and concurrences on the Court as a whole.

Overall, what is most striking about the data in table 6.2 is the high level of consensus on the Supreme Court across the thirty-four years examined. There was no dissent in three-quarters of all cases, and there were no concurring opinions in five-sixths of decisions. When the Court failed to reach consensus, the level of disagreement was generally modest, with most divided decisions involving one or two dissents. Separate concurring opinions were even less frequent: only 4 per cent of all cases had more than one concurrence. There was some variation over time in the frequency of both dissents and concurrences but no clear temporal pattern. The last four years under study had the fewest concurrences; the lowest rates of dissent were between 1984 and 1990. One might have expected the number of both dissents and concurrences to increase after the Charter as the perceived political stakes increased, yet the trends in table 6.2 provide no support for that conjecture.

Further insight into justices' tendencies to write separately is provided by the simultaneous occurrence of dissents and concurrences. Table 6.3 further emphasizes how strongly the justices tend to agree. When a decision is unanimous, there is a strong tendency for the justices to unite behind a single opinion. In fact, in almost seven out of

Table 6.2
Number of dissents and concurrences on the Supreme Court of Canada, 1970–2003

Frequency of number of dissents over time
Number of dissents per case

Time period	0 (%)	1 (%)	2 (%)	3 (%)	4 (%)	N
1970–75	66.7	8.7	15.4	5.5	4.6	584
1976–83	79.7	5.0	6.0	5.7	3.5	680
1984–90	81.8	6.0	7.1	4.4	0.7	588
1991–99	73.6	8.7	9.3	5.3	3.1	923
2000–03	74.8	7.4	5.0	7.1	5.7	282
Overall	75.1	6.3	7.8	4.7	2.9	3057

Frequency of number of concurrences over time
Number of concurrences per case

Time period	0 (%)	1 (%)	2 (%)	3 (%)	4 (%)	N
1970–75	84.1	13.1	2.8	0	0	458
1976–83	89.4	9.1	1.2	0.4	0	577
1984–90	85.6	10.0	2.7	1.3	0.4	521
1991–99	78.4	14.7	5.0	1.5	0.5	804
2000–03	90.6	7.3	1.2	0.4	0.4	246
Overall	84.4	11.5	3.0	0.8	0.3	2,606

Table 6.3
Number of concurrences for decisions with varying numbers of dissents on the Supreme
Court of Canada, 1970–2003

Frequency of number of dissents over time
Number of concurrences per case

Number of dissents	0 (%)	1 (%)	2 (%)	3 (%)	4 (%)	N
0	86.9	9.8	2.1	0.9	0.4	1943
1	79.6	13.1	6.8	0.5	0	191
2	80.5	14.3	4.8	0.4	0	251
3	69.2	23.1	7.0	0.6	0	156
4	76.1	20.4	1.1	2.3	0	88
Overall	84.3	11.6	3.0	0.8	0.3	2,629

eight cases with unanimous outcomes, there has been a single opinion. The other notable finding is that dissents and concurrences tend to go together. When the Court is split on a case, it is more likely that the majority has been unable to agree on a single majority opinion. When there have been at least three dissents, the majority has been split, with multiple opinions 28 per cent of the time – more than twice the rate of concurrences for cases with unanimous decisions.

Table 6.4 presents the number of dissents and concurrences for six major categories of issues. There is a low rate of dissent and a low rate of concurrence in all issue categories; that said, civil liberties cases stand out from the rest. The rate of dissent in those cases is over 40 per cent higher than the rate in the next most contentious area. The civil liberties category is also distinctive in that far more such cases generate multiple dissents. Over 18 per cent of civil liberties cases have at least three dissents – almost double the rate for criminal cases. Similar differences are evident for concurrences. Almost twice as many civil liberties cases as any other category of cases have at least one concurring opinion, and the proportion of cases with three or more concurrences is three times higher for civil liberties cases than for any other category of cases. These data suggest that civil liberties cases evoke the most controversy on the Court and perhaps produce the greatest passion among the justices.

During the interviews, the justices indicated that they saw it as the Court's role to 'balance' the federal judicial system – that is, to watch over the top appellate courts in each province and to ensure national uniformity in interpretations of the law and the constitution. In this regard, McCormick (1992) compared the success of appeals coming from different provincial courts beginning in 1949, when Privy Council appeals were abolished and the Supreme Court of Canada was firmly established as the ultimate arbiter of conflicting legal interpretations. He found a rather strong variation in terms of provinces, ranging from a low of 36.4 per cent for appeals from Prince Edward Island to a high of 59.8 per cent for appeals from New Brunswick. Below, this analysis is extended to the present (McCormick had taken it only to 1990), and trends over time are examined.

To say that appellants from a given province have a low success rate is the same as saying that that province's appellate court is more often upheld. When we extend McCormick's analysis to 2003, we find that little has changed: the Court of Appeal of New Brunswick remains the court whose judgments are most often overturned by the Supreme Court; Prince Edward Island, as before, is still the least often overturned.

Table 6.4
Number of dissents and concurrences by issue areas, Supreme Court of Canada, 1970–2003

Frequency of number of dissents by issue area
Number of dissents per case

Issue	0 (%)	1 (%)	2 (%)	3 (%)	4 (%)	N
Criminal	73.4	7.5	9.4	6.2	3.6	1,235
Civil liberties	61.8	7.6	12.4	11.8	6.5	170
Government regulation	75.6	7.7	8.5	5.0	3.1	480
Tax	81.4	6.2	6.8	4.5	1.1	177
Torts	73.2	6.4	13.0	4.4	3.0	299
Private economic	78.4	7.0	7.6	3.8	3.2	527

Frequency of number of concurrences by issue area
Number of concurrences per case

Issue	0 (%)	1 (%)	2 (%)	3 (%)	4 (%)	N
Criminal	82.8	12.2	3.5	1.1	0.4	1218
Civil liberties	65.9	22.2	8.4	3.0	0.6	167
Government regulation	87.6	9.7	2.0	0.4	0.2	444
Tax	89.3	9.5	0.6	0.6	0	168
Torts	86.7	10.0	2.9	0.4	0	279
Private economic	89.8	9.3	0.9	0	0	344

However, for the entire period studied in the current analysis (1970 to 2003), the Court of Appeal of Ontario reaps the honour as the court whose judgments are most consistently sustained by the Supreme Court. Overall, though, the differences between provinces in success rates for litigants are relatively modest. No provincial court has been overturned as much as three out of five times, and every court has been overturned in more than one-third of its judgments. Remember here that in every province, a large majority of appellate court judgments are never reviewed by the Supreme Court.

A detailed breakdown by period (not displayed in table 6.5) highlights several interesting features. First, from 1970 to 1975 the Supreme Court overturned the courts from almost every province fairly frequently. Alberta, with a 40 per cent rate of decisions overturned, did the worst among courts with any substantial number of decisions

Table 6.5
Proportion of appeals allowed from different Canadian provinces
by the Supreme Court of Canada, 1970–2003

Province	Appellant wins (%)	N
Alberta	40.8	262
British Columbia	43.2	442
Manitoba	48.5	171
New Brunswick	56.8	95
Nova Scotia	50.9	114
Ontario	36.0	739
Quebec	48.5	588
PEI	38.1	31
Saskatchewan	50.4	121
Nfld & Lab.	49.1	57

reviewed. All other provinces were overturned at least 45 per cent of
the time. New Brunswick suffered the highest rate of reversal of any
province for any of the time periods examined, with appeals allowed
from its decisions in nearly 71 per cent of the cases accepted for review.
After 1975, the Court of Appeal of Ontario was consistently sustained
by the Supreme Court. Petitioners were never successful more than
36 per cent of the time between 1976 and 2003, and the petitioners' success rate of only 25.8 per cent between 1984 and 1990 stands as the lowest rate of success in our data. In contrast, petitioners from British
Columbia seem to be enjoying increasing rates of success over time.
Between 1976 and 1990, their appeals were allowed in only 35 per cent
of cases accepted for review. However, BC's success rate increased to
almost 49 per cent between 1991 and 1999, then climbed again to over
55 per cent between 2000 and 2003.

New democracies have been springing up around the world for the
past quarter-century, and this has renewed interest in judicial independence. Without substantial freedom from government interference and
public opinion, the rule of law is impossible. During the interviews, all
of the justices expressed confidence that the appellate courts had a
very substantial degree of independence in practice and that legal safe-
guards to prevent political interference were strong. In subsequent
interviews that the author conducted with judges on four of the

provincial appellate courts, the same confidence in Canadian courts' independence was always expressed. There is no completely satisfactory way to test empirically whether this confidence is warranted. One indicator, perhaps, that a court is sufficiently independent to make the ideal of the rule of law a reality is that it is free to rule against the government even in cases with important political ramifications. Thus, as a partial confirmation of the justices' confidence that they are indeed independent, the next step in the analysis is to examine the government's success, both in the total aggregate of cases in which the federal government was one of the formal parties and in a subset of cases in which the political stakes for the government were especially high.

Unfortunately, there is no completely objective answer to the question of how high a rate of government success needs to be in order to indicate that the courts' independence may be limited. Certainly, if the government's success rate were to approach 100 per cent either in all cases or in the most important cases, one would suspect that the courts had limited independence. Yet a series of studies applying party capability theory have found that in other countries widely reputed to have strongly independent courts, including Australia, England, and the United States, the government often wins more than 60 per cent of the cases it litigates in appellate courts. Governments win much of the time in part because they often have better lawyers than their litigation opponents and in part because as the ultimate 'repeat player,' they are skilled at managing their dockets, appealing only decisions in which they have a better than even chance of success (see Galanter 1974; McCormick 1993a; Songer, Sheehan, and Haire 1999; Atkins 1991; Kritzer 2003).

Given this ambiguity, what can one say about the trends in government success displayed in figure 6.4? Certainly the government wins more often than it loses – overall, about five-eights of all cases. In the absence of a readily available measure of how much the government cares about the outcome of each case, two indicators of political salience were employed. It seems reasonable to suppose that the government is generally more concerned with constitutional challenges to its authority than to many non-constitutional cases. Also, one can assume that cases that attract the participation of one or more interveners (usually either interest groups or other governments) are more politically salient than cases without interveners. Using these indicators of 'importance,' it seems that the government has a slightly higher success rate in 'important' cases than in all cases. Should we be concerned that these rates of success point to limits on judicial independence? While

Figure 6.4
Change over time on the Supreme Court:
Government wins in all cases and salient cases before
and after the Charter

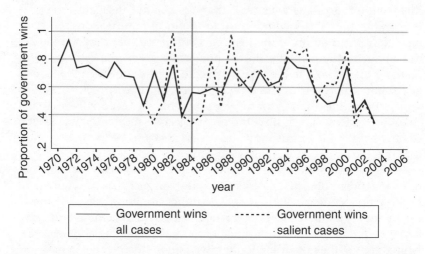

| Government wins all cases | ------ Government wins salient cases |

the author's evaluation admittedly is somewhat subjective, my answer would be a resounding 'no.' Given the findings of party capability studies, one would expect the government to win significantly more than half of decisions even if the courts were completely independent. Thus the success rates displayed in figure 6.4 do not seem to indicate a lack of independence. One can argue that if the government consistently loses from 30 to 40 per cent of its cases – including the cases it cares the most about – then judges must feel free to rule against the government. And in some periods, the government wins barely half its cases. Thus the confidence expressed by the justices in their independence to follow the law without government interference seems justified by the actual outcomes.

Trends in Policy Making on the Supreme Court

While much of the discussion of the Court's policy output has had a doctrinal focus, some empirical accounts also exist. Most of those focus on the Charter's impact rather than on more general policy trends. Russell (1992) demonstrated that in the first two years of the Charter, those asserting that their Charter rights had been violated won an astounding two out of three cases. But those initial success rates quickly dropped, and by the late 1980s Charter claimants were winning slightly less than 30 per cent of their appeals.

Similar figures are supplied by Morton, Russell, and Walker (1992), who report the initial high success rate of Charter claimants but then note that overall, in the first hundred Charter decisions, rights claimants won only 35 per cent of the time. This success rate is more than double that of rights claimants in the thirty-two cases adjudicated by the Court under the Canadian Bill of Rights and is almost identical to the success of rights claimants in the U.S. Supreme Court for the same period.

In response to the criticism of Morton and Knopff that the Court has usurped parliamentary supremacy, Monahan (1999) notes that 55 per cent of the Charter cases have involved challenges to police actions rather than to statutes. Moreover, of the sixty-four instances of judicial review of legislation, just over half (thirty-four) involved federal legislation; in the rest, the Court was applying the Charter to restrain provincial actions. Moreover, of the thirty-four federal statutes struck down under the Charter, twenty involved only procedural rules.

Before examining Charter outcomes, we next examine the more general trends in the policy outcomes of Court decisions over the entire period studied. As a summary indicator of the output of the Court in policy terms, figure 6.5 charts the change over time in the percentage of decisions that could be considered 'liberal.' Here, *liberal* is defined as a pro-defendant outcome in criminal appeals; as support for an expanded concept of rights in civil liberties issues; as the position of the federal government in the application of other public law; and as support for the government in tax cases, for the plaintiff in tort cases, and for the economic underdog in private economic disputes.

Overall, there has been a slightly conservative tendency in Supreme Court decisions over the past third of a century. These moderately conservative outcomes have characterized the Court throughout the period examined. Figure 6.5 indicates that there has been only a modest degree of change over time. Furthermore, there is no linear trend in the data, though in general the Court has given more support to conservative outcomes in the post-Charter era. In most years, support for liberal outcomes has fluctuated between 40 and 60 percent, which is consistent with the general theme that the Supreme Court of Canada has been politically moderate.

There is greater variation when one examines outcomes in different issue areas (see figure 6.6). Decisions are most conservative for crimi-

Figure 6.5
Changing decisions on the Supreme Court:
Support for liberal outcomes before and after the Charter

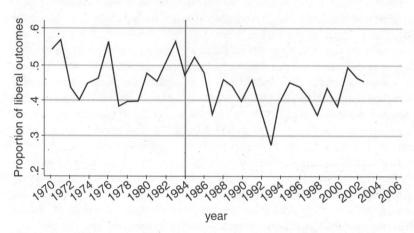

year

nal appeals, with fewer than one-third of all outcomes favouring the accused. Support for civil liberties claimants is higher, but overall only 41 per cent of the decisions have supported a liberal outcome. The Court appears to be modestly liberal in all other areas, each of which has a substantial economic component. The Court's record is most liberal in public law cases involving economic regulation and welfare state benefits; nearly three-fifths of all decisions have supported liberal outcomes. Outcomes have been almost as liberal in tort cases, where the Court has supported the claims of the plaintiff 57 per cent of the time. Given these differences, it appears that any overall categorization of the Court as liberal or conservative is misleading; rather, the direction of policy support depends on the issue area.

Perhaps more revealing than the aggregate support for liberal versus conservative outcomes has been the trends over time. In the early 1970s the Supreme Court had a strongly conservative record for criminal appeals, with fewer than one-fifth of decisions favouring criminal defendants. Then in late 1970s and early 1980s, support for the accused nearly doubled, to over 35 per cent. In each of the three periods after the adoption of the Charter, this new, less conservative pattern was basically maintained.

Trends in the resolution of civil liberties cases appear to be strongly related to the Charter. One could easily argue that the purpose of those

Figure 6.6
Proportion of liberal decisions
by the Supreme Court of Canada 1970–2003 by issue

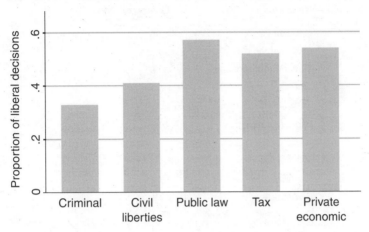

who urged the adoption of the Charter was to provide greater support for civil liberties claims. This seems to be borne out by the dramatic change in support for civil liberties claimants since the Charter came into effect. Before the Charter, the Court heard few civil liberties cases and supported liberal outcomes in only one-fourth of decisions. In the first seven years of Charter litigation, support for civil liberties claimants jumped to nearly 48 per cent – more than double the Court's level of support in the previous eight years. The proportion of liberal decisions dipped somewhat in the next time period; even so, it remained substantially above the highest pre-Charter level. Then in the most recent period examined, support for civil liberties rose to 50 per cent.

As might be expected, other issue areas were much less affected by the Charter's provisions; thus trends in the level of liberalism of the Court in those areas showed less change. Yet even without a direct Charter effect, increasing liberalism was apparent in the disposition of private economic disputes. Support for the economic underdog averaged only 44 per cent in the early 1970s, then increased to 50 per cent in the next time period, remained relatively constant at 48 per cent in the first Charter period, and increased to nearly 66 per cent over the two most recent periods.

One recent study appears to contradict nearly all previous analyses of Charter politics. Among the critics of the Charter from both the right

Table 6.6
Trends over time in support for liberal policy outcomes in decisions of the Supreme Court of Canada, 1970–2003

Time period	Issue area	Liberal decision (%)	N
1970–75	Criminal	17.8	90
	Civil liberties	33.3	12
	Government regulation	62.8	86
	Tax	66.1	56
	Torts	58.9	107
	Other private econ.	44.3	106
Time period	Issue area	Liberal decision (%)	N
1976–83	Criminal	35.2	233
	Civil liberties	23.1	13
	Government regulation	57.1	133
	Tax	52.4	42
	Torts	62.1	58
	Other private econ.	50.5	97
Time period	Issue area	Liberal decision (%)	N
1984–90	Criminal	34.8	290
	Civil liberties	47.9	48
	Government regulation	52.5	80
	Tax	56.2	16
	Torts	54.3	35
	Other private econ.	48.1	52
Time period	Issue area	Liberal decision (%)	N
1991–99	Criminal	31.6	484
	Civil liberties	39.4	71
	Government regulation	60.6	104
	Tax	38.5	39
	Torts	55.1	49
	Other private econ.	58.9	56

Table 6.6 (*continued*)
Trends over time in support for liberal policy outcomes in decisions of the Supreme Court
of Canada, 1970–2003

Time period	Issue area	Liberal decision (%)	N
2000–2003	Criminal	37.6	117
	Civil liberties	50.0	22
	Government regulation	55.0	40
	Tax	20.0	10
	Torts	45.8	24
	Other private econ.	65.5	29

and the left, and among its supporters as well, there seems to be a consensus that the Charter has had a strong effect on the Court's agenda as well as on its substantive impact. In stark contrast, one scholar suggests that the Charter has actually made very little difference. Epp (1996, 1998) argues that the Charter has not had a major impact on either the Court's agenda or on its level of support for civil liberties. Using data on Court decisions at five-year intervals, he notes (1998) that the proportion of the Court's agenda devoted to 'civil liberties and civil rights' increased dramatically between 1960 and 1990; but then he argues that this trend began well before the Charter and that it seemed to be related more to increases in the support structure for rights litigation than to the Charter itself. He concludes that 'contrary to expectations, the Charter had no sustained effect on the Court's level of support for the rights claims on its agenda' (1996, 773). Perhaps even more surprising, he finds no increase in the proportion of cases decided on constitutional grounds since the adoption of the Charter. These surprising conclusions seem to contradict most previous empirical and more doctrinal analyses of the Charter's effects, yet Epp's results have yet to be seriously challenged. Though his findings were published in one of the most prestigious journals of political science, there are some potentially serious flaws in the methods he applied to reach his surprising conclusions. First, he doesn't explain how he coded 'civil rights and liberties,' and the number of cases produced by his coding seems to be at odds with the numbers of cases arrived at in other studies of Court decisions for the same period. Second and more seriously, he only examines the cases in one year in each five (i.e., 1960, 1965, 1970) and thus runs the risk that his data are not representative. Finally, his analysis of Charter outcomes ends in 1990.

Remember here that chapter 3 raised serious questions about the validity of Epp's claims regarding agenda change. It was shown that there was a dramatic increase in the proportion of the Court's docket devoted to civil liberties cases after the adoption of the Charter. The proportion of cases raising constitutional challenges also increased rapidly. In the following analysis, Epp's claims about outcomes in civil rights and liberties cases and his conclusions about the exercise of judicial review are subjected to a more extensive analysis, one that involves all cases decided by the Court (instead of just those decided every five years). Also, the analysis will be carried forward to 2003 in order to obtain a fuller account of Charter adjudication.

Refer again to table 6.6. As noted earlier, when all of the Court's civil liberties decisions from 1970 to 2003 are considered, Epp's claim that the Charter had no sustained effect on the Court's support for rights claims appears to be contradicted. In the eight years immediately before the first Charter cases came to the Court, rights claimants won only 23 per cent of the cases decided by the Court. Over the next eight years, the success of rights claimants more than doubled. Those figures are as far as Epp extends his analysis. His conclusion that the Charter's effect was not 'sustained' was based on an analysis of just two years' worth of data after the adoption of the Charter (1985 and 1990). He did not look at any outcomes after 1990. Yet table 6.6 indicates that besides dramatically increasing its support for rights claims in the first eight years after the Charter, the Court continued to provide much higher rates of support for rights claimants for the thirteen post-Charter years that Epp did not examine than in the pre-Charter years.

Perhaps even more surprising was Epp's claim that the proportion of constitutional cases did not increase after the Charter was adopted. Instead, he suggests that there may simply have been a substitution – that is, the Charter was used as a basis for decisions instead of an alternative constitutional argument. Table 6.7 presents a computation of the proportion of cases in each of five periods with no constitutional issue versus those with constitutional challenges to laws and executive decisions.

The data show unambiguously that before 1984, the Supreme Court considered constitutional challenges in only a very small percentage of cases (fewer than 7 per cent in both pre-Charter periods). But after the adoption of the Charter, the proportion of cases raising constitutional

Table 6.7
Changes over time in frequency of judicial review by the Supreme Court of Canada, 1970–2003

Time period	No const. issue (%)	Law challenged		Executive action challenged		
		Struck (%)	Upheld (%)	Struck (%)	Upheld (%)	N
1970–75	96.8	0.3	1.7	0.5	0.7	584
1976–83	93.7	1.8	2.5	1.2	0.9	679
1984–90	75.3	2.7	8.9	5.1	8.0	587
1991–99	72.0	3.9	7.1	6.3	10.8	920
2000–03	78.8	4.0	9.0	4.0	4.3	278
Overall	82.8	2.5	5.5	3.6	5.5	3048

issues exploded, contributing more than three times the proportion of constitutional issues in each of our three post-Charter periods than in either of the two pre-Charter periods. Moreover, the rate at which the Court struck down both challenged laws and challenged actions of the executive branch also increased after the Charter. These same trends hold both for the period immediately after the Charter that Epps examined (in part) and for the thirteen subsequent years not included in Epp's analysis.

Besides refuting Epp's claims, table 6.7 shows that though the frequency of constitutional issues increased dramatically after the Charter, they still comprise less than one-third of the Court's agenda. Moreover, while many of the cases in which federal and provincial laws and actions have been struck down as violations of the Charter have received extensive media coverage, they remain a small proportion of the Court's output. Since the Charter, fewer than 4 per cent of all Supreme Court decisions have struck down either a federal or a provincial law, and decisions striking down executive actions have been only slightly more frequent.

In the next table, consideration of the impact of the Charter on the output of the Court is continued with a comparison of the basis of decisions in constitutional cases. Before 1984, of course, all constitutional challenges were based on the Constitution Act of 1867. After the Charter, constitutional challenges under that earlier act continued to be within the jurisdiction of the Court and continued to be brought to the Court along with Charter cases. Tables 6.7 and 6.8 indicate that the

Table 6.8
Basis of constitutional challenges resolved by
the Supreme Court of Canada, 1970–2003

Time period	Basis of constitutional challenge		N
	BNA Act (%)	Charter (%)	
1970–75	100	0	17
1976–83	100	0	40
1984–90	16.9	83.1	142
1991–99	14.1	85.9	256
2000–03	18.0	82.0	61
Overall	23.8	76.2	516

number of cases raising constitutional questions increased dramatically after 1984 and that the basis of the challenge changed dramatically as well. After 1984, more than four-fifths of all constitutional
cases raised claims under the Charter rather than the Constitution Act.
This proportion has remained nearly constant across the three post-
Charter periods.

The Charter of Rights has thirty-four sections, and both the frequency of litigation and the success of Charter claimants have varied
dramatically according to which sections of the Charter are being
'called out.' Also, appellants sometimes raise issues relating to multiple provisions of the Charter and scholars disagree over which of the
several provisions litigated is really the 'most important' issue in the
case at hand. Usually there is no completely objective way to determine which of the Charter issues raised in the case is the most important. The analysis below of the success of Charter claimants relies on
the judgment of the Court's professional staff. For each case, those people prepare a series of 'tag lines' – which appear at the top of each
opinion – that abstract the key legal issues from their perspective.
These tag lines are widely used by lawyers and legal scholars to search
for cases of interest. For the analysis below, the first two Charter provisions that were mentioned in the tag lines were used and the case outcome was coded as to whether the opinion supported or opposed the
position of the Charter claimant on each of these two Charter issues.[8]

The tag lines for the cases indicate that that just eleven Charter sections have accounted for the bulk of claims resolved by the Supreme

Table 6.9
Support for Charter claimants by the Supreme Court of Canada for selected sections
of the Charter of Rights

Charter section	Pro-rights claimant (%)	N
1 Reasonable limits to rights	62.5	164
2 Fundamental freedoms	35.5	62
6 Enter and leave Canada	38.5	13
7 Life, liberty, and security of person	35.1	151
8 Search and seizure	37.7	69
9 No arbitrary detention	42.9	14
10 Right to counsel and habeas corpus	57.5	40
11 Criminal procedure rights	33.3	81
12 No cruel and unusual punishment	27.3	11
15 Equality rights	28.6	42
24 Exclusion of evidence	50.8	65
— Other rights	46.5	43
Total	39.5	607

Court. Table 6.9 displays the results for all sections of the Charter with decisions by the Court in at least ten cases. Overall, through the end of 2003, Charter claimants have been successful in just under 40 percent of the challenges that have reached the Court. Whether one takes this as evidence that the Court is 'liberal' or 'conservative' depends on one's frame of reference. By a conventional calculus, one could say that the Court has made a conservative decision in a substantial proportion of its decisions; thus the Court is 'conservative' and the Charter has advanced a conservative rather than a liberal agenda. Alternatively, one might take the pre-Charter status quo as the point of reference. From that reference point, one would conclude that on 240 occasions, litigants have challenged the status quo, been able to take their rights claim all the way to the Supreme Court, and achieved the validation of a right previously not recognized.

Moreover, the Charter's impact has been much greater than the simple success rate might suggest, because presumably there has been a ripple effect, with both the lower courts and the executive taking account of each successive rights decision of the Court and altering their subsequent behaviour accordingly. There is, then, a multiplier effect from each rights decision by the Supreme Court that affects many more people than the litigants in the Court. The nature of the ripple effect can be guessed by noting the pattern over time. As noted above (see Morton, Russell, and Withey 1992), in its first two years of Charter litigation, close to two-thirds of Charter rights claimants were successful, but subsequently the success of rights claimants dropped significantly. Table 6.9 indicates that the success of those claimants continued at near these lower rates through 2003. One might interpret these findings as indicating that there was an initial period in which challenges were brought to practices and laws whose origin was prior to the Charter and that the Court sought to bring these prior practices into conformity with the Charter's new requirements. In these initial challenges, rights claimants were often successful. These early Charter decisions were presumably watched carefully both by lower-court judges and by government administrators, who then tried to adjust their own behaviour to conform to the Supreme Court's initial interpretations of the Charter. Subsequently, interest groups and other rights claimants sought to expand their initial gains by bringing 'second generation' rights claims, which sought to push the interpretation of the Charter towards even greater protection of rights. It is likely that the second- and third-generation issues brought to the Court typically asked either that the Court extend the protection of the Charter into new areas or that the Court give a more expansive reading of the rights guarantees than had been provided in earlier cases. As Justice J noted in an interview with the author, litigants (especially those supported by organized groups) tend to 'flex their muscles' after being encouraged by a previous pro-rights decision with the result that the 'Charter is pled in everything' that comes to the Court over the following few years. In such a scenario, it would be likely that the proportion of cases in which rights claimants were successful would be relatively modest even if the Court was steadily expanding rights (i.e., moving policy in a liberal direction) at the margins.

For example, in R v. Brydges[9] a unanimous court ruled that the Charter required police to notify suspects of their right to retain counsel and that police must refrain from eliciting information from the detainee until he or she had had a reasonable opportunity to exercise that right. This was an easy win for rights claimants because the result seemed mandated in a fairly straightforward manner by the words of the Charter itself. Then, four years later, in R v. Prosper,[10] the courts faced a more difficult 'second generation' question: Did the Charter require the government to provide free and immediate counsel to indigent detainees?

Here it was possible to make a reasoned argument in favour of the position advocated by the rights claimants, but a pro-claimant outcome was certainly not mandated in an unambiguous manner by the Charter's text (see Kelly 2005, 116).

Similarly, a recent analysis indicates that most of the statutes struck down before 1990 had been passed before the Charter's adoption. In the 1990s and the twenty-first century, however, most statutes challenged on Charter grounds have been passed *since* the Charter, and these statutes have undergone extensive Charter screening by Cabinet before passage (and thus the rights protected in these 1990s decisions have been more expansive than many of the rights in the decisions in the 1980s). The pre-1982 legislation 'was designed in a policy context that placed less emphasis on protected rights' (ibid., 144). Thus, though the percentage of pro-rights decisions made by the Supreme Court in the late 1990s and the early part of the twenty-first century is lower than the analogous percentage of decisions in the period immediately after the Charter, it is plausible that the Court may now be supporting an even more expansive interpretation of rights because the recent laws struck down have been the ones that have undergone extensive vetting by Cabinet to ensure that they protect Charter rights. This vetting process includes consideration of past Charter decisions by the appellate courts.

Table 6.9 also indicates that rights claimants have had different degrees of success litigating different provisions of the Charter. The lowest rates of success for rights claimants have come in cases raising a series of criminal procedure rights listed in Sections 11 and 12, which include a prohibition of unreasonable delay in being brought to trial, protection against self-incrimination, prohibition of unreasonable bail, and prohibitions against double jeopardy and cruel and unusual punishment. Rights claimants have also had low success rates litigating under Section 7, which is similar to the 'due process' clause of the U.S. Bill of Rights. Section 7 states: 'Everyone has a right to life, liberty and security of the person and the right not to be deprived thereof except in accordance with the principles of fundamental justice.' The relatively broad and vague language of this section perhaps invites rights claimants to challenge a wide variety of well-established practices, with the low success rate indicating that these claims often ask the Court to depart from the status quo to a greater extent than the justices are willing to permit. Finally, given the nature of the criticism of Charter politics offered by critics such as Morton and Knopff, one might expect that claimants under the equality rights provisions of Section 15 would have a high rate of success. Instead, table 6.9 indicates that claims of denial of equal rights succeeded less than one-third of the time.

Conclusions

While the proportion of the Supreme Court's docket devoted to criminal appeals and civil liberties claims has increased substantially over the past third of a century, the success of criminal defendants and rights claimants remains relatively low. Yet there appears to be little support for Epp's controversial claim that bills of rights do not have any appreciable impact on the policy outcomes of high courts. Since the Charter, in percentage terms, there has been a substantial increase in constitutional challenges – an increase driven by rights claims. Moreover, while the overall success rate of rights claimants remains below 50 per cent, that rate has increased substantially since the Charter. It may also be inferred that changes in policy brought about by litigation under the Charter have been quite substantial in the aggregate if one focuses not on the percentage of successful appeals but rather on the number of changes in the status quo that have been brought about both directly and indirectly by the Charter of Rights.

7 Decision-Making Models of Individual Voting

The previous chapter focused on the patterns of decisions by the Supreme Court as a whole and on how the patterns of decisions changed over time. In this chapter the focus shifts from that aggregate level of analysis to the level of individual justices. The particular concern is to explain differences among the justices that may reflect differences in backgrounds and experiences. Thus, instead of examining all decisions as in chapter 6, the following analysis limits itself to the decisions of the justices in non-unanimous decisions. To understand the patterns of decisions that will be explored, it may first be helpful to think about *why* justices make the decisions they do. What factors influence their decisions? This question has been the central interest of social scientists who have studied the courts for most of the past half century. This chapter begins by exploring the most prominent theories of judicial decision making suggested by legal scholars. After that, evidence in support of those theories in Canada and in other appellate courts will be assessed. Following this overview of previous studies, the chapter will begin analysing the actual patterns of votes on the Supreme Court of Canada.

Explanations of Judicial Decision Making

In most traditional accounts of courts, judges are viewed as skilled scholars who apply well-settled legal rules to settle concrete disputes. This way of thinking about courts and judges has been described by scholars as the 'legal model' of judicial decision making. However, one of the central concerns of both social scientists and journalists is the role of politics in those decisions. Scholars are concerned both with the political role of courts – especially 'who wins and who loses' – and with the potential impact of political factors on court decisions. The question of who wins and who loses was explored in chapter 4. Here the analysis focuses more on the second question: Do political factors influence justices' decisions? The most prominent approach to understanding the decisions of appellate courts in the United States has been the 'attitudinal model,' whose basic contention is that judges' decisions are influenced by their political preferences and ideology. Most of the empirical support for the attitudinal model comes from the United States, but in recent years it has also been used to explain judicial behaviour across a wide spectrum of courts, including the Supreme Court of Canada. A final approach to understanding judicial decision making is known as the 'strategic model,' in which the propensity of judges to make judicial policy that is consistent with their personal policy preferences is constrained by institutional arrangements as well as by the possible reactions of other political actors. However, little evidence in support of a strategic interpretation of Canadian judicial politics has been produced in previous studies, so it will be given only brief attention in this chapter.

The Legal Model

The legal model is based on the view that judges are neutral arbiters who apply objective statements of the law to resolve disputes. Judges 'find' the law, they do not 'make' it (Hart 1961). Richardson and Vines (1970) suggest that in the United States (and, one might presume, in most other common law countries as well) there is a 'legal subculture' in the larger society that is strongly reinforced by the socialization that future judges receive in law school and throughout much of their legal practice prior to taking their place on the bench. According to the legal model, judges apply established legal doctrine from previous cases, statutes, constitutions, and so on to determine outcomes in cases. Adjudicating under the legal model allows both litigants and society predictability in the outcomes of cases and provides continuity in the law (Carter 1998; Klein and Lindquist 2002).

Most social scientists believe that a purely legalistic approach to judicial decision making in appellate courts does not exist. Few believe that judges are capable of applying the law in a mechanistic way without at least the subconscious influence of their personal preferences and expectations. Even in England, where the idea of a non-political judiciary is perhaps most deeply rooted, political scientists question the utility of the purely legal model (Robertson 1982, 1998).

In high courts, a straightforward application of the legal model is difficult; justices are often confronted with 'hard' cases in which the law is unclear and in which precedent cannot easily be applied in a straightforward, 'objective' manner. When this happens, judges must apply their own interpretations of how existing law fits the present case. In such situations, complete objectivity is difficult. Thus one might suggest that justices' actual behaviour looks a lot like what is predicted by the legal model in 'easy' cases, but that politics intrudes when 'hard' cases are being considered. Alternatively, instead of thinking of the legal model and the attitudinal model as competing explanations of judicial behaviour, one might adopt the perspective of Richardson and Vines (1970) – that judges often face tugs from multiple sources within the legal subculture while at the same time experiencing the pull of attitudinal preferences and attitudes as well as expectations emanating from the larger cultural and political subculture in which they live.

The Supreme Court of Canada, which has a largely discretionary docket (see chapter 3), but which still must decide some appeals that come to the Court 'as of right,' may face a mixture of 'easy' and 'hard' cases. In hard cases, where the law is unclear, justices have a great deal of discretion, whereas they may feel more constrained by clearer manifestations of law in some easy cases coming as of right. Thus it will be no surprise if the analyses below discover evidence of some influences from both the legal model and the attitudinal model in the Court's decision-making patterns.

The legal model still has considerable support among both the general public and some legal practitioners, yet it has been difficult to establish objective empirical support for it. A key problem is that legal variables are difficult to measure in a way that is both reliable and valid. Nevertheless, some empirical analyses have developed innovative ways of overcoming these measurement problems. The most widely cited support for the legal model comes from a study of search-and-seizure decisions in the United States. Segal (1984) derived a set of case facts that could be objectively measured from legal doctrine on the standards for upholding a search and then demonstrated that these indicators of precedent had strong predictive power for the outcomes of cases even after one controlled for the Court's ideology. Follow-up studies have found that similar indicators of precedent have substantial predictive power for explaining decisions of the Supreme Court of Canada (Ostberg and Wetstein 1998; Wetstein and Ostberg 1999).

Other studies have found that elements of the legal model have had at least some impact on appellate courts' decision making. For example, based on a reading of the papers of U.S. Supreme Court justices, Knight and Epstein (1996) have found evidence of a norm favouring respect for precedent – a norm that affects both the nature and the substance of the legal rules established by the Court. In a somewhat more interpretative analysis, Epstein and Kobylka (1992) conclude from their study of death penalty decisions in the U.S. Supreme Court that 'law matters dearly' (1992, 302). Brenner and Stier (1996) have found evidence that precedent, rather than policy preferences, often sway centre justices whenever the two collide; and Richards and Kritzer have found strong evidence that both judicial ideology and legal doctrine matter in the justices' free-speech decisions (2002). Similarly, Songer and Lindquist (1996) have found evidence of the influence of precedent in the 'progeny' of landmark decisions; and Klein and Lindquist (2002), from a study of circuit conflict cases, have found evidence of the influence of legal reasoning on the decisions of justices on the U.S. Supreme Court.

The Attitudinal Model of Judicial Decision Making

Unlike the legal model, the attitudinal model holds that justices make legal decisions based on their own 'ideological attitudes and values' (Segal and Spaeth 1993, 73; see also Segal and Spaeth 2002) without the constraints of law and precedent. The attitudinal model holds that the political ideology of the justices is a complete explanation of their votes in all cases. Even when the plain meaning of the text of the law or precedent is clear, 'they are easily avoided' (Segal and Spaeth 1996, 973). As one analysis of the British House of Lords suggests, 'judges form a view of what result they want, and then employ complex and subtle arguments from precedent or from interpretive rules to provide ex post facto "justifications" for these preferences' (Robertson 1998, 13).

The attitudinal model is now the dominant paradigm among scholars who engage in empirical research on the U.S. Supreme Court and has been found to be useful as an explanation of top appellate courts in a number of other countries. As one review of the state of knowledge on judicial behaviour stated, 'in scholarship on the Supreme Court ... the view that policy considerations are dominant over legal considerations has been taken by the most prominent work' (Baum 1997, 22).

Another assessment echoes this view by concluding that 'the attitudinal model's systematic empirical shattering of the myth of mechanical
jurisprudence permeates virtually all our work on judges and courts
today' (Lawrence 1994, 3). Even critics of Segal and Spaeth concede
that while judicial attitudes may not tell the whole story of judicial decision making, 'empirical scholarship has now firmly established that
the ideological values ... of Supreme Court justices have a profound
impact on their decisions' (Songer and Lindquist 1996, 1049).

Glendon Schubert (1965) was the first to develop a well-delineated
theory of judicial decision making based on the attitudinal model. His
approach to judging showed that by scaling the individual votes of justices in prior cases, he could predict the likely voting blocs of the justices in future cases. In this model, justices have ideal points, i *points*, in
multidimensional ideological space, which represent their attitudes.
Case stimuli are represented by j *points* and these are also measured in
the same multidimensional space. According to Schubert, 'the decision
of the Court in any case will depend upon whether the case dominates,
or it is dominated by, a majority of i-*points*' (1965, 38).

Schubert found that the votes from the divided decisions of the
Court form Guttman scales with high degrees of reproducibility and
concluded that this is evidence that there is an important attitudinal dimension in judicial votes. Simple statistical tests have demonstrated
that the probability of the resulting scales is so low that the ordering of
the justices can be due neither to chance nor to any effect predicted by
the legal model. Schubert also found that there is not a single scale; instead there are separate scales: the 'E scale' for economic cases and the
'C scale' for civil liberties cases. Justices' positions on these two scales
are not necessarily the same (e.g., a justice who is a liberal on the E
scale might be a conservative on the C scale). Between these two scales,
one can accurately predict the votes of the justices in more than 80 per
cent of all non-unanimous decisions of the Supreme Court. Later research (e.g., Rohde and Spaeth 1976) has found that these two attitudinal scales have retained their predictive power for the U.S. Supreme
Court for many decades.

Beyond the evidence from scaling studies, other attempts have been
made to demonstrate the impact of judicial attitudes on votes. One approach is the attribute model (Ulmer 1973; Tate 1981; Tate and
Handberg 1991). In this approach, the social background characteristics of judges are used to predict their votes. An obvious strength of
this approach is that it avoids the problem of circularity inherent in

analyses based on scaling. Some of these characteristics include the party of the appointing president, the type of law school attended, race and gender, region, social class, religion, and prior employment. While this approach solves Schubert's problem of a priori independent variables, there are problems with this approach as well. One problem is that these demographic variables provide only an imprecise measure of judicial attitudes. Despite this criticism, a body of research over the past few decades has clarified which variables are more accurate in predicting judges' votes and which can be omitted from models. The consensus from this body of work is that at least in the United States, party and region are the most significant factors in predicting judicial votes, though with increases in the number of women and minorities on the bench, the importance of race and gender variables can also be demonstrated (Brace and Hall 1997; Tate 1981; Tate and Handberg 1991; Tate and Sittiwong 1989; Songer and Haire 1992; Songer, Davis, and Haire 1994).

A third approach to measuring judicial attitudes is through content analysis of newspaper articles. Segal and Cover (1989) measured the attitudes of justices prior to appointment by using newspaper editorials from four national newspapers (two liberal and two conservative). When judicial attitudes are defined a priori, they argue, votes cast in cases are truly independent of ideology in a statistical sense, unlike when votes are used to predict votes. This approach also avoids the problem of imprecision because same-party, same-region justices still vary in their scores. Moreover, at least for the U.S. Supreme Court, the results are quite robust, demonstrating a strong relationship between judicial attitudes and votes.

While much of the support for the attitudinal model has been developed from analyses of the U.S. Supreme Court, several quantitative studies have found attitudinal or ideological voting to be present in appellate courts around the world. Following up on his pioneering work on the U.S. Supreme court, Schubert (1968; 1969a; 1969b; 1985a; 1987) utilized scaling techniques to discover ideological voting in the high courts of Australia, South Africa, and Switzerland. A series of studies by other scholars applying Schubert's methods have found similar results in a number of other countries. For instance, scalogram analyses of the Supreme Courts of India, the Philippines, and Japan have found systematic ordering of the justices that indicates attitudinal patterns in decision making (Becker 1970; Danelski 1969; Gadbois 1969; Samonte 1969; Kawashima 1969). And even in the face of a strong tradition of parliamentary supremacy and non-political courts, Robertson has found evidence of attitudinal voting in the judicial decisions of the British House of Lords (Robertson 1998). These studies from multiple areas of the world suggest that attitudinal voting by the courts often goes hand in hand with judicial policy making.

Strategic Models

According to strategic accounts, justices pursue their policy goals, not within just the constraints of the law, but also within the constraints of their colleagues and the political/institutional environment. Strategic models of judicial voting have recently generated considerable interest among scholars, though the seminal work applying a strategic model was written more than forty years ago (Murphy 1964).

Two recent works have brought the strategic approach to the forefront. Both Epstein and Knight (1998) and Maltzman, Spriggs, and Wahlbeck (2000)[1] have utilized unique data sources in order to provide an account of judicial behaviour inside the U.S. Supreme Court. They argue that justices are constrained by one another; that is, they strategically accommodate the preferences of their colleagues without veering too far from their own preferences. Maltzman, Spriggs and Wahlbeck (2000) have found that Supreme Court justices are strategic at several stages. During opinion assignment, chief justices, acting within Supreme Court norms, assign majority opinions in an attempt to influence the content of the opinion. Justices also use conference voting norms to gauge one another's preferences. After that, opinion writers may use bargaining and accommodation with their colleagues to increase their majority size, but also, more important, to maintain the majority coalition. While less rigorous in their methodological approach, Epstein and Knight (1998) describe a similar process of judicial behaviour. Using papers of Justices Brennan, Marshall, and Powell, they provide support for the argument that justices strategically modify their positions in order to achieve their preferred policy goals.

Courts may also be strategic in the sense that they seek to maximize policy preferences while being constrained by external forces.[2] A substantial literature suggests that State Supreme Courts in the United States are responsive to external political pressure, especially in states where the justices face re-election. Langer (2002) has shown that State Supreme Courts use their agenda-setting powers to avoid salient political issues. This might occur out of fear of retaliation by the governor and state legislatures, which in turn, depends on the method of selection of state judges and the relative powers of the state's political actors. Because judicial selection and retention practices vary among states, judges must be strategically aware of the political environment in which they operate. One case study (Hall 1987) provides strong evidence that electoral incentives may at times compel judges to disregard their personal preferences and instead vote for positions favoured by their constituents.

When scholars have turned their attention to courts outside North America, strategic accounts have often been concerned with limitations on judicial independence imposed by the political contexts in which courts operate. For example, Helmke (2002) has found that judges on the Supreme Court of Argentina have often adopted a forward-looking strategic posture, reducing their support of the current government in anticipation of a likely regime change in the near future. In Helmke's account it is not clear whether in such 'strategic defections' the judges were departing from their own political preferences to avoid sanction from a future government or whether the perception of the coming demise of the current government freed them from past restraints on their decision making (or possibly both). Nevertheless, her evidence provides strong support that judicial decision making is responsive to perceptions of changes in the political environment.

There is abundant evidence that when faced with authoritarian governments or interludes of emergency rule in otherwise democratic governments, the decision making of appellate judges is constrained. Toharia (1975) found that while pre-revolution Spanish courts were able to continue to operate independently under Franco, that independence was possible only as long as they strategically refrained from challenging the government in its core concerns and refrained from challenging the authority of the special courts and court martial system set up by Franco to handle the issues it considered most politically salient. Similarly, Haynie (2003) discovered that the courts inherited from the period of English rule were allowed to function with considerable independence on most cases under the apartheid government of South Africa as long as they did not attempt to challenge the basic tenets of apartheid. These examples from Europe and Africa may be symptomatic of a more widespread pattern. Tate (1993) has argued that, at least for 'crisis regimes' in Asia, the trend has been for the new regimes to maintain the basic structure of the judicial system because the authoritarian rulers 'need to maintain an *appearance of respect for constitutionality* [emphasis in the original] ... Yet judges cannot be left free to challenge the power of the crisis regime. Consequently, ways are found to emasculate the power of judges without abolishing or directly attacking the judiciary' (1993, 317). Similarly, in much of common law Africa, there are instances of overt efforts by revolutionary governments to substantially constrain or repress attempts to implement the rule of law[3] (Widner 2001).

Studies of Decision Making by Individual Justices on the Supreme Court of Canada

There are relatively few studies of decision making on the Supreme Court of Canada. Those that do exist generally support the conclusion that the political attitudes of the justices have a strong effect on their decisions. The first support for an attitudinal understanding of judicial behaviour closely followed Schubert's development of a theory of attitudinal voting in the United States (1965). These initial studies focused mainly on judicial decision making on the Supreme Court of Canada in the 1950s and 1960s (see Fouts 1969; Peck 1969; Russell 1969).

Peck (1969) and Fouts (1969) found voting blocs to exist on the Court in the 1950s and 1960s, even before the Court was granted control of its docket and even before the expansion of a civil rights and liberties agenda as a result of the Charter of Rights and Freedoms. Using the scalogram methods developed by Schubert, Peck's analysis of the 1958 to 1967 period found voting blocs to exist on the Court across five dimensions: crime control versus due process, pro-versus anti-economic regulation, pro- versus anti-economic underdog, pro- versus anti-taxpayer, and pro- versus anti-provincial authority. In each of these areas the consistency of the alignments among the justices on their divided votes provided strong evidence that the cleavages were related to attitudinal differences among the justices. Using a similar approach, Fouts (1969) uncovered two scales for years 1950 to 1960: a criminal/civil liberties scale and a public law scale, similar to those suggested by Schubert (1965) for the U.S. Supreme Court. These conclusions were reaffirmed by Russell (1969), who also found substantial evidence of attitudinal voting by justices in this early period.

Since these early studies suggested the presence of attitudinal voting in the 1950s and 1960s, several studies have provided additional support for an attitudinal explanation from more recent Courts. Looking at the early Dickson Court (1984 to 1988), factor analytic techniques employed by Wetstein, Ostberg, and Ducat (1999) suggested two ideological dimensions underlying Charter decisions, the first being a traditional liberal versus conservative dimension, and the second, a government regulation versus societal interest dimension. Statistical analyses of the scales demonstrated strong evidence that the patterns could not have happened by chance. Their findings reinforced the conclusions of Peck and Fouts that the consistency of the alignments among the justices was so extensive that their existence could not be easily explained by anything other than an assumption that the political attitudes of the justices motivated their choices. However, the uncovering of these separate scales suggests that ideology in Canada might not be constituted in the same way as ideology in the United States among political elites since a government-regulation versus societal[interest dimension has not been found in U.S. Bill of Rights cases.

Regarding the late Dickson Court (1989 to 1990), Wetstein, Ostberg, and Ducat (1999) noticed a shift in the dimensionality of Charter decisions, finding that the justices tended to decide these cases in either a crime-control versus due-process dimension or an ethic-of-care versus ethic-of-justice dimension. Thus, scaling techniques indicate that though the specific structuring of attitudes may be changing over time, the attitudes of the justices continue to have a significant impact on their choices. By the beginning of the Lamer Court (1991 to 1995) the ethic-of-care versus ethic-of-justice dimension had replaced the crime-control versus due-process dimension as the most prominent underlying factor in Charter decisions (Ostberg, Wetstein, and Ducat 2002). Furthermore, it was suggested that in terms of judicial attributes, the communitarian ethic-of-care dimension was gender based rather than region based. Most recently, Ostberg and her colleagues (2004) have analysed the 1984–2002 terms of the Court and have found additional support for an attitudinal explanation of judicial voting.

The consistency of the results using methods similar to those developed by Schubert (1965) to lay the groundwork for the attitudinal model is impressive. In at least seven studies spanning Supreme Court decisions from 1950 until close to the present, when the divided decisions of the Court are examined, the alignments of the justices consistently support an attitudinal explanation for the cleavages.

Other attempts have been made to assess ideological decision making in Canada. The most innovative approach involved creating a measure of ideology that was independent of judicial voting and then examining whether this measure correlated with the justices' votes. Ostberg and Wetstein (1998) were the first outside the United States to replicate the highly successful methods developed by Segal and Cover (1989) to measure ideology. They created newspaper ideology scores based on editorial comments published in the *Globe and Mail* concerning the justices' ideological orientations prior to appointment to the Supreme Court. Examining a sample of search-and-seizure cases, they found that even after controlling for a detailed set of case characteristics, these independent measures of ideology provided part of the explanation for judicial decisions. In a subsequent study, a more reliable measure of ideology was developed by extending the content analysis of articles and editorials on appointments to the Supreme Court to Canada's nine leading national and regional papers. According to the authors, 'the results provide substantial support for the general proposition that the political preferences of the justices are related to their overall pattern of support for liberal versus conservative outcomes in the cases before them' (Ostberg et al. 2004, 19). Both the cumulative ideology measure and the score derived from the *Ottawa Citizen* were found to be related to the voting behaviour of the justices in civil liberties cases, criminal appeals, and in cases involving labour and economic issues.

Judicial attribute models have also been effective in measuring judicial preferences. In a study of the Supreme Court from 1949 to 1985, Tate and Sittiwong (1989) found that judicial attributes could be used to predict voting patterns in two issue areas: criminal and civil liberties cases, and economic cases. Specifically, they found that individual justices' votes on the merits could be predicted using region, religion, party of the appointing prime minister, political experience, and judicial experience. In an extension and update of their attribute model, McCormick and Greene (1990) also found social-class background to be a reliable predictor of pro-Charter rulings by the justices.

Other studies have also concluded that Canada's Supreme Court justices are ideological in their decisions and that the Charter of Rights has had a strong impact on the potential for judicial policy making. McCormick (1998) found voting blocs on the Supreme Court. In a more extensive analysis, McCormick (2000) traced the voting decisions of the justices for the half century since the Court became 'supreme at last' in 1949. In every time period, he found stable voting blocs of justices that seemed consistent with differences in judicial policy preferences. Similarly, after examining the first hundred Charter decisions,

Morton, Russell, and Withey (1992a) found clear patterns of bloc voting and concluded from this that there was 'no doubt about the ideological nature of the cleavage within the Court' (1992, 39). However, they went on to add that these differences in judicial philosophy at the heart of divisions over the Charter did not seem to be the result of conscious choices when justices were selected. Rather, they concluded that 'there has thus far been no evidence that the federal government has let ideological criteria influence its Supreme Court appointments' (ibid., 46). In interviews with the justices, Greene and his colleagues (1998) found that none of them admitted to ideological voting, though by the same token, none denied that the Court could be divided into ideological camps.

Some scholars are not surprised that justices are reluctant to admit that their decisions are ideologically based. Court decisions rarely reference the justices' attitudinal preferences; however, Gold (1985) has argued that in key Charter decisions the Court has managed to 'camouflage' its political calculations behind a veil of legal reasoning. Heard (1991) appears to agree, arguing that the 'broad and ringing phrasing of many rights contained in the Charter gives free rein to judicial discretion' (1991, 293). Having studied the voting patterns in 121 Charter cases, he provides strong evidence that in many Charter cases the outcome depends on which judges hear the case. Some justices are more than twice as likely to support Charter rights as their colleagues, and there have been consistent patterns of alignment among the justices that are too regular to have arisen from chance.

In summary, the evidence that the justices' political preferences have some influence on their votes seems strong. This does not mean that those preferences are the sole or even the principal influence on judicial choices. Almost all of the analyses discussed above are limited to the minority of cases in which the Court has been divided. Much less is known about those cases (the majority) in which the justices have reached a unanimous decision. Moreover, even in divided decisions, while the evidence shows that judicial attitudes matter, that evidence is not inconsistent with the view that attitudes interact with judicial perceptions of legal constraint and the nature of the facts to produce the ultimate decision. As Morton, Russell, and Withey (1992a) suggest, it is the justice and not the law that decides many Charter cases, but only because those cases have generally tended to be 'borderline' – that is, without clear violations of well-established rights and thus without clear, unambiguous law on either side.

Two questions remain. First, given the evidence for attitudinal influence on the divided decisions, what is the basis for the cleavages? Several scholars have concluded that the Court's ideological diversity is linked neither to ideological selection criteria, to party politics, or to gender (McCormick and Greene 1990; Heard 1991; Morton, Russell, and Withey 1992). Beyond this, in order to obtain a fuller political understanding of the Court one would want to know whether its divisions at all reflect the political cleavages in the broader society. Differences in judicial philosophy may result from a partisan selection system even when the choosers are not consciously seeking those with similar ideology; this is because differences in the ideological preferences of the government may affect whom it looks to for advice and may even subconsciously affect which people it views as 'qualified.' Second, given the near absence of studies of unanimous decisions, what explains the high rate of unanimity on the Court? The first question is addressed in the following analysis. The second is the focus of the subsequent chapter.

A First Look at Divisions on the Supreme Court

We begin our analysis of the voting divisions on the Supreme Court by looking at the patterns in four distinct issue areas for five different periods of time. The time periods employed in the analysis of agenda change are used again. In the first period, 1970–75, the Supreme Court lacked substantial agenda control and there was no Charter of Rights. Table 7.1 displays the proportion of pro-defendant decisions in criminal cases, the proportion of decisions supporting the rights claimant in civil rights and liberties cases, the proportion supporting the economic underdog in private economic disputes,[4] and the proportion supporting the government in other public law cases (i.e., cases not involving a civil liberties claim or a criminal appeal). In keeping with the focus on the basis of cleavage, only the votes of the justices in the non-unanimous decisions are included. To facilitate comparison of voting across issue areas, the justices are listed in order of their support for criminal defendants. Justices who cast fewer than five votes in divided cases in a given issue area are excluded.

The behaviour of the justices in this period in the Court's history has yet to receive much empirical study. McCormick (2000) has examined the propensity of each justice to join the majority or to dissent and his or her proclivities in opinion writing. But he does not delve into the

Table 7.1
Proportion of non-unanimous votes in favour of different policy positions by justices
on the Supreme Court of Canada, 1970–75

Justice	Party	Pro defend. (%)	Civ lib. liberal (%)	Pro underdog (%)	Pro government (%)
Fauteux	Lib.	4	–	27	–
Judson	Con.	11	14*	30	100*
Martland	Con.	14	25*	27	00*
Ritchie	Con.	17	29*	28	40*
Abbott	Lib.	20	0*	27	100*
Pigeon	Lib.	21	29*	44	67*
Dickson	Lib.	43	80*	67	–
Beetz	Lib.	50	–	58	–
Spence	Lib.	93	100*	67	17*
Hall	Con.	94	–	76	17*
Laskin	Lib.	100	100*	85	17*
Cartwright	Lib.	100*	–	60*	–
Min.		04	00	27	00
Max.		100	80	85	100

* Indicated percentage based on at least five but fewer than ten decisions.

directionality of their voting. According to McCormick, the voting in the late 1960s and early 1970s can best be understood in terms of two highly cohesive blocs, a 'Diefenbaker trio' (Judson, Martland, Ritchie) and a 'Quebec trio' (Fauteux, Abbott, Pigeon). Though table 7.1 only partially overlaps the period discussed by McCormick, it can be said that the Diefenbaker trio (appointed by Prime Minister John Diefenbaker, a Conservative) formed a cohesive conservative bloc. The justices were solidly anchored at the conservative end of the voting alignment on criminal cases: all three supported the defendant in only 11 to 17 per cent of non-unanimous votes. In addition, each supported rights claimants in fewer than one-third of their votes; similarly, all three supported the economic underdog in fewer than one-third of their votes. Thus, Diefenbaker seems to have appointed a solidly conservative cohort of justices.

At the other end of the spectrum, there were three consistent liberals (small 'l') across the same three issue areas. Justice Hall (the 'odd one out' among the Diefenbaker appointees, according to McCormick [2000, 39]) was joined by Justices Laskin and Spence, both of them appointees of Prime Minister Lester Pearson, a Liberal. Each returned a resounding 93 per cent or better level of support for criminal defendants; and two-thirds to five-sixths of the time, they favoured the economic underdog. Their record on civil issues is harder to assess with confidence because there were few such cases before the Court, but on those in which they did vote, all three appeared to be solid supporters of rights claimants.

It seems that the 'Quebec trio' was only slightly less conservative on both criminal cases and private economic cases than the 'Diefenbaker trio.' Moreover, they adopted a conservative stance on the few civil liberties cases on the agenda, with Abbott opposing the rights claim in every case. Though appointed by a Liberal prime minister, all three Quebec justices seem to have been more conservative than all of the other Liberal Party justices on the Court. Public law was the only issue on which they appeared to break with the 'Diefenbaker trio.' The Quebec judges, perhaps reflecting a more communitarian approach, had the most pro-government record of any of the justices. Of course, the small number of divided votes in this area suggests one should exercise some caution in interpreting these results.

Overall, the voting in this period has two notable characteristics. First, there seems to have been a high level of ideological cleavage on the Court. In all four of the areas examined, the range of scores among the justices is more than 60 percentage points from high to low, and in two of the areas it ranges from 4 and 0 per cent at one end to 100 per cent for at least one justice at the other end. Moreover, as you look at the total distribution, there appear to be two distinct clusters in each area, one concentrated at the conservative end of the spectrum and the other at the liberal end, with few justices in the middle range. The other feature of the voting patterns is that many of the justices are consistent across at least the three areas of criminal law, civil liberties, and private economic cases (for the other public law cases, analysis is hampered by a small number of divided votes). So the Court during that period seems to have been characterized by a relatively cohesive bloc of consistent liberals facing a relatively cohesive bloc of consistent conservatives.

Voting in the 1976 to 1983 period is described in table 7.2. This period represents the portion of the Laskin Court after the Court gained greater

Table 7.2
Proportion of non-unanimous votes in favour of different policy positions by justices
on the Supreme Court of Canada, 1976–83

Justice	Party	Pro defend. (%)	Civ lib. liberal (%)	Pro underdog (%)	Pro government (%)
Martland	Con.	14	–	40	70
Ritchie	Con.	14	–	65	50
Pigeon	Lib.	16	–	50	25*
Judson	Con.	20	–	50*	–
Beetz	Lib.	26	–	53	30
Pratte	Lib.	31	–	67*	17*
McIntyre	Lib.	37	–	67*	67*
Chouinard	Con.	40	–	–	–
Lamer	Lib.	57	–	–	–
Estey, w.z.	Lib.	60	–	67	33*
Wilson	Lib.	67*	–	–	–
Spence	Lib.	68	–	54	–
Dickson	Lib.	69	–	65	62
Laskin	Lib.	83	–	58	60
Min.		14	–	40	17
Max.		83	–	67	70

* Indicated percentage based on at least five but fewer than ten decisions.

control of its agenda. It seems that overall, ideological cleavages on the Court were not as great as in the previous period, but they are still substantial. In criminal cases, four justices supported the criminal defendant less than one-quarter of the time; at the other end, four justices cast pro-defendant votes in at least two-thirds of the divided decisions. This division appears to have had a clear partisan dimension, in that three of the four pro-prosecution justices were Conservative appointees (the 'Diefenbaker trio,' who anchored the conservative end of the Court in the previous period) while all four of the most pro-defendant justices were Liberal appointees. Chief Justice Laskin now emerged as the most liberal justice, joined frequently by two new justices (Dickson and Wilson) as well as by Justice Spence, who continued his support from the previous period for the appeals of criminal defendants.

McCormick (2000, 87) notes that before 1975, nearly 85 per cent of the appeals heard by the Court came 'as of right,' with just 15 per cent coming as the result of successful leave petitions. After 1975 these proportions almost reversed themselves. In chapter 3 it was noted that the justices' power to select which issues they heard resulted in a substantial decline in the number of private economic appeals heard, and it may be assumed that the nature of those appeals also changed. One might ask whether the change in the nature of the private economic cases coming to the Court resulted in any changes in the decisional trends of the Court. The answer appears to be yes. In the previous period, private cases were marked by sharp differences in the tendency to support the economic underdog – differences that reflected the same ideologically based partisan cleavages that characterized the criminal and civil liberties cases. This tendency appears to have been much less pronounced after 1975. While Justice Martland continued to hew to a solidly conservative line in this area, all the other justices developed moderate records ranging between 50 and 67 per cent support for the economic underdog.

The decisions in the remainder of the public law cases defy an easy political explanation, though again the small number of divided decisions makes generalizations difficult. The greatest support for the government came from the opposite ends of the ideological spectrum apparent in other issue areas. Justice Martland, who anchored the conservative end of the 'Diefenbaker trio,' was joined by Justice Dickson and Chief Justice Laskin, the two most liberal members of the Court, as the trio who most consistently supported the government. In contrast, while Quebec justices provided the greatest support for the government before 1975, now two of the justices from Quebec (Pigeon and Pratte) appear to have been among those providing the least support to the government position.

The third period examined, 1984 to 1990 (see table 7.3), corresponded roughly with the tenure of Brian Dickson as chief justice and marked the beginning of Charter of Rights litigation in the Court. There was an increase in the number of cases raising civil liberties issues. Also, the criminal appeals docket was transformed, with many criminal cases including Charter challenges to police or prosecution practices. As noted in chapter 3, this period witnessed a continued drop in the number of private economic cases heard by the Court, making analysis of decisional trends in that area difficult.

Criminal appeals continued to provide a number of cases in which the Court was divided. And table 7.3 indicates, there continued to be

Table 7.3
Proportion of non-unanimous votes in favour of different policy positions by justices on the Supreme Court of Canada, 1984–90

Justice	Party	Pro defend. (%)	Civ lib. liberal (%)	Pro underdog (%)	Pro government (%)
McIntyre	Lib.	20	17*	–	80*
L'Heureux–Dubé	Con.	22	–	–	–
Le Dain	Lib.	25	–	–	–
McLachlin	Con.	27	–	–	–
Beetz	Lib.	36	33*	–	–
Gonthier	Con.	36	40*	–	–
Dickson	Lib.	47	46	67*	33*
Chouinard	Con.	50	–	–	–
La Forest	Con.	58	62*	40*	40*
Wilson	Lib.	62	50	83*	43*
Estey, w.z.	Lib.	64	–	–	–
Lamer	Lib.	64	29*	–	20*
Sopinka	Con.	67	–	–	–
Cory	Con.	67*	–	–	–
Min.		20	17	40	20
Max.		67	62	83	80

* Indicated percentage based on at least five but fewer than ten decisions.

sharp divisions on the Court. However, turnover on the Court had changed the identity of those at the opposite ends of the ideological divide. By 1984, the 'Diefenbaker trio' was gone, and so were Justices Laskin and Spence, who had been the most consistent liberals during earlier periods. Replacing the 'Diefenbaker trio' at the conservative end of the spectrum on criminal appeals were two female Conservative Party appointees (Justices L'Heureux-Dubé and McLachlin) and two male Liberal Party appointees (Justices McIntyre and Le Dain). All four supported the prosecution between 73 and 80 per cent of the time when the Court divided. At the other end of the Court, no justice supported criminal defendants as consistently as Justices Laskin and Spence had in the previous periods, but a cluster of five justices

(Wilson, Estey, Lamer, Sopinka, Cory) supported the defence in slightly more than three of five cases. The partisan and gender backgrounds of this group were also mixed, with the most obvious common element being that four of the five came from Ontario. Overall, the difference between the most liberal and most conservative judicial record (47 percentage points) in criminal cases was much smaller than it had been in the previous two periods.

Regarding the other three issue areas, the small number of divided decisions makes it difficult to detect trends. It does appear that the justices' positions on criminal cases roughly corresponded with their positions on civil liberties. The lone exception was Justice Lamer, who had one of the most liberal records on criminal appeals but the second most conservative record in civil liberties cases. In private economic cases, Justice Wilson stood out as a stout defender of economic underdogs, but little else can be gleaned from the small number of divided decisions.

The period 1991 to 1999 corresponds roughly to the Lamer Court.[5] For our purposes, the period has the fortunate circumstance that there were abundant divided decisions in all four of the issue areas examined. Once again, there were sharp differences among the justices in their tendency to support the prosecution rather than the accused in criminal appeals. One justice stands out at the conservative end: Justice L'Heureux-Dubé supported the criminal defendant in less than 10 per cent of all divided decisions, substantially less than half as often as the next most conservative justices (Justices Gonthier and Bastarache). At the other end of the spectrum, five justices cast more than 70 per cent of their votes for the defendant (Justices Sopinka, Binnie, Wilson, and Major and Chief Justice Lamer). Justices Wilson and Major topped the liberals, voting for the defendant more than eight times as often as Justice L'Heureux-Dubé. These five most consistent supporters of the defence were split along lines of party, region, and gender.

There was also a strong split on the Court over civil liberties, with two Conservative Party appointees scoring below 15 per cent support for rights claimants and two other Conservative Party appointees (Justices McLachlin and Cory) supporting rights claimants more than half the time. In contrast to the previous period, however, there does not appear to have been a strong correspondence between the liberalism of justices on criminal appeals and their liberalism on rights claims. Justices L'Heureux-Dubé and Bastarache compiled far more liberal records on rights claims than on criminal appeals, while justices La

Table 7.4
Proportion of non-unanimous votes in favour of different policy positions by justices
on the Supreme Court of Canada, 1991–99

Justice	Party	Pro defend. (%)	Civ lib. liberal (%)	Pro underdog (%)	Pro government (%)
L'Heureux–Dubé	Con.	9	50	75	71
Gonthier	Con.	26	24	60	69
Bastarache	Lib.	29	50*	60*	–
La Forest	Con.	49	14	55	77
McLachlin	Con.	49	61	39	33
Stevenson	Con.	53	00*	–	–
Iacobucci	Con.	55	50	40	64
Cory	Con.	58	58	59	60
Lamer	Lib.	72	41	44*	33*
Sopinka	Con.	75	43	46	38
Binnie	Lib.	75	–	–	–
Wilson	Lib.	80*	–	–	–
Major	Con.	80	38	38	60
Min.		0	14	38	33
Max.		80	60	75	77

* Indicated percentage based on at least five but fewer than ten decisions.

Forest, Stevenson, and Major were much more likely to support criminal defendants than rights claimants.

There was also an absence of correspondence between the positions of justices on criminal appeals and their positions on private economic cases. The three justices who were least likely to support criminal defendants (generally underdogs both economically and socially) were also the three justices most likely to support the underdog in private economic cases. Yet Justice Major showed the opposite trend, being more than twice as likely to support criminal defendants than economic underdogs.

The most successful coalition on the Court was a five-member bloc dubbed the 'gang of five' by Monahan. Indeed, according to McCormick, the firmness of this group, consisting of Justices Lamer, Sopinka, Cory, Iacobucci, and Major, was the 'single most important

factor in understanding the voting dynamics of the Lamer Court'
(2000, 135). As might be expected, table 7.4 indicates that this group
(with the notable exception of Justice Major) constituted a centre or
centre-left coalition on all four of the issue areas. While as noted above,
many of the justices flipped between strong support for the liberal and
conservative positions when the issue changed from criminal appeals
to civil liberties claims to economic cases, four of the justices (all except
Justice Major) in this 'gang of five' adopted positions that were consistently near the ideological middle of the Court on all four issues.

In the most recent period examined (2000 to 2003), the Supreme
Court of Canada became the first major Court in the common law
world to be presided over by a female chief justice. Table 7.5 indicates
that in the first four years of the McLachlin Court, the justices took a
wide range of positions in the divided decisions. In criminal cases, the
three justices with the most conservative records on the Lamer Court
(L'Heureux-Dubé, Bastarache, and Gonthier) again were the most reliable supporters of the prosecution, supporting the criminal defendant
in less than 15 per cent of all divided decisions. At the other end of the
spectrum, the most liberal justice on criminal appeals in the Lamer
Court fell to second place in support of defendants behind a new justice, Louise Arbour.

Continuing the trend of the Lamer Court, there was little correspondence between the positions of the justices on different issues. Arguably the most variable among the justices was Justice Binnie, who was
the most conservative justice (i.e., the least supportive of the underdog) on private economic cases, the most liberal justice on the Court in
civil liberties cases, and squarely in the middle of the Court on criminal cases. Other justices, too, had records that varied substantially
across issue areas. Justice L'Heureux-Dubé had the most conservative
record on the Court in criminal cases (supporting the prosecution in
every divided case) but the most liberal record in private economic
disputes. Similarly, Chief Justice McLachlin was an infrequent supporter of criminal defendants but had one of the strongest records on
the Court in support of rights claimants and economic underdogs.
Justice Iacobucci remained near the middle of the Court on all three
issues, and Justice Arbour was a classic liberal across the board, providing strong support for criminal defendants, rights claimants, and
economic underdogs.

How is one to make sense of this variation? Both the substantial variations among the justices in all three issue areas and the relatively high
consistency for most justices from one time period to the next suggest

Table 7.5
Proportion of non-unanimous votes in favour of different policy positions by justices on
the Supreme Court of Canada, 2000–3

Justice	Party	Pro defend. (%)	Civ lib. liberal (%)	Pro underdog (%)	Pro government (%)
L'Heureux–Dubé	Con.	0	17	100*	–
Bastarache	Lib.	13	43*	40*	–
Gonthier	Con.	15	17*	57*	–
McLachlin	Con.	26	71*	80*	–
Binnie	Lib.	48	83*	20*	–
Iacobucci	Con.	67	50*	67*	–
Lebel	Lib.	67	–	50*	–
Major	Con.	72	43*	50*	–
Arbour	Lib.	85	67*	80*	–
Min.		00	17	20	–
Max.		85	83	100	–

* Indicated percentage based on at least five but fewer than ten decisions.

that the divisions on the Court are a product of differences in judicial philosophy or ideology. However, when combined with differences across issue areas, the data imply that the philosophical differences cannot be neatly captured by the traditional liberal versus conservative continuum. Rather, many of the justices have more complex policy preferences. As Ostberg and Wetstein (2007) have recently demonstrated, the voting of the Canadian justices tends to be ideologically 'consistent' but the differences cannot be explained simply by placing the justices along a single ideological dimension. To more adequately represent the ideological differences among the justices, one must locate them in a more complex, multidimensional space. Ostberg and Wetstein suggest that such an ideological space must be oriented in terms of separate dimensions relating to order, freedom, and equality. Moreover, few of the justices are located at the extremes of any of these dimensions. Thus the analysis of the nature of these cleavages on the Court reinforces the conclusion introduced earlier – that the Supreme Court of Canada must in some important sense be understood as a political court, yet it is nonetheless a moderate court rather than a sharply divided ideological court.

Judicial Backgrounds and the Bases of Cleavages on the Court

Having examined individual differences among the justices, the analysis now shifts to exploring whether there are any consistent commonalities in the backgrounds of the justices that are associated with the differences in the patterns of votes discovered in the last section. Tate and Sittiwong (1989) analysed voting patterns on the Supreme Court in the 1950s, 1960s, and 1970s and suggest that over that extended period, the justices' votes were strongly related to three factors: the political party of the appointing prime minister, the region from which the justice was appointed, and the religion of the justice.[6] The continuing relationship between these factors and voting patterns on the Supreme Court for the period 1970 to 2003 is explored next. The present analysis retains the dichotomy between Catholics and other religions (overwhelmingly Protestant Christians in the period studied) used by Tate and Sittiwong as well as the dichotomy for the party of the prime minister. However, the subsequent analyses depart from the Tate/Sittiwong dichotomy of Quebec/non-Quebec for capturing regional effects. To gain a fuller understanding of regional cleavages on the Supreme Court, judicial origins have been categorized as follows: Quebec, Ontario (by law and practice, each of these provinces has three justices on the Court), the 'East' (i.e., the Atlantic provinces), and the 'West' (i.e., all provinces west of Ontario).

Critics of some studies that establish support for the attitudinal model (see above) object to methods such as Guttman scaling and to factor analyses that rely on the justices' votes to infer attitudes. These critics have suggested that scholars ought instead to search for indicators that are independent of and prior to the justices' voting behaviour. One of the most obvious a priori measures utilized in the discipline is the party affiliation of the appointing chief executive. (For examples in the United States, see Tate and Handberg 1991; Wasby 1993. For Canada, see Tate and Sittiwong 1989; Songer and Johnson 2007; Ostberg and Wetstein 1998; Wetstein and Ostberg 1999.) The presumption here is that political conflict in other arenas is often structured along party lines; in other words, policy-oriented chief executives are likely to appoint justices to the high court who mirror their own ideological beliefs. In line with past research in this area, a measure of the party of the prime minister is included in the analysis, which has been coded as a dichotomous variable (1 = Conservative appointee, 2 = Liberal appointee). The expectation of an attitudinal interpretation of cleavages on the Court is that appointment by a Liberal prime minister should be associated with more 'liberal' policy choices by the justices, including support for criminal defendants, rights claimants, and economic underdogs.

The relationship between the decisional trends of the justices and the political party of the appointing prime minister is presented in table 7.6. The results suggest that over the thirty-four-year period studied, when it comes to divided decisions, there has been a moderately strong relationship between the appointing party and the policy positions supported by the justices. That is, justices appointed by Liberal prime ministers have been more likely to support both criminal defendants and economic underdogs to a statistically significant extent. However, the magnitude of party differences is moderate – an 11-percentage-point differential in criminal cases and slightly less than a 10-point differential in economic cases. Differences in civil liberties cases are in the predicted direction (i.e., Liberal appointees support rights claimants more frequently) but are not statistically significant.

The results parallel those reported by Tate and Sittiwong (1989) for an earlier period. Thus, in spite of continuing disclaimers by both government officials and earlier studies that there are no partisan-based ideological criteria for selecting justices, empirical studies suggest that throughout the more than half century since the Supreme Court of Canada became the court of last resort in 1949, there have in fact been party-based differences in the policy-relevant decision making of the justices. Also paralleling the earlier findings of Tate and Sittiwong, the magnitude of the differences between parties, while too large to have occurred by chance, are relatively modest. That is, there are definite party-based differences, but party cohorts on the Court are far from monolithic; the average members of each party tend to be different, but there is considerable variation within each party as well.

The logic behind assessing differences among justices in terms of political parties has been extended to include other judicial attributes. Since regional conflict permeates Canadian politics, it is natural to ask whether regionally based political differences have extended to policy-relevant behaviour on the Supreme Court.

An examination of the regional origins of the justices reveals statistically significant differences in three different policy areas. Regarding criminal cases, Ontario justices have been twice as likely as Western justices to support criminal defendants, and the propensities of justices from Quebec have been only marginally different from those of Western justices. Justices from the Atlantic provinces land in

Table 7.6
Differences in policy positions supported by justices appointed by Liberal vs Conservative prime ministers in non-unanimous votes in different policy areas on the Supreme Court of Canada, 1970–2003

Prime minister's party	Pro defend. (%) (n)	Civ. lib. liberal (%) (n)	Pro underdog (%) (n)	Pro government (%) (n)
Conservative	42.3	41.7	47.1	54.0
	(1352)	(297)	(340)	(187)
Liberal	53.1	48.7	56.6	48.4
	(1024)	(160)	(373)	(157)
Chi Square[1]	27.37***	2.06	6.15**	1.07

[1] Calculated from contingency table
*P < .05
**P < .01

Table 7.7
Differences in policy positions supported by justices appointed from different regions in non-unanimous votes in different policy areas on the Supreme Court of Canada, 1970–2003

Religion	Pro defend. (%) (n)	Civ. lib. liberal (%) (n)	Pro underdog (%) (n)	Pro government (%) (n)
East	50.3	48.6	48.6	51.0
	(702)	(138)	(177)	(100)
West	33.1	33.3	42.7	57.5
	(263)	(54)	(82)	(40)
Ontario	66.3	56.9	60.3	50.0
	(605)	(102)	(209)	(90)
Quebec	34.1	36.2	49.5	50.9
	(806)	(59)	(204)	(114)
Chi sq.[1]	167.48**	14.51**	9.91*	0.68

[1] Calculated from contingency table
*P < .05
**P < .01

the middle. The magnitude of these regional differences is substantial – roughly three times the magnitude of party-related differences.

Regarding civil liberties, the differences are also substantial, albeit not as great as the regional differences for criminal appeals. Once again, justices from Ontario have been the most liberal, with justices from both Quebec and the West supporting rights claims only 60 per cent as often as the justices from Ontario. The Atlantic provinces again fall in the middle.

Regarding private economic cases, the pattern is only slightly different, though the magnitude of regional differences is smaller than in the other two areas. Justices from Ontario again have stood out as the most liberal, supporting the economic underdog in 60 per cent of divided decisions. Justices from the other provinces have supported the underdog at rates varying from 42 to 49 per cent. There are no apparent regional differences in voting on other public law cases.

Tate and Sittiwong assumed, consistent with most academic writing on Canadian politics and with most journalistic accounts, that the regional effect that matters most is between Quebec and 'English' Canada. Yet table 7.7 suggests that in terms of actual differences in judicial behaviour on the Supreme Court, it is Ontario that stands apart. In three important areas of judicial policy making, the justices from Ontario on average have been much more likely to support liberal outcomes than the justices from other provinces. In contrast, the voting behaviour of justices from Quebec has been largely indistinguishable from the voting of justices from at least one of the other two regions in each of the three policy areas examined.

When asked, particularly in reference to Tate and Sittiwong's study, the justices interviewed for this project were unanimous that religious differences may at one time have shaped judicial philosophy but that religion no longer mattered. Table 7.8 suggests that the justices are wrong! Both in criminal appeals and in civil liberties cases, the differences between the voting records of Catholic versus non-Catholic justices continue to be statistically significant. Non-Catholic justices have been moderately more likely than Catholic ones to support criminal defendants and have been much more likely to support rights claimants in civil liberties cases. While the magnitude of the differences is not as great as can be associated with regional origins, the relationship between religion and voting seems about as strong as the one between political party to voting.

Table 7.8
Differences in policy positions supported by Catholic vs non-Catholic justices in
non-unanimous votes in different policy areas on the Supreme Court of Canada,
1970–2003

Religion	Pro defend. (%) (n)	Civ. lib. liberal (%) (n)	Pro underdog (%) (n)	Pro government (%) (n)
Non-Catholic	48.1	51.9	51.2	54.1
	(1212)	(212)	(406)	(183)
Catholic	42.7	36.8	53.6	49.0
	(1047)	(220)	(250)	(145)
Chi sq.[1]	6.62*	9.94**	0.35	0.85

[1] Calculated from contingency table
*P < .05
**P < .01

In summary, when the justices cannot achieve unanimity on the case before them, the cleavages seen to be related to party, region, and religion. Of these three, region seems to have the greatest impact.

Change over Time in Models of Judicial Behaviour

It has been established that cleavages on the Supreme Court are related to party, region, and religion. The following analysis develops models of judicial behaviour in three policy areas.[7] In each of these three, the effects of these sources of cleavage is examined in a multivariate model that allows us to examine the impact of each variable while controlling for the effects of all other variables. Moreover, since there has been some hint of its relevance in the examination of the behaviour of individual justices (see tables 7.1 to 7.5), separate models are run for the pre-Charter (i.e., 1970–83) and post-Charter (1984–2003) eras. Since the dependent variable is dichotomous and ordinary least squares models are inappropriate, logistic regression is used to model the likelihood of a 'liberal' vote in each policy area (Aldrich and Nelson 1984). Four dummy variables have been created to permit the assessment of regional effects. The variable 'East' has been excluded from each table, so one may interpret the coefficients for 'Quebec,' 'Ontario,' and 'West' as indicating the effect of being from that region compared to being a justice from the Atlantic provinces. Comparison of the two models in each area will provide some insight into whether cleavages on the Court have changed over time.

A comparison of the models of judicial behaviour before and after the onset of Charter litigation (see table 7.9) suggests that there has not been any fundamental change in the basic cleavages on the Court in criminal cases over the past third of a century. This may be somewhat surprising, given that the Charter changed the nature of the legal issues argued in many of the criminal cases coming to the Court. However, the results in table 7.9 suggest that there may be more basic orientations towards defendants and prosecutors that influence the interpretation of the legal issues involved in the 'hard' cases (i.e., those without clear precedent that divide the court). And this basic orientation or judicial philosophy appears to remain relatively constant whether the issues are statutory and factual (as in the 1970–83 period) or involve the interpretation of the Charter (since 1984).

The findings suggest that the effects of party, region, and religion are independent of one another and operate jointly. Even after controlling for region and religion, Liberal appointees have been more likely than their colleagues appointed by Conservatives to support criminal defendants. This was true before the Charter and it remains true.

Regional effects are similar but not identical over the two eras. Justices from Ontario have always been significantly more likely than those from Quebec to support criminal defendants. The evident change is that in the pre-Charter era, and by a wide margin, justices from Quebec were the most likely to support the prosecution. In post-Charter litigation, however, the behaviour of justices from Quebec has been indistinguishable from that of justices from the Atlantic provinces.

Catholic justices are *more* likely than non-Catholics to support criminal defendants after controlling for the effects of party and region. The results are consistent across time, yet they are also directly opposite to the apparent relationship between religion and behaviour in criminal cases observed in table 7.8, where the relationship between religion and voting was examined in isolation from other influences on the justices. When these results are taken together with the effects of the other variables, it seems that Catholics from Quebec may be more conservative than Protestants, whereas Catholics outside Quebec may be more liberal in criminal cases than their Protestant colleagues.

Table 7.9
Logistic regression models of the likelihood of pro-defendant vote by justices on the
Supreme Court of Canada, pre- and post-Charter periods

Variable	Pre-Charter (1984–2003) MLE	SE	Post-Charter (1970–83) MLE	SE
Party of PM	0.638***	0.121	2.141***	0.229
Quebec	−0.238	0.181	−4.057***	0.653
Ontario	1.538***	0.260	0.630#	0.344
West	1.191***	0.223	−0.181	0.348
Catholic	0.911***	0.167	2.608***	0.481
Intercept	−5.399	0.932	−2.702	1.142
	N = 1,469 −2Log L = 1929.56 Chi sq. = 93.63***		N = 827 −2Log L = 886.76 Chi sq. = 179.50***	

* P < .05
** P < .01
*** P < .001
# .05 < P < .10

Table 7.10
Logistic regression models of the likelihood of a pro-rights claimant vote in civil liberties
cases by justices on the Supreme Court of Canada, pre- and post-Charter periods

Variable	Pre-Charter (1984–2003) MLE	SE	Post-Charter (1970–83) MLE	SE
Party of PM	0.087	0.237	3.052***	0.746
Quebec	0.246	0.357	−5.632***	1.713
Ontario	0.880#	0.492	−0.120	0.930
West	0.432	0.447	−0.447	0.921
Catholic	−0.354	0.313	2.761*	1.217
Intercept	−1.729	1.825	−1.403	3.078
	N = 372 −2Log L = 497.53 Chi sq. = 12.55*		N = 95 −2Log L = 92.06 Chi sq. = 25.12***	

* P < .05
** P < .01
*** P < .001
# .05 < P < .10

In contrast to the findings for criminal cases, it appears that there has been substantial change over time in the nature of the cleavages in the divided civil liberties decisions of the Court. Before the Charter, party, region, and religion were all significantly related to the justices' voting choices. Liberal appointees were much more likely than Conservative ones to support rights claims. Similarly, Catholics gave more support to rights claims than did Protestants. And finally, just as in criminal cases, justices from Quebec in the pre-Charter era stood out as more hostile to rights claims than justices from other regions. But in the post-Charter era these cleavages have largely disappeared. There are no differences in voting on civil rights cases that can be associated with either party or religion, and regional differences have been sharply reduced.

The preceding analysis has pointed to strong differences among individual justices with regard to rights claims. This suggests that a new cleavage has arisen in the post-Charter era. The final section of this chapter explores one possible new cleavage.

Table 7.11 suggests that there has been substantial change over time in the bases of cleavages in divided private economic cases. This is somewhat surprising, since the issues in these cases should not have been affected much by the Charter. Yet for the pre-Charter era a pattern is evident that is very similar to the patterns of judicial behaviour in the other two issue areas for the same period. Party, region, and religion are all strongly related to voting choice even when the effects of the other variables are controlled. Moreover, the directionality of the effects is very similar. In the pre-Charter era, Liberal appointees were much more likely than Conservative ones to support the economic underdog. Similarly, Catholics were more likely than non-Catholics to support the underdog. Finally, as in the other two issue areas, justices from Quebec were significantly different from justices from all of the other regions and were more likely than others to support the conservative (i.e., not the underdog) position.

In sharp contrast to these findings for the pre-Charter period, none of the variables in the model has a statistically significant effect when it comes to the post-Charter era. Neither party nor region nor religion seems to be related to the pattern of judicial voting. Since individual differences among the justices remained substantial, it must be that there are new bases of cleavage that have divided the Court in the post-Charter era. One possible basis for the new cleavages is investigated below.

Table 7.11
Logistic regression models of the likelihood of a pro-underdog vote in private economic cases by justices on the Supreme Court of Canada, pre- and post-Charter periods

Variable	Pre-Charter (1984–2003) MLE	SE	Post-Charter (1970–83) MLE	SE
Party of PM	−0.402	0.300	1.468***	0.287
Quebec	0.122	0.434	−2.617***	0.630
Ontario	0.656	0.586	−0.124	0.380
West	−0.458	0.523	−0.266	0.368
Catholic	0.123	0.354	1.681***	0.444
Intercept	0.152	2.138	−0.634	1.174
	N = 245 −2Log L = 330.42 Chi sq. = 7.97#		N = 447 −2Log L = 568.39 Chi sq. = 45.36***	

* P < .05
** P < .01
*** P < .001
# .05 < P < .10

Taken together, these three models of judicial voting behaviour demonstrate that in the pre-Charter era, cleavages on the Court were related to party, region, and religion. Each of these factors seems to have had an independent effect on judicial decisions in all three of the issue areas examined. Potential regional effects were disaggregated to see whether Quebec origin was an 'outlier.' The findings confirm that Quebec origin had a distinct and largely conservative impact on all three issue areas. In addition, when decisions in criminal cases and civil liberties cases were examined separately, it was found that in the pre-Charter period, the cleavages in all three issue areas were remarkably similar. This suggests that a single overarching judicial philosophy quite similar to the traditional liberal/conservative continuum characterized most of the disagreements on the Supreme Court in those years.

In the post-Charter era, pre-Charter cleavages seem to remain at the heart of disagreements on the Court, but *only* for criminal appeals. Yet even in criminal appeals, there is evidence that it is the distinctiveness of Ontario origins rather than that of Quebec origins that is driving the significance of region for the structuring of conflict. There is also some evidence of this Ontario distinctiveness in civil liberties cases, and perhaps a slight hint of it when it comes to private economic conflicts. Perhaps more important, the bases of cleavages are definitely not similar across the three issue areas: party, region, and religion seem to have lost their power to structure conflict in either civil liberties or private economic conflicts.

The Emergence of Gender as a Basis for Cleavage on the Supreme Court

The most obvious change in the composition of the Supreme Court since the first Charter litigation in 1984 began with the appointment of Bertha Wilson, its first female justice. Since then, seven women in all have been appointed. As of the middle of 2005, the Court was composed of five men and four women. The final section of this chapter begins to explore the impact of this gender diversity on cleavages on the Court.

The basic question is this: Have the Court's decisional patterns changed since female justices began to be appointed? Justice Wilson (1990) has argued that female justices have had an impact. According to her, there is 'overwhelming evidence that gender-based myths, biases, and stereotypes are deeply embedded in the attitudes of many male judges [and that] gender difference has been a significant factor in judicial decision-making, particularly in the areas of tort law, criminal law, and family law' (1990, 512). In contrast, the first woman appointed to the Supreme Court of the United States has argued that gender makes no difference in judging (Woodruff 2003).

Justice Wilson argues that women view the world differently from men and that female judges often bring this alternative perspective to bear on the cases they decide (Wilson 1990). She argues that the addition of more women to the bench could make a difference in the law, if 'women judges, through their differing perspectives on life, can bring new humanity to bear on the decision-making process' (ibid., 522). Supreme Court justice L'Heureux-Dubé points to her own opinions as evidence. In *R v. Seaboyer*[8] she argued in dissent that the 'rape-shield' law under consideration was the product of decades of myths and stereotypical thinking about sexual assault. Similarly, in *Symes v. Canada*[9] she disagreed with her male colleagues about whether income tax law provisions regarding what constituted a valid business expense were based on the experiences of male businessmen and whether those provisions neglected to consider the experiences of professional women (L'Heureux-Dubé 1997).

Not everyone agrees that women produce different decisions than men on the bench. Several analyses of O'Connor's voting behaviour on the U.S. Supreme Court have failed to provide much support for the position that O'Connor's decision making was distinctive solely because of her gender (Davis 1993; O'Connor and Segal 1990). However, Davis did find that O'Connor was more supportive of claims involving equality than she was of claims brought against criminal defendants.

Unfortunately, larger-scale studies of gender disparities in other appellate courts have been limited primarily to judicial behaviour in the United States. This research has generally produced mixed results. Some scholars have found evidence that the effects of gender vary across issues – specifically, that female judges are more likely to support women's rights claimants (Allen and Wall 1987; Cook 1981; Kuersten and Manning 2000; Martin 1993; Palmer 2002; Songer, Davis, and Haire 1994). An analysis of female decision making on the U.S. District Courts, however, found that female judges tend to be less supportive of personal liberties and positions advanced by minority groups than are their male colleagues (Walker and Barrow 1985). Women were found, however, to be more sympathetic to economic regulation. The same study found no difference between male and female judges in their consideration of criminal and women's rights cases (Walker and Barrow 1985). Another study of the U.S. Courts of Appeals found significant differences between male and female judges in cases involving employment discrimination, but no evidence of a gender effect in obscenity and search-and-seizure cases (Songer, Davis, and Haire 1994).

Two studies of gender in Canadian courts have also come to different conclusions. White (2002) examined the Charter opinions of women on the Supreme Court between 1993 and 1996. Based on this limited sample, she concluded that no gender difference existed in Charter cases dealing with legal rights but that the female justices were more supportive than their male colleagues of rights claimants in cases involving fundamental freedoms and equality rights. In contrast, in their analysis of criminal cases in Alberta, McCormick and Job (1993) found few differences between the decisions of male and female judges, even across issues such as sexual assault. The differences that *were* found suggested that women are slightly more conservative in criminal cases than their male colleagues.

To explore the impact, if any, that gender diversification has had on cleavages in the Court, the logistic regression models of judicial voting described above were re-run for the post-Charter era, but with a control added for gender in each model. As in chapter 4, for each independent variable we calculated the maximum likelihood estimate (MLE) along with its standard error. The MLEs represent the change in the logistic function that occurs from one unit change in each independent variable. Since these coefficients are difficult to interpret intuitively, in the last column we provide a measure of the change in the estimated probability of a liberal vote caused by a one unit change in the independent variable when all other variables are held at their median value. The results are presented in tables 7.12 through 7.14.

For criminal appeals, the addition of a control for gender of the justices has little impact on the effects of the other variables. Cleavages remain strongly related to political party as well as to region of origin and religion, though the impact of party is marginally decreased. For example, when all other variables are held at their median value, the probability that a justice appointed by the Conservative Party will support a liberal outcome is 48 per cent. But the last column of table 7.12 indicates that in the same situation, the probability of a justice appointed by a Liberal prime minister increases by over 12 percentage points to just over 60 per cent. What is most significant about the results in table 7.12 is that a justice's gender is also strongly related to judicial decisions. Female justices appear to be strongly supportive of the position of the prosecution when one first controls for party, region, and religion. The results are statistically significant and stronger in magnitude than the effects of the political party of the appointing prime minister. More specifically, the probability of a liberal vote by a female rather than a male justice decreases by almost 19 points (from 48 to about 29 per cent) when the values of all other variables are set at their median value.

In contrast, table 7.13 suggests that in civil liberties cases, the female justices are substantially more likely than their male colleagues to support rights claimants. When other variables are set at their median, there is only a 44 per cent chance that male justices will support a liberal outcome, but that increases by slightly over 12 points to just over 56 per cent for a female justice. Party and religion continue to exert negligible impacts on judicial decisions, and Ontario origins appear to increase the likelihood of a pro-rights claimant decision, but the regional differences are not statistically significant. For example, the last column indicates that there is only a 4-point difference in the chances of a liberal vote by justices appointed by prime ministers of different parties and a 9-point difference based on religion. Overall, though, the impact of gender seems to be more significant than the impact of either party or religion or region on decisions in civil liberties cases.

Table 7.12
Logistic regression models of the likelihood of a pro-defendant vote by justices on the
Supreme Court of Canada, post-Charter period

Variable	MLE	SE	Change in estimated probabilities
Party of PM	0.515***	0.122	+.128
Quebec	−0.034	0.184	−.009
Ontario	1.781***	0.259	+.444
West	1.355***	0.226	+.338
Catholic	0.865***	0.165	+.215
Female	−0.754***	0.134	−.188
Intercept	−5.007	0.921	

N = 1469
−2Log L = 1897.34
Chi sq. = 123.13***

* P < .05
** P < .01
*** P < .001
# .05 < P < .10

Table 7.13
Logistic regression models of the likelihood of a pro-rights claimant vote in civil liberties
cases by justices on the Supreme Court of Canada, post-Charter period

Variable	MLE	SE	Change in estimated probabilities
Party of PM	0.156	0.241	+.038
Quebec	0.093	0.366	+.023
Ontario	0.672	0.507	+.165
West	0.279	0.457	+.069
Catholic	−0.368	0.318	−.091
Female	0.500*	0.247	+.123
Intercept	−1.782	1.845	

N = 372
−2Log L = 493.41
Chi sq. = 16.26**

* P < .05
** P < .01
*** P < .001
# .05 < P < .10

Table 7.14
Logistic regression models of the likelihood of a pro-underdog vote in private economic cases by justices on the Supreme Court of Canada, post-Charter period

Variable	MLE	SE	Change in estimated probabilities
Party of PM	−0.340	0.305	−.084
Quebec	−0.034	0.444	−.009
Ontario	0.454	0.603	+.113
West	−0.594	0.531	−.148
Catholic	0.138	0.359	+.034
Female	0.506*	0.299	+.126
Intercept	0.022	2.161	

N = 245
−2Log L = 327.53
Chi sq. = 10.64#

* P < .05
** P < .01
*** P < .001
# .05 < P < .10

While previous studies have not suggested that private economic issues are likely to produce gender-specific responses, the addition of a variable to indicate a justice's gender appears to have a significant effect (see table 7.14). Female justices are much more likely than their male colleagues to support the underdog in a private economic dispute. As in the other two areas, the last column of table 7.14 indicates that the magnitude of the gender difference is about 12 points. For example, holding other variables at their median, the probability of a vote in support of the economic underdog rises from 53 per cent for male justices to almost 66 per cent for female justices. In contrast, the difference between justices of different parties is only 8 points, which is not statistically significant. Similarly, neither region nor religion has any significant relationship to judicial votes, leaving gender as the only characteristic of justices considered in the model that affects judicial voting decisions.

In summary, gender has emerged as a significant new basis for cleavages on the Supreme Court of Canada in the Charter era. In the pre-Charter era, conflict on the Court was structured by political party, region, and religion. In the post-Charter era, conflict is more frequently structured by gender, and the effect of gender on judicial choices remains strong even after one controls for all of the traditional bases of conflict that dominated the pre-Charter courts. The results seem to confirm, at least in the Canadian context, the early prediction of Justice Wilson that the addition of women to the Court would make a difference.

The evidence of this chapter and of earlier studies (reviewed above) provides strong evidence that whether one calls them judicial philosophies or political ideologies, the attitudes and policy preferences of the justices are strongly related to the decisions they make. Notwithstanding disclaimers that judicial ideology is not actively considered in judicial selection, the evidence is clear that the actual behaviour of the justices is related to the party of the appointing prime minister. Now that the relevance of religion to justices' decisions seems to have waned in the post-Charter era, gender has emerged as a substantial basic force in judicial decision making. One very strong caveat is in order, however: all of the above analyses are based only on cases in which the Supreme Court was divided. Since a large majority of all cases decided by the Court result in unanimous decisions, one should not jump to the conclusion that what has been found to explain the divided decisions necessarily serves as an explanation of decision making in all cases. To round out our understanding of decision making on the Supreme Court, it is also necessary to closely examine the Court's unanimous decisions. That investigation forms the heart of the next chapter.

8 The Unanimous Decisions of the Supreme Court of Canada

In the previous chapter we examined the divisions on the Supreme Court with regard to divided decisions. The results were consistent with the expectation that on many politically salient issues, the Court often divides along lines that are somewhat similar to the cleavages in the broader political system. Many scholars and former clerks, as well as the justices themselves, have argued that judicial ideology is not actively considered in judicial selection, yet the evidence is clear that the actual behaviour of the justices is related to the party of the prime minister who appointed them. Additionally, in the post-Charter era, gender has emerged as a substantial basic force in judicial decision making. But such an analysis falls far short of telling the whole story of the voting decisions of the justices. One of the most obvious characteristics of the Court has been that its decisions are often unanimous.

Figure 8.1 indicates that the rate of agreement on the Supreme Court has remained consistently high since 1970. Overall, almost three-quarters of decisions have been unanimous, and in fewer than 10 per cent of cases has the Court been split so sharply that there has been a minimum winning coalition.[1] Perhaps more noticeable has been the consistency with which the Court has maintained this high level of agreement. Most decisions in every year have been decided by a unanimous vote; indeed, the rate of unanimity has fallen below 60 per cent in just one year (1973).

One might have expected the Court to have had higher rates of agreement in the years before it gained control of its docket, because in those years there were presumably more cases coming to the Court 'as of right' that raised no substantial issues that might divide the justices.

Figure 8.1
Unanimous decisions and minimum winning coalitions:
Change over time on the Supreme Court

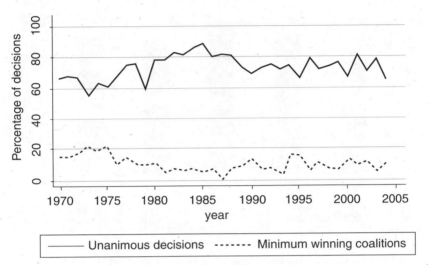

But in fact, the data suggest that such was not the case. Some of the lowest rates of unanimity and highest rates of minimum winning coalitions actually occurred before the Supreme Court Act of 1975 gave the Court greater control over its docket. In all six years from 1970 to 1975, the rate of unanimity was under 70 per cent; that rate dipped below 70 per cent in only four of the subsequent twenty-eight years. Similarly, the proportion of cases decided by a minimum winning coalition was at least 14 per cent in the first six years examined but reached that rate in only three of the subsequent years.

Looking at the entire sequence, there is no clear linear trend in the data. The proportion of unanimous decisions is lowest in the early 1970s. Then it rises steeply in the late 1970s and early 1980s and remains above 80 per cent unanimous throughout the 1980s. Finally, it drops below 80 per cent beginning in 1990. It has remained below 80 per cent ever since.

To step back a bit from the detailed trends in figure 8.1 to gain a better perspective on broader trends, the rates of unanimous decisions and minimum winning coalitions are summarized by chief justice in figure 8.2. While the proportion of unanimous decisions is

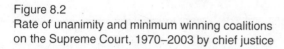

Figure 8.2
Rate of unanimity and minimum winning coalitions
on the Supreme Court, 1970–2003 by chief justice

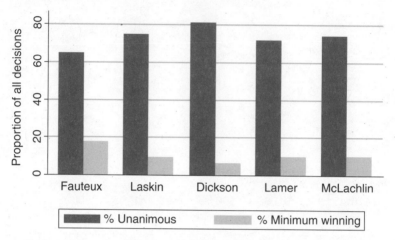

high under every chief justice, there is a substantial degree of variation. The lowest rates by far occurred when Joseph Fauteux was
chief justice and the highest rates of agreement occurred when Brian
Dickson was chief justice.

One caution is needed when interpreting these figures. Before 1975,
not all of the decisions of the Supreme Court were published with
opinions. Though we don't know for sure, it seems likely that most of
the unpublished decisions were unanimous, which means that their
exclusion may artificially lower the rate of unanimity and inflate the
rate of minimum winning coalitions for that period. One piece of evidence that supports this conclusion is that during the first three years
when Bora Laskin was chief justice the proportion of unanimous decisions was under 70 per cent; this quickly rose to over 75 per cent for
virtually the rest of his term as chief justice.

The high rate of agreement on the Supreme Court evident in
figures 8.1 and 8.2 is apparently not a recent phenomenon. Other writing about earlier periods in the Court's history suggests that it was
high long before 1970. For example, McCormick (2000) reports that the
average justice dissented only 16.6 per cent of the time in the Rinfret
Court (1949–54), 15.9 per cent of the time in the Kerwin Court (1954–
63), and 24.7 per cent of the time between 1963 and 1973.

Table 8.1
Variation in the proportion of unanimous decisions for different types
of issues on the Supreme Court of Canada, 1970–2003

Issue	Unanimous (%)	No. of cases
Criminal	72.9	1306
Civil liberties	60.3	509
Other public law	75,1	179
Tax	80.2	182
Torts	73.3	311
Other private economic	77.8	555
Family law	79.5	117
Other	86.4	88
Total	74.4	3247

This tendency towards unanimous agreement apparently characterizes the entire agenda of the Court, though there is some variation
across types of cases. Table 8.1 shows that the proportion of unanimous
decisions is high in every major category of issue heard by the Court.
Nonetheless, some differences are apparent. Most notably, the justices
have been least likely to reach agreement in civil liberties cases. But
even in that most conflictual area, the justices have agreed in three out
of five cases. In all other areas, the rate of unanimity has been above 70
per cent. Further analysis (not shown) indicates that civil liberties was
the most contentious area between 1970 and 2003. So the Charter of
Rights has increased the frequency of civil rights issues on the agenda
of the Court (as chapter 3 indicated), and those issues have been a major source of conflict throughout the Court's recent history.

This continuing high rate of unanimity is in marked contrast to what
is found in the U.S. Supreme Court. Analyses in the United States have
indicated that over the past half century the proportion of decisions
without dissent has oscillated between 30 and 40 per cent of the total
docket (Spaeth 1989; Hensley and Johnson 1998). At the other extreme,
close to 15 per cent of the decisions have involved minimum winning
coalitions[2] – a rate 50 per cent higher than the comparable rate in Canada noted earlier. At the other end of the spectrum, Britain's top appellate court has even higher rates of agreement than those found in
Canada. Between 1970 and 2003 the House of Lords announced a
unanimous decision in 81.8 per cent of the cases it decided and had a
minimum winning coalition in only 8.3 per cent of its decisions.

Figure 8.3
Rate of unanimity and minimum winning coalitions
on the Supreme Court, 1970–2003, by panel size

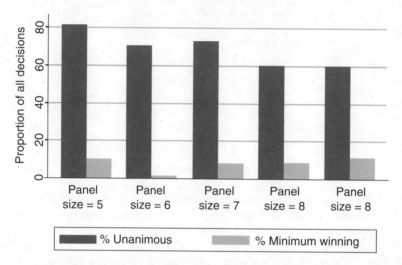

These differences in other common law courts may be due in part to differences in panel size. All else equal, it will always be easier for smaller groups to reach agreement. The U.S. Supreme Court, like its counterpart in Canada, has nine justices, but it always sits *en banc*, whereas most cases in the Canadian court are decided by panels of five or seven. For their part, the Law Lords in Britain almost always sit in panels of five. To explore the plausibility of the argument that differences in rates of agreement may be a function of panel size, one needs to look at how rates of agreement vary by panel size in Canada. Figure 8.3 indicates that the frequency of unanimous decisions declines sharply as panel size increases. Note that for five-justice panels the proportion of unanimous decisions is almost exactly the same in Canada as in England. However, even when all nine justices sat, the likelihood of a unanimous decision was substantially higher in Canada than in the United States.

What accounts of this high degree of unanimity that has persisted for at least the past half century? The starting point for our investigation was to ask the justices themselves. During the interviews, the interviewer commented on the high rate of unanimity that has persisted on the Court and asked the justices what they thought contributed to this phenomenon.

Explanations of Unanimity: The Justices' Perspective

Two themes emerged in almost all the interviews. First, the justices believed that unanimity was the end result of serious discussion and debate about the meaning of law and precedent for a particular decision. In addition, most of them suggested that informal norms of collegiality and respect for the opinions of colleagues often resulted in deliberate efforts to find compromise solutions that everyone on the Court could accept. No justice reported that anything like the behaviour predicted by the attitudinal model had a substantial effect on the rate of unanimity. Nor did strategic reactions to external actors.[3]

All of the justices maintained that law and precedent figured into their decision making. While social scientists might be wary of accepting such statements at face value, when asked about *process*, all described specific things that they routinely did that were consistent with the proposition that they took the law seriously and inconsistent with expectations that one would derive from the unconstrained version of the attitudinal model. For example, every justice, without prompting, emphasized that he spent a great deal of time during preparations for oral argument attempting to master the legal arguments in the factums.[4] Moreover, all of them asked their clerks to do additional research on the key legal issues raised by the litigants, and especially to analyse the precedents cited in the factums that they were not familiar with. Finally, all of the justices discussed the legal issues with their clerks prior to oral argument but only occasionally discussed the policy aspects of the case. None of these approaches to preparation would seem to make a lot of sense for a justice who plans to make a decision solely on the basis of political considerations. Moreover, no justice mentioned asking a clerk to prepare legal justifications for a position he had already arrived at (which would be the rational way to utilize the talents of law clerks for a justice deciding purely on political grounds). Justices B, C, and G explicitly made the point that they never told their clerks which way they were leaning before the clerk completed the legal research because it was important to them for their clerks to approach the legal issues with 'a fresh mind.' Finally, Justice F said that he was only sure which way he would vote on about half the cases before oral argument, and Justice E indicated that he switched the side he favoured 'moderately often' after hearing oral argument. Such statements do not provide absolute refutation to the attitudinal model, yet it is difficult to believe that a justice who is concerned only with whether a decision for the appellant rather than for the respondent is more consistent with his personal political position would ever doubt which way he was going to vote after reading all the factums *plus* the lower court decision *plus* a clerk's memorandum analysing the issue. In sum, then, the way the justices talk about their decision-making processes suggests that law and precedent do affect their decisions to at least some non-trivial degree.

The justices' comments on the decision-making process in conference and on the opinion-writing stage (see chapter 5) suggest that a second reason for unanimity may have to do with informal norms related to collegiality. Justices E and H reported that there was informal pressure to work out differences that were initially expressed (Justice E characterized this as 'gentle' pressure). Justice F recalled that in conference, the person designated to write the majority opinion often says something like, 'If I write the opinion in thus and such a way, would that satisfy the concerns that have been expressed?' Similarly, Justice B indicated that he believed that most of his colleagues share his belief that it is important for the Court to 'get a blend of individuality and collegiality.' He said that he constantly reminds himself that 'we are not just soloists' but a choir. Thus, while he feels free to dissent when his differences on principle are 'major,' he 'looks first to try to get consensus.' Justice G agreed: 'Justices have a commitment whenever principle doesn't require them to divide to give a little and take a little to try to reach agreement.' These sentiments were echoed by Justice F when he was asked to describe the typical process in the opinion-writing stage. He said that there is often a deliberate attempt to increase consensus and that the person originally selected to write the opinion of the Court will frequently moderate his original draft in order to get unanimous support for his opinion. When asked directly about this view expressed by Justice F, Justice A agreed and went on to add that the chief justice makes it clear that she favours consensus when possible. Significantly, no justice indicated that he ever sought to create only a minimum winning coalition, which would be the rational approach of justices if they were motivated solely by policy preferences.

When asked more generally about how they approached decision writing, both Justice C and Justice D indicated that the process is characterized often by fairly direct bargaining. Justice C said that though the justices generally approach one another tactfully, one often receives a memo after the initial draft of the opinion has been circulated that says something like, 'I think that the analysis in Section 3 could be strengthened if you approached it in the following way.' And he said that everyone understands that such a memo indicates that an implicit bargain can be reached wherein the responding justice drops his initial opposition to the opinion in return for the indicated change in the opinion. Moreover, he added, most of the time such implicit bargains are accepted by the opinion writer unless he has very strong feelings about his original position. Justice D agreed that implicit bargaining goes on, but added that sometimes the bargaining is explicit; that is, a justice's memo explicitly says that unless such and such a change is made he will have to write separately. One result of such bargaining, according to several justices, is that the scope of the original opinion is often limited in order to gain unanimous support. In the words of Justice G, 'opinions are sometimes *"fudgier"* ... or more limited than the opinion writer initially preferred in order to obtain a unanimous decision.'

Related to the acceptance of such bargaining, several justices indicated that especially on complex cases, the give and take in conference and in opinion writing often leads justices to change their personal positions; that is, discussion of the legal issues often results in the justices sincerely agreeing about the proper outcome even when there was initial disagreement in conference. Justice D said that he is more often convinced to change his mind on the meaning of precedent by discussion with his colleagues than from listening to the arguments of counsel. Justice A indicated that even on hard cases, the justices often eventually comes to a consensus that the lower court should be reversed after they have spent the time to carefully work through all the legal issues. And at least two of the justices noted that sometimes one realizes that an initial dissenting position 'just won't write' and thus accepts the legal reasoning of the majority.

In summary, the justices freely admit that their political attitudes do have some impact on their decision making. But then they all add that the unconstrained version of the attitudinal model does not describe the behaviour of the Court. In both direct and indirect ways, they indicated that law and precedent matter and that unanimity is sometimes the result of agreement on what the law means. In addition, the justices are often willing to compromise, not just to produce a 'minimum winning coalition' but more often to achieve unanimity.

Are Unanimous Decisions Consistent with Attitudinal Explanations of Judicial Decision Making?

In chapter 7 we saw that the most widely accepted explanation for decisions on the U.S. Supreme Court is the attitudinal model. According to the strongest supporters of the attitudinal model, justices on the U.S. Supreme Court decide *all* cases based solely on their political preferences and ideology. Law and precedent, these people say, provide no more than convenient rationalizations (Segal and Spaeth 1993, 2002; Robertson 1998). And the analysis in chapter 7 suggested that such judicial attitudes do have a substantial effect on the divided decisions of the Supreme Court of Canada. In contrast, the justices' own views are not consistent with an attitudinal explanation of their high rate of unanimity. In the rest of this section we take a further look at empirical data on case outcomes and judicial votes to see whether the attitudinal models or the alternative view advanced by the justices themselves provides a better understanding of unanimous outcomes in Canada.

Schubert (1965) is generally credited with developing the psychometric model that provides the essential theoretical underpinning of subsequent claims that judicial policy attitudes provide a complete and unconstrained explanation of decision making by Supreme Court justices. In Schubert's model (see figure 8.4), justices have ideal points, the *i-points*, in multidimensional ideological space, which represent their attitudes. Case stimuli are represented by the *j-points*, and these are also measured in the same multidimensional space. According to the unconstrained attitudinal model of Supreme Court decision making developed from Schubert's psychometric model, a decision should be unanimous only when the choices presented by the case stimulus (the *j-points* in Schubert's terminology) are extreme relative to the attitudinal preferences (the *i-points*) of all nine justices. Even in unanimous decisions, the work of Schubert (1965) and Segal and Spaeth (1993, 2002) leads to the prediction that the votes of all justices reflect their sincere attitudinal preferences. That is, all nine justices agree ideologically on the case because the *j-point* exceeds the *i-point* of all nine justices. But, as Kritzer, Pickerill, and Richards (1998) suggest, 'unanimity results pose problems for the unconstrained attitudinal model' (1998, 9).

The key to understanding unanimous decisions from the perspective of the attitudinal model is that the policy position taken in the decision reviewed is 'extreme.' In the analysis below, several tests are used to explore this central tenet of the attitudinal explanation for unanimous decisions.

As noted earlier, according to the attitudinal model the Supreme Court should be unanimous only when the *j-point* of the case reviewed is extreme compared to the *i-points* of all the justices. Several empirical

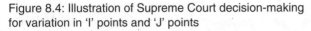

Figure 8.4: Illustration of Supreme Court decision-making
for variation in 'I' points and 'J' points

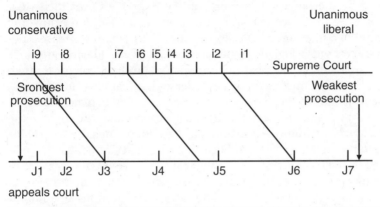

i - represents the ideological positions of the Supreme Court justices
J - case facts and issues
* each of the 'J' points also represents how liberal you have to be at each
  of the point to make a liberal decision.

predictions flow directly from this position. First, the ideological space
for a single issue dimension in which judicial policy decisions are
made may be represented by a line of finite length. For issues debated
by appellate courts, many theoretically possible political positions are
excluded from consideration as a practical matter; likewise, the nature
of the judicial selection process means that only potential candidates
holding policy positions within a somewhat limited range of possible
positions are seriously considered for selection. In figure 8.4 we represent these practical limits on the range of *j-points* that can be considered by any Canadian appellate court in practice as '*j1*' and '*j7*.' Thus
the greater the proportion of this finite space (i.e., *j1* to *j7*) that is occupied by the range of the *i-points* on the Supreme Court, the less space is
'available' for a case to be 'extreme.' In fact, if the range of *i1* to *i9* is
equal to the range of *j1* to *j7*, then no cases can be 'extreme' and all decisions will be divided according to the attitudinal model. This logic
leads to the expectation that if the attitudinal model is correct, one
would expect that the greater the range of ideological space occupied
by the current justices on the Supreme Court, the less likely a given
case will be decided unanimously.

The test of the first prediction derived from the attitudinal model is straightforward. We tested the basic idea that as the ideological space occupied by the range of positions on the Supreme Court increased, thus reducing the space available for an 'extreme' decision below, the likelihood of a unanimous decision by the Court would decrease. Specifically, we used a logistic regression model of the likelihood that a given case would be decided unanimously with the ideological range on the Supreme Court as the main independent variable. In addition, we added a control for the size of the Supreme Court panel, since, as figure 8.4 indicates, the smaller the size of the panel the greater the likelihood of a unanimous decision (all else equal). Thus the criteria for determining panel size may reflect variables that are related to unanimity. For the measure of the ideological range we used a measure of the voting behaviour of the justices in non-unanimous votes.[5] For each justice we used all votes that could be categorized as either unambiguously liberal or conservative over their career on the bench and computed the percentage of those votes that were liberal. Then, to construct our measure of the ideological range on the panel deciding each case, we simply subtracted the value of the most conservative member from the value for the most liberal member on each panel.

Table 8.2 suggests that a substantial change in the behaviour of the justices occurred after the adoption of the Charter. Regarding the post-Charter era, the analysis provides no support for the first hypothesis derived from the attitudinal model. The coefficient for panel size is negative and statistically significant as predicted, indicating that smaller panels are more likely to be unanimous than larger panels. However, once panel size is taken into account the ideological diversity of the panel has no effect on the likelihood that a decision will be unanimous. In fact, the sign of the relationship is even in the opposite direction from the prediction of the attitudinal model.

However, regarding the pre-Charter era the model is consistent with the predictions of the attitudinal model. The effect of panel size remains the same: smaller panels are much more likely than larger ones to be unanimous. But prior to 1984, the ideological diversity of the panel is strongly related to the probability that the decision will be unanimous. The more similar the ideologies of the justices on the panel are to one another, the more likely a unanimous decision.

To further the analysis of the implications of the high degree of unanimity on the Supreme Court of Canada for attitudinal explanations of judicial voting, attention is turned to unanimous reversals[6] of lower-court

Table 8.2
Logistic regression models of the influence of the ideological diversity on the Court
on the likelihood of a unanimous decision by the Supreme Court of Canada, for
pre- and post-Charter periods

Variable	Pre-Charter (1984–2003)		Post-Charter (1970–83)	
	MLE	SE	MLE	SE
Ideological Range	0.232	1.120	−2.756**	1.047
Panel Size	−0.281***	0.043	−0.198***	0.045
Intercept	3.039	0.356	3.365	0.401
	N = 1,639		N = 1,058	
	−2Log L = 1,779.30		−2Log L = 1,209.58	
	Chi sq. = 50.48***		Chi sq. = 54.65***	

* P < .05
** P < .01
*** P < .001

decisions. These analyses are limited to unanimous reversals because it is
impossible to make firm predictions from the attitudinal model about the
expected ideology of appellate court decisions that are unanimously affirmed by the Supreme Court. For example, a very liberal appellate court
panel might make a conservative decision that is inconsistent with its policy preferences either because the judges believed that existing precedent
requires such a decision or because they were acting strategically to avoid
reversal by the Supreme Court. A conservative panel might make a conservative decision in an identical case for these same reasons or because
such a decision is consistent with the judges' private preferences. Thus a
conservative decision unanimously affirmed by the Supreme Court
might have been produced by either a liberal or a conservative appellate
panel, making it impossible to predict the lower court's ideology for a
unanimous affirmance. In unanimous reversals, however, it is possible to
make a set of precise predictions from the attitudinal model about the
ideology of the panel below because it is implausible to suggest that a
very liberal panel would make a decision so conservative that it would be
reversed in a unanimous liberal decision that was consistent with the ideology of the most conservative member of the Supreme Court.[7]

The attitudinal model suggests that the Supreme Court will only reverse unanimously a decision of the appellate court when the policy
position announced in the decision below meets two criteria: (1) it is

contrary to the preferences of the *majority* of the Supreme Court, and (2) the policy position is 'extreme' relative to the policy preferences of *all* members of the Supreme Court.

To understand the implications of the attitudinal model, one must consider the range of theoretically possible outcomes in the appellate courts. Existing studies suggest that decisions of appellate court judges will be determined by three factors: the political preferences of the judges, constraints from law and precedent, and/or strategic calculations. Appellate court judges are faced with some cases in which the relevant law and precedent are clear and well settled. In other cases there is either no clearly relevant law or there is considerable ambiguity as to the meaning of the existing law for the current controversy. Consider each of these situations in turn. First, both existing studies and interviews with the justices suggest that when the law is clear, all lower court judges will follow it and thus produce a decision that is not outside the preferences of all Supreme Court justices. Hence there will be very few cases (if any) with clear law in which the appellate court is unanimously reversed by the Supreme Court.

The second possibility is that appellate court judges will be faced with a case in which the law is not clear (e.g., precedent is ambiguous or it is a question of 'first impression'). The consensus in the literature on lower court behaviour is that when the law is not clear in such 'hard cases,' the policy preferences of the judges will strongly influence the policy they announce in the case (Carp and Rowland 1983; Goldman 1975; Greene et al. 1998; Hall and Brace 1992, 1994; Howard 1981; Richardson and Vines 1970; Songer, Sheehan, and Haire 2000). In these hard cases, liberal decisions will be produced only by panels on which a majority of the judges have liberal policy preferences. Even in these hard cases, appellate court judges may be constrained in part either by precedent (e.g., precedent may limit the extent of discretion even when it does not dictate a precise outcome) or by strategic concerns. If, for example, liberal judges are constrained in part by precedent, then the policy position adopted will be less extremely liberal than the sincere preferences of the liberal majority. But all existing empirical studies predict that if such a 'hard' case were heard by a panel with conservative preferences, the decision would be conservative.

If neither the attitudes of the judges in the lower courts nor the legal constraints determine the decision of the judges, then the consensus of empirical scholarship is that the decision will be based on strategic calculations. If the judges are constrained by their strategic perceptions of the Supreme Court, then the policy adopted will also be closer to the median position of the Supreme Court than the preferred position of the panel. Thus it would be very unlikely that even in hard cases, lower court judges would adopt an extremely liberal (or conservative) policy position unless the policy views of the panel majority were at least as liberal (conservative) as the 'extreme' policy position adopted by the appellate court. To the extent that legal constraints or strategic calculations affect the decision, they will make the appellate court decision less extreme than a decision produced solely in accordance with the attitudes of the justices. It is reasonable to expect instead that an extreme lower court decision will only be adopted by judges whose personal policy preferences are 'extreme' relative to the position of either the current Supreme Court justices or the positions of other lower court judges. That is, the decision of the lower court will be extreme only when the majority of that court has policy preferences that are either far to the right or far to the left.[8] This logic leads to two predictions from the attitudinal model, one related to the composition of the Supreme Court panel and the other related to the composition of the appellate court panel.

The attitudinal model leads to the prediction that the more extreme the members on the Supreme Court panel are, the *less* likely it is that their reversal of a decision below that is contrary to the preferences of the Court's majority will be arrived at by a unanimous decision. The logic is that when the Court has a very liberal member it will be much less likely that any case will be so extreme that even that very liberal member will be able to agree to a conservative decision. Thus, the proportion of reversals that are unanimous should decrease the more extreme the views of the political outlier on the Court. For example, the extremity of the ideology of the most liberal member of the panel should be negatively related to the likelihood of a unanimous decision in a reversal of a liberal decision below.

This prediction of the attitudinal model is tested in table 8.3. The results are presented using the same measure of ideology employed in the previous table (but now using just the score of the most extreme member). From the attitudinal model one would expect that the sign of the coefficient for the degree of extremity[9] of the most extreme member should be negative and statistically significant. But it isn't. In fact, during the post-Charter era the sign of the coefficient is in the opposite direction (i.e., positive), suggesting that contrary to the predictions of the attitudinal model, the more liberal or conservative the most extreme

Table 8.3
Logistic regression models of the influence of extreme ideological preferences on the like-lihood of a unanimous decision in reversals by the Supreme Court of Canada for pre- and post-Charter periods

Variable	Post-Charter (1970–83) MLE	SE	Pre-Charter (1984–2003) MLE	SE
Extremity of Preference	1.208	1.807	−1.825	1.917
Panel size	−0.336***	0.060	−0.196**	0.064
Intercept	2.575	1/143	3.371	1.314
	N = 697 −2Log L = 787.81 Chi sq. = 31.59***		N = 431 −2Log L = 523.15 Chi sq. = 12.47**	

* P < .05
** P < .01
*** P < .001

member of the Supreme Court, the more (rather than less) likely a reversal of the court below is to be unanimous. While the results for the pre-Charter era are signed in the predicted direction (i.e., negative), the magnitude of the relationship falls far short of statistical significance. Thus the results fail to confirm the predictions derived from the attitudinal model for both time periods.

The same logic about unanimous reversals derived from the attitudinal model also leads to a prediction about the nature of the appellate court panels that are unanimously reversed. Most directly, the prediction from the attitudinal model is that the panels whose decisions are reversed by a unanimous liberal decision should be extremely conservative and that the panels reversed by a unanimous conservative decision should be extremely liberal. But Songer and Tantas (n.d.)[10] found that contrary to the predictions of the attitudinal model, the ideology of the panels unanimously reversed by the Supreme Court was not in any sense 'extreme.' Instead, judges reversed in unanimous decisions by the Supreme Court of Canada appeared to be essentially a cross-section of all appellate court judges. Their most telling test was a comparison of the means of the ideology of the panels unanimously reversed to the mean ideology of all judges on the appellate courts. Their results are reprinted below as tables 8.4 and 8.5.

Songer and Tantas summarize their findings as follows: 'The results are dramatically different from what would be predicted from

Table 8.4
Median ideology of Court of Appeal panels whose criminal decisions were reversed
unanimously by the Supreme Court of Canada compared to ideology of all Appeals
Court judges

	Mean App Ct ideology	Std dev	Difference	P
Panels with unanimous liberal Supreme	0.352	0.072		
Court reversal			0.017	NS
All Court of Appeal judges	0.379	0.197		

	Mean App Ct ideology	Std dev	Difference	P
Panels with unanimous conservative Supreme	0.393	0.084		
Court reversal			0.014	NS
All Court of Appeal judges	0.379	0.197		

the Attitudinal Model. In both criminal and Charter cases, there is
virtually no difference at all between the mean ideology of panels reversed by a unanimous decision and the mean ideology of all judges
on the courts of appeal. Panels whose decisions are unanimously reversed look very much like "normal" rather than "extreme" panels in
terms of ideology.' In summary, the analyses of the unanimous reversals of the Supreme Court of Canada provide no support for the unconstrained version of the attitudinal model. Judicial attitudes do not
appear to provide a useful explanation for unanimous decisions.

   An analysis of unanimous affirmances of decisions below also raises
questions about attitudinal explanations of unanimity. A recent paper
has challenged the notion that the attitudinal model, unconstrained,
can explain unanimous decisions in the U.S. Supreme Court. Kritzer,
Pickerill, and Richards (1998) argue that in any explanation of unanimous decisions it is 'extremely helpful to think of law as a constraint'
(1998, 3). After noting that no one to date has systematically analysed
unanimous decisions to determine whether they are in fact 'extreme' as
postulated by the unconstrained attitudinal model, they express doubt

Table 8.5
Median ideology of Court of Appeal panels whose Charter of Rights decisions were reversed unanimously by the Supreme Court of Canada compared to ideology of all Appeals Court judges

	Mean Appeal Court ideology	Std dev	Difference	P
Panels with unanimous liberal Supreme Court reversal	0.360	0.056	0.017	NS
All Court of Appeal judges	0.377	0.225		

	Mean Appeal Court ideology	Std dev	Difference	P
Panels with unanimous conservative Supreme Court reversal	0.370	0.079	0.007	NS
All Court of Appeal judges	0.377	0.225		

that one-third or more of the cases chosen by the Court for review are in fact extreme. They concede that the Court sometimes might need to correct (i.e., reverse) extreme decisions below; then they add that the logic of the attitudinal model leads to the conclusion that a unanimous affirmation of the lower courts should almost never occur (ibid., 6). If, given the facts of the case, the petitioner in the lower court were to request an extreme decision from the Court (e.g., one that either goes far beyond any precedent and/or that is far from the attitudinal preferences of all the justices), and if the lower court were to reject that request, announcing a decision firmly grounded in existing law, there would be little reason for a policy-oriented Supreme Court to even hear the case. More likely, it would simply refuse to hear that case. Only rarely does a policy-oriented Court feel the need to grant the petition for certiorari so that it can affirm the obviously correct lower-court decision for symbolic purposes. Yet Kritzer and his colleagues have found that 28.9 per cent of unanimous cases selected by writs of certiorari have been affirmed and that the affirmance rate is not lower when the analysis is

Table 8.6
The frequency of decisions by the Supreme Court that unanimously affirm the decision by a lower court, by chief justice, 1970–2003

Chief justice	No. of all cases that affirm unanimously	% of all cases that affirm unanimously	Total all cases
Fauteux	134	37.5	357
Laskin	390	43.9	888
Dickson	271	47.0	577
Lamer	406	39.5	1,029
McLachlin	144	43.5	331
Total 1970–2003	1,372*	42.2	3,247

Unanimous decisions only		
Number affirmed	Percentage affirmed	Total number of unanimous decisions
1,372	56.7	2,417

*Note: this total includes cases during the brief periods of time between the death and resignation of one Chief Justice and the appointment of another.

limited to cases without circuit conflicts (ibid., 8–9). Next, they argue that support for the unconstrained attitudinal model should be greatest in civil liberties cases, especially those arriving at the Court through cert that do not contain any circuit conflicts. Yet even among these cases, they have found that 24 per cent are affirmed unanimously. Thus, they are unable to test directly whether the cases producing unanimous decisions are extreme; but they also argue that the patterns they *have* found could not plausibly occur if the unconstrained attitudinal model explained all judicial votes even in areas such as civil liberties, where attitudes are thought to be most influential.

Repeating the analysis of Kritzer and his colleagues suggests there is even less support for an attitudinal explanation of unanimous decisions in the Supreme Court of Canada than in the U.S. Supreme Court. As table 8.6 indicates, decisions that unanimously affirm a lower court's outcome are approximately 50 per cent more common in Canada. Overall, 42.2 per cent of all judgments of the Court have unanimously affirmed the decision below. Moreover, while there have been some variations relating to who the chief justice is at the time, in every period the frequency of unanimous affirmances has been substantially above the rate in the United States. In civil liberties cases, which supporters of the attitudinal model suggest are most likely to be decided attitudinally, the proportion of cases with a unanimous reversal of the decision below has been somewhat lower, albeit still surprisingly high: almost one-third of all decisions (32.4 per cent). Kritzer's logic would seem as applicable to Canada as to the United States. It is hard to believe that a Court that cared only, or even primarily, about advancing its policy preferences would unanimously affirm decisions of the lower courts 1,372 times over one-third of a century.

A Model of Unanimous Decisions of the Supreme Court

The results of the multiple tests above provide strong evidence that on the Supreme Court of Canada, justices' votes are not solely ideologically driven. While both previous research and the analysis in chapter 7 provide abundant evidence that justices' political attitudes sometimes have a measurable impact on their decisions, the analyses above demonstrate that those attitudes fall far short of explaining completely all of the Court's publicly announced votes. Most specifically, the results suggest that the justices' policy preferences do not adequately explain the Court's unanimous decisions, which account for three-quarters of all cases formally decided. The only evidence inconsistent with this conclusion is the finding that in the pre-Charter (but not post-Charter) period, panels with greater ideological diversity have been less likely to be unanimous. But even the support this finding provides for an attitudinal explanation of unanimity is limited by lack of evidence for a similar effect of ideological diversity when analysis is limited to specific policy areas (i.e., instead of all cases together). These results do not negate the findings of chapter 7 that attitudes are at least an important part of the explanation for the significant minority of cases in which the Court's decision is non-unanimous; they do, however, suggest that attitudes are not useful for explaining roughly 75 per cent of the Court's decisions. Thus, one must conclude that in the Supreme Court of Canada, attitudes provide only a partial explanation of judicial behaviour; that is, attitudes are only one of several factors that influence justices' decisions.

Given that political preferences do not adequately explain unanimous decisions, is there an alternative explanation? The analysis above supports in part the reasons for unanimity suggested by the interviews with the justices in that both the interviews and the empirical analysis suggest that political attitudes do not predict when a given decision will be unanimous. Unfortunately, some of the suggestions offered in the interviews cannot easily be tested with empirical data derived from case outcomes. Some concepts suggested by the justices, such as collegiality, are difficult to measure; others, such as perceptions of the degree of constraint imposed by precedent in a given case, and the willingness to accept specific compromises offered by other justices to a first opinion draft, are simply not available from the final opinions. However, some of the implications of the perspective offered by the justices can be tested. The following model attempts to provide such a partial test of the justices' perspective on unanimity.

The dependent variable is whether the decision is unanimous or divided. Thus we again employ logistic regression to estimate the likelihood of a unanimous decision. Separate analyses are provided for the pre- and post-Charter eras.

One of the consistent themes that came through the interviews was that collegiality on the Court and mutual respect for the views of colleagues encouraged justices to work towards compromise opinions. However, that willingness to compromise was usually qualified. All of the justices said something to the effect that they would go along or work towards mutual accommodation 'when they could' or when such a compromise 'did not go against strongly held principles.' This suggests that unanimous decisions are most likely when the perceived stakes are not as high. To capture this element, the model includes three measures of the salience of the issues in each case. First, justices may care most about constitutional issues, especially since the Charter of Rights. In addition, many Charter issues have come to the Court as questions of first instance, making it less likely that there is clear precedent that might constrain all of the justices in the same way. So the first independent variable is simply whether or not a constitutional issue was discussed in the opinion.

While perhaps not perceived as raising quite as high stakes as constitutional issues, cases that involve the construction of a federal statute might be perceived as having higher stakes than cases that do not. To test this possibility, a dichotomous variable noting the presence or absence of an issue of statutory construction has been added to the model.

An alternative way to assess the political stakes in a case is whether or not non-parties (e.g., interest groups or other governments) appear as interveners. So the model includes the number of interveners listed as appearing before the Court.

The justices also indicated that one way in which they tried to achieve unanimity was by narrowing the scope of the opinion, deleting issues that some justices wanted to address but that the justices decided after some give and take were not essential for the appeal's resolution. To assess this possibility, the tag lines of the opinion have been used to identify the number of paragraphs raising separate legal issues.

Finding reliable empirical indicators of the influence of precedent and other legal factors to use when analysing judicial voting has been a stumbling block for years. While no completely satisfactory indicator is available, one partial indicator may be agreement among different levels of the courts. The fact that two or more sets of judges ultimately reach the same conclusion about the proper resolution of the legal issues in a case may be at least a rough indicator that law or precedent has constrained the justices. This may be more likely in the case of a Court that controls its own docket, since the decision to grant leave to appeal is often based in part on a first impression of the justices that the lower court has decided the case incorrectly. When that initial presumption is overcome after further consideration and deliberation on the case, it may indicate that the justices have concluded that the law constrains their ability to overturn. Thus the model includes a dichotomous variable indicating whether or not the Court has affirmed the decision below.

Alternatively, the interviews with the justices indicate that panel size may indicate both the legal complexity and the political salience of a case. The justices agreed that five-justice panels are usually set to hear a case when the initial perception of the justices is that the case is relatively straightforward from a legal perspective. Conversely, the chief justice is expected to have the entire Court sit when an especially important or controversial issue is being considered. To test these observations, panel size has also been included as a variable in the model.

Finally, the variable used in the initial test of the impact of attitudes on unanimity (i.e., the ideological diversity on the panel) is included in the model as a control. As in the analyses in chapters 4 and 7, for each independent variable we have calculated the maximum likelihood estimate (MLE), along with its standard error. The MLEs represent the change in the logistic function that occurs from one unit change in each independent variable. Since these coefficients are difficult to interpret intuitively, we provide a measure in the table's final column of the change in the estimated probability of a liberal vote caused by a one unit change in the independent variable when all other variables are held at their median value. The results are presented in table 8.7.

Table 8.7
Logistic regression models of the likelihood of a unanimous decision by the Supreme Court of Canada, for pre- and post-Charter periods

A Post-Charter

Variable	Post-Charter (1984–2003) MLE	SE	Change in estimated probabilities
Constitutional issue	−0.259*	0.144	−.048
Statute interpretation	−0.260*	0.135	−.048
No. of interveners	−0.258*	0.153	−.048
Narrow opinion	0.214*	0.129	+.039
Affirm	0.221*	0.120	+.040
Panel size	−0.253***	0.047	−.046
Ideological range	1.070	1.360	+.192
Intercept	2.550	0.406	

N = 1,599
−2Log L = 1,706.76
Chi Sq = 76.26***

* P < .05
** P < .01
*** P < .001

B Pre-Charter

Variable	Pre-Charter (1970–1983) MLE	SE	Change in estimated probabilities
Constitutional issue	0.066	0.372	+.012
Statute interp	−0.266#	0.180	−.054
No. of interveners	0.298	0.393	+.055
Affirm	0.280*	0.142	+.056
Panel size	−0.194***	0.047	−.038
Ideological range	−2.991**	1.060	−.589
Intercept	3.299	0.411	

N = 1,058
−2Log L = 1,202.23
Chi Sq = 51.97***

* P < .05
** P < .01
*** P < .001
# .05 < P < .10

At least in the post-Charter era, the results provide some support for the perspectives of the justices. All three indicators of the salience of the issue are strongly and significantly related to the likelihood of a unanimous decision. Unanimous decisions are less likely when either constitutional or statutory interpretation is involved. For example, we can see from the figures in the last column of table 8.7a that the probability of a unanimous vote drops by 5 points (i.e., from 76 to 71 per cent) when either a constitutional issue or an issue of statutory interpretation is present. Moreover, the more interest the case attracts from interest groups and other interveners, the less likely the judges are to resolve the dispute unanimously.

The data also support the justices' suggestion that initial conflicts are sometimes resolved by finding a narrower resolution that all can accept. Narrow decisions are about 4 points more likely than broader ones to be unanimous.

The two rough indicators of possible legal constraints are also statistically significant: the Court is more likely to be unanimous when it is affirming than when it is reversing a lower court's judgment, and unanimous decisions are more likely the smaller the panel size. Specifically, the data in the last column of table 8.7a indicate that when the Supreme Court is affirming a lower court's decision, the chances of a unanimous decision increase by 4 points, from 76 to 80 per cent. The same column also indicates a 4.5 point change for each unit change in the size of the panel. In other words, while the chances for a unanimous decision are about 76 per cent for a panel with five members, the probability drops to 58 per cent when all nine justices sit (i.e., $76\% - [4 \times -.045] = 58$).

The results for the pre-Charter era are more ambiguous. Neither the presence of a constitutional issue nor the involvement of interveners seems to have affected the likelihood of a unanimous decision. In part this may reflect that both constitutional issues and the presence of interveners were relatively rare in pre-Charter times. And perhaps the types of constitutional issues (mainly involving questions of federalism) before 1984 were less likely to be those on which the justices embraced strong principles. The presence of a question of statutory interpretation has a negative affect on the chances of unanimity in both periods, but that relationship is only marginally significant in the pre-Charter era (though the magnitude of the change, about 5 percentage points, is similar in both eras).

Unfortunately, data on the number of legal issues is not available for the pre-Charter era. However, the other indicator of legal constraint –

whether the Court affirmed the opinion below – seems to have a significant effect on unanimity in both eras and has a magnitude that is marginally greater in the pre-Charter era (5.6 percentage points pre-Charter versus 4.0 points post-Charter). Finally, the impact of panel size remains constant for both periods.

Though the analysis earlier in the chapter indicated that the Court has achieved high levels of unanimity throughout the thirty-four years examined, it is possible that the factors that encourage unanimity have changed. In particular, we are limited in understanding whether there has been substantial change by the nature of the interviews with the justices. Only justices serving under Chief Justice McLachlin were available for interviews, and all of those justices had served primarily during the Charter era.

Lack of Agreement in Unanimous Decisions

So far, this chapter has focused solely on agreement on decisions. In other words, were the justices unanimous, whether they dismissed the appeal (i.e., sustained the lower court's decision) or allowed it (i.e., rejected the lower court's decision)? One might extend this investigation by asking how often the justices were in agreement on the *reasoning* supporting the judgment as well as on the *outcome*. The answer to this question is provided in table 8.8, which presents the number of separate concurring opinions written in each case in which the outcome was unanimous.

Table 8.8 indicates that the level of total agreement on the Supreme Court of Canada is remarkably high. Unanimous decisions usually have only a single opinion on which all of the participating justices agree. In seven out of eight times that the Court announces a unanimous decision, it does so with a unanimous opinion as well. Moreover, when the Court fails to unite behind a single decision, rarely is there more than one alternative concurring opinion. It is rare for the Court to be fractured with multiple explanations for the unanimous outcome. Fewer than 4 per cent of unanimous decisions have had multiple concurring opinions (and the vast majority of cases in the 'multiple' category have had only two concurring opinions).

When we break this finding down by chief justice, no trend over time is apparent. The two most recent chief justices had the lowest and the highest rates of concurrence in the thirty-four-year period analysed. Indeed, little variation is apparent generally. Under all but one of the chief justices, the proportion of unanimous decisions with no

Table 8.8
The frequency of concurring opinions in the unanimous decisions of the Supreme Court, by chief justice, 1970–2003

| Chief justice | Unanimous decisions with concurrence | | | |
| | Number of concurrences | | | |
	None % of cases	One concur % of cases	Multiple concur % of cases	N
Fauteux	89.2	8.7	2.2	185
Laskin	89.2	9.4	1.4	553
Dickson	89.8	7.8	2.3	384
Lamer	80.9	12.6	6.5	629
McLachlin	93.0	5.7	1.3	158
Total 1970–2003	86.9*	9.8	3.7	1,943

*Note: this total includes cases during the brief periods of time between the death and resignation of one chief justice and the appointment of another.

concurring opinions has ranged between 89.2 to 93 per cent. Only the Lamer Court had a conspicuously higher rate of concurrences.

When we combine these results with figure 8.2 (proportion of unanimous decisions), we find that in 64.6 per cent of all cases[11] heard by the Supreme Court of Canada, all of the justices on the panel agreed on both the outcome of the case and on the supporting reasons. From this, it is easy to conclude that the normal outcome on the Court is agreement.

Conclusions

Empirically, the results of our analysis are easily summarized. For the past thirty-four years the Supreme Court of Canada has been characterized by very high levels of agreement. There has been some variation over time and across issues, and agreement has been higher on small panels than on large ones, but the differences have been small compared to the consistency in the high rate of agreement.

What has caused this high rate of agreement? The conventional explanation derived from studies of the U.S. Supreme Court is that unanimity is largely the result of attitudinal agreement among the justices that the case presents an extreme stimulus. However, the analysis above provides no support for this explanation derived from the attitudinal model. The finding that judicial policy preferences do not adequately explain the unanimous decisions of the Supreme Court of Canada is important because the Court is so often unanimous. The inescapable conclusion is that whatever the findings for the United States, judicial attitudes and policy preferences provide only a partial explanation of Supreme Court decision making in Canada. The findings in chapter 7 indicate that those preferences are sometimes important influences on judicial choices; the findings in this chapter suggest that they may not be the most important influence on most decisions. Judicial attitudes may play a critical role in a number of important, politically significant decisions of the Court, but they 'do not tell the whole story' of judicial decision making in Canada (Songer and Lindquist 1996).

In contrast to the attitudinal explanation of the high rate of unanimity, the justices suggested that serious grappling with the legal issues, and a willingness to listen carefully to the views of colleagues, sometimes led all of the justices to ultimately reach the same sincere conclusion about the proper legal solution to the case. Often this consensus did not exist when the justices as individuals first examined the factums and case facts. Instead it emerged during the oral arguments, the written and oral exchanges among the justices in conference, and the opinion-writing process. This process of gradually emerging consensus seems to be related in part to the fairly high degree of collegiality on the Court. It can only happen if justices deliberately reject closure before discussing the case with their colleagues and if they respect their colleagues enough to consider their views carefully when those are different from their own first impressions.

A high degree of collegiality produces unanimous decisions in another way as well. Most of the justices talked about an informal norm that everyone should try to find a basis on which all can agree if this can be done without sacrificing strongly held principled positions related to the appeal. Some of the justices were uncomfortable with the terms 'bargaining' and 'compromise,' but to a social scientist who does not share the negative connotations that these words seem to have developed among many of the public (who are disgusted with the seamier side of politics), it appears that bargaining is common. Sometimes it is implicit in the responses that one justice makes to the conference statements of another or to an opinion draft; at other times it is quite explicit. It should be emphasized that there seems to be absolutely no 'logrolling' – that is, trading of votes on one case for future concessions on another. Rather, bargaining is confined to reaching an agreement on each case considered separately. The justices appear to value 'speaking with one voice' and are therefore willing to decide a case on narrower grounds than they would if they had only their preferences to consider, and to accept language that goes only part of the way to the doctrinal position they consider ideal.

It is impossible to argue that by themselves these interview results provide conclusive 'proof' that the process works the way the justices assert; it is also impossible to provide a completely objective empirical test of most of the key points made by the justices. Nevertheless, I believe that the interview results should be taken seriously. Confidence that the interview results provide credible evidence rests on several considerations. First, all scholars conducting elite interviews must make judgments about the honesty and trustworthiness of the respondents and their answers based on the sort of demeanour cues used by all sorts of people in everyday life. Such judgments, unfortunately, cannot easily be demonstrated to be reliable. Nevertheless, my judgment is that our respondents passed this test. Second, the guarantee that they would not be identified in any accounts of the interviews and the fact that they were being interviewed by a scholar from a foreign country, who would likely publish the results outside Canada, reduced any potential gain they might have received from being less than honest. Third, the justices did not describe their behaviour in a manner that might be expected from those trying to support the traditional myths of a non-political judiciary. For example, they admitted the influence of political attitudes in some cases, and they admitted engaging in activities – such as bargaining – that are not part of the stereotypical myth of judicial behaviour.[12] Their willingness to admit to these behaviours makes their insistence that legal factors also influence many decisions more credible. Finally, they described a number of specific behaviours that are logically inconsistent with the behaviour that would be rational for a judge whose decisions are based on the unconstrained version of the attitudinal model. The fact that they were describing specific behaviours related to process, sometimes using examples from specific cases they had decided, instead of providing more general philosophical descriptions of the bases of their decisions, also adds credibility to the findings.

While a complete external test of the position of the justices was not possible, an exploratory model of the factors that produce a unanimous decision did add plausibility to the interview results. Those results suggested that unanimity was less likely in highly salient cases and more likely when there were some objective indicators of constraint from 'legal' influences such as precedent.

9 Continuity and Change in the Role of the Supreme Court of Canada

The account provided in the chapters above documents how the Supreme Court of Canada has changed from a relatively obscure court focused on private law disputes to an important policy maker. Since 1970 there has been a remarkable transformation in the role of the Court as well as in the way it operates. But some things have remained constant. This chapter traces the themes that underlie both the continuity and the change that define the Court's role at the beginning of the twenty-first century.

The Supreme Court has always had some impact on politics, though for much of its history it operated largely outside public interest and scrutiny. That veil began to lift in the mid-1970s and early 1980s as the Court gained substantial control over its own agenda and as some of the justices began to push for a more activist role. The policy-making role of the Court then increased dramatically with the adoption of the Charter of Rights and Freedoms in 1982. Since then, the Court has played an increasingly important role in the resolution of some of the most divisive issues in Canadian politics (e.g., Quebec independence, abortion, child pornography, gay rights, the role of women, the meaning of equality, and increased protection of those accused of heinous crimes). Many of its decisions have provoked both passionate support and intense disagreement. It is widely expected that the Court will continue to play an important role in some of Canada's most significant policy debates for the foreseeable future.

In Canada, most of the attention produced by this changing role of the Court has focused on studies analysing doctrinal development on the Court and providing normative commentary on the appropriateness of the Court's actions. For example, Morton and Knopff

(2000, 0149) argue that since the adoption of the Charter, the Court has become a willing adherent of the 'Court Party' and has ignored the majoritarian preferences of Parliament. Others have seen a tendency of the Court to use the Charter to further entrench the interests of a wealthy elite (Mandell 1994). Still others have been supportive of the Court's increasing role in protecting rights and liberties found in the Charter as a critical counterpoint to legislative and executive excesses (see Roach 2001). But few of these rival claims about the changing role of the Court have been subjected to systematic empirical analysis. While the normative debates will almost certainly continue, the empirical analyses presented in the preceding chapters will help place some of those debates in a broader perspective.

At the beginning of this study it was suggested that the evolution of the Supreme Court could be understood in terms of four themes that highlighted both continuity and change on the Court. To summarize the findings of this study and to place the many disparate concrete trends discovered in a broader perspective, the rest of this chapter returns to those four themes.

A Thematic Summary of Continuity and Change

First, there has been a major transformation of the Court's role in Canadian law and politics, largely a result of the Charter of Rights. Most obviously, since 1984 the Court's agenda has undergone a radical revision. As noted in chapter 3, the Court no longer concerns itself mainly with the resolution of private disputes between individuals and businesses and with routine, fact-driven public law cases such tax disputes; it is now a public law Court with a special interest in constitutional issues and the interpretation of widely applicable statutes. As one of the justices noted, the orientation of the current Court is that 'we won't take cases on which the law is well settled ... and we are generally not interested in cases that are "fact driven" – "who done it" is a question for the lower courts.' Thus, cases like the 1971 inheritance and tax disputes (see chapter 1) would simply not be selected for review by the current Court because the issues in such cases revolve largely around 'who done it.'

Some of this agenda change has been brought about by the end of many categories of cases – those that before 1975 would have come to the Court 'as of right.' The Court's increased discretion over its docket since 1975 has had the biggest impact on the types of cases chosen for review, especially now that the Charter has presented the Court with a number of fundamentally new and important issues with potentially far-reaching impact. The most dramatic changes in the Court's agenda were the major increases in the number of civil liberties and criminal appeals heard by the Court after the adoption of the Charter. Perhaps as important, there has been a change in the *kinds* of criminal cases coming to the Court. Since the Charter, the Court rarely hears appeals that primarily raise questions of innocence or guilt or that raise narrow questions about individual misconduct by police or prosecutors. Instead, criminal appeals heard by the Court are now dominated by possible Charter violations and by statutory interpretations – matters with broad policy significance.

During the interviews, the justices suggested that on the current Court the issue of the uniformity of law looms large. The justices seemed unanimous that it is important for federal law to mean the same thing throughout a highly diverse country. This means they are especially interested in accepting a case for review when there is a question of statutory interpretation that has national implications – particularly when the law has been interpreted differently by the appellate courts in different parts of the country. The empirical analysis of the Court's changing agenda confirmed this perspective from the interviews. That agenda has come to be dominated by questions of constitutional and statutory interpretation that have profound implications for Canadian society. The proportion of cases raising questions of statutory construction increased slightly after 1975, then increased *dramatically* after the Charter of Rights was adopted. In recent years the Court has heard almost twice as many cases involving statutory construction as it did prior to 1984. One might not have expected the rate of statutory construction to be affected by the Charter, but a close reading of the cases demonstrates that constitutional challenges to legislation have forced the justices to take a hard look at statutory language and that they often search for plausible constructions of statutes that will make judicial review unnecessary. So besides increasing the number of constitutional challenges heard by the Court, the Charter has enhanced the Court's more traditional role, which is to interpret statutes and promote the uniform interpretation of the law across a diverse nation.

Less surprising to almost anyone who has been following the evolution of the Supreme Court is the finding that the proportion of cases on the Court's docket involving constitutional interpretation rose sharply after the Charter was adopted. This increase was due almost entirely to litigation directly involving the Charter. The Supreme Court of Canada has always exercised the power of judicial review in some cases, but as chapter 3 indicated, the proportion of the docket devoted to constitutional interpretation has more than tripled since the Charter. The Court's increased power to control its agenda through the expanded use of leave-to-appeal petitions had little effect on the number of rights claims reaching the Court until the Charter became a reality. Since the Charter, a large range of new constitutional issues have emerged. These have not displaced earlier constitutional issues from the Court's agenda; they have simply taken their place on that agenda beside older issues.

Virtually all scholars who have written about the Supreme Court have recognized that its policy-making role, especially in rights adjudication and other constitutional issues, is dramatically different now than it was in the 1960s or early 1970s. Some have applauded this new role, and others have sharply criticized the Court for embracing it, but both friends and critics of the Court agree that the adoption of the Charter was pivotal to it. In sharp contrast, one article in North America's leading political science journal argued that 'the Charter's influence is overrated' (Epp 1996, 775). Epp contends that the Charter was not what made this 'rights revolution' possible. Given this striking disagreement in the literature over the impact of the Charter, the analyses in chapters 3, 4, and 6 explored its impact in depth. The results strongly reaffirmed the view that the Charter has done a great deal to change the Court's role. For example, when the proportion of rights cases on the Court's agenda was examined year by year, a sharp break was discovered in 1984, the year the first Charter cases came before the Court. Both the proportion and the raw number of rights cases increased dramatically after the Charter.

In addition, the data suggest that the Charter has had a strong impact on the Court's exercise of judicial review – an impact that made itself felt immediately after the first Charter cases reached the Court. Before the Charter there had been only three years in which the Supreme Court considered six or more cases requesting judicial review; since the Charter, the Court has considered at least that many constitutional challenges every year. The effect is even more dramatic when one examines constitutional challenges to administrative actions as well as demands for judicial review of legislation. Immediately after the Charter was adopted, there was a sharp increase in judicial review of the constitutionality of executive actions.

The Charter's impact on outcomes was less strong but still significant. A criminal defendant's appeal was far more likely to succeed when he or she was able to contest a conviction or sentence on Charter grounds.

The analysis in chapter 6 demonstrated that trends in decisions for civil liberties cases seem to be strongly related to the Charter. Before it was adopted, the Court heard few civil liberties cases and supported liberal outcomes in only one-quarter of its decisions. In the first seven years of Charter litigation, support for civil liberties claimants jumped to nearly 48 per cent, more than double the Court's level of support in the previous eight years. Moreover, this result almost certainly understates the impact of the Charter. First, since the number of cases raising rights claims increased dramatically after the Charter, the number of people whose rights claims were vindicated increased by much more than just the increase in the proportion of victories. And as noted in earlier analyses (e.g., Russell 1992), rights claimants were highly successful in the first two years of Charter litigation; moreover, the effect of these new precedents rippled through the entire society. Consequently, in later years the Court began to deal with a second generation of rights issues in which claimants sought to extend rights substantially further than had ever been attempted before. In this second wave of rights litigation, even victories by rights claimants in one-third of their cases meant the addition of many rights that the Court had not sanctioned in the pre-Charter era.

None of this is meant to suggest that the Charter was the sole cause of either the rights revolution or the expanded policy-making role of the Court. These changes would not have been possible without determined actions by litigants and the appointment of judges who did not back away from sometimes aggressive interpretations of the Charter. That said, the sudden shifts in the trends of Court decisions noted in the analysis above – shifts that correspond so closely to the time when the Charter was adopted – provide strong evidence that the adoption of the Charter was an event of huge importance. Clearly, constitutions do matter.

While it thus seems clear that there was major change in the role of the Court that corresponded to the adoption of the Charter, there was also considerable continuity. For one thing, the highly collegial pattern of decision making on the Court seemed to be unaffected by the increasing political contentiousness of the issues on its agenda. Both before and after the Charter, a large majority of the decisions were decided by unanimous vote. In addition, the Court continued to play a role quite consciously in the development of the law governing private economic relations. Interviews with the justices and a close look at the empirical data on agenda change indicate clearly that the Court has continued to resolve disputes relating to contracts, torts, property, and family law. These disputes no longer dominate the agenda, but it appears that there is no danger that they will disappear altogether.

A Legal and Political Court

A second theme that emerged from both the analysis of the data and the interviews with the justices was that the Supreme Court of Canada must be thought of as both a political and a legal institution. Some social scientists scoff at the notion that top appellate courts are constrained by law; at the same time, some doctrinal analyses seem to lack all appreciation for the role of politics in the evolution of legal rules. This study has found that both law and politics must be understood if one is to appreciate fully the reality of the Supreme Court.

At one level, the Court is obviously a 'legal' court. In form and reality, it is the court of last resort in the Canadian legal system, and its rulings provide the authoritative interpretations for all provisions of the constitution, provincial and federal statutes, and legal precedents. Since 1949 its decisions cannot be formally appealed, and in practice it enjoys substantial independence that guarantees that its interpretations of the law are almost always the 'supreme law of the land.'

Chapter 5 demonstrated that even when carrying out its traditional legal function, the Court inevitably plays an important role in determining the winners and losers in society. Its dispute resolution function ensures that its decisions will have significant political consequences. Moreover, chapter 3 left little doubt that the Court's agenda has been transformed in such a way that any Court in the foreseeable future is going to be called on to decide a large number of issues that are politically salient and highly charged. It is not as if the justices have decided that the Court will play a political role; that role is basic to its mandate.

There has been considerable debate about whether the Court is political in a different sense. Given that the Court must decide a number of politically important issues, it becomes important to ask whether the justices' political preferences determine the outcomes or whether those outcomes solely reflect the letter of the law. Those who support the attitudinal model (e.g., Schubert 1965; Segal and Spaeth 2002) insist that though the Court's decisions prominently cite law and precedent, those decisions are actually framed by the political attitudes of the justices. There is strong empirical evidence that in the United States, Australia, and Britain, the political preferences of high court justices do much to shape their behaviour on the bench (e.g., see Segal and Spaeth 2002; Galligan 1987; Robertson 1998).

The review in chapter 7 of recent scholarship indicated that over the past half century, the 'attitudinal model' has become the dominant one in studies of courts in the United States. That model holds that justices make legal decisions based on their own 'ideological attitudes and values' (Segal and Spaeth 1993, 73), largely free from the constraints of law and precedent. It holds, as well, that justices' votes can be explained almost completely by their political ideology.

While there have not been as many empirical studies of decision making by the Supreme Court of Canada, the consensus in the literature reviewed in chapter 7 was that at least in divided decisions, there have been consistent alignments among the justices which suggest that differences in political attitudes are in play. This evidence of attitudinal voting on the Canadian Court is present as far back as the 1950s and 1960s (see Fouts 1969; Peck 1969; Russell 1969). A series of more recent studies found similar patterns of attitudinal divisions among the justices during the Charter era (Wetstein, Ostberg, and Ducat 1999; Ostberg, Wetstein, and Ducat 2002; Ostberg and Wetstein 2007). Other studies have used alternative methods to assess the impact of the political attitudes of the justices, re-enforcing the conclusion that attitudinal differences among them have been reflected in their divided decisions.[1] In summary, the evidence that the political preferences of the justices have some influence on their voting choices seems to be extremely well established.

The current study has built on this earlier work to examine the nature of the cleavages among the justices and to explore whether they have changed over time. The finding here is that both the substantial variation among the justices in multiple issue areas, and the relatively high consistency for most justices from one time period to the next, suggest that divisions on the Court are a product of differences in judicial philosophy or ideology. Notwithstanding disclaimers that ideology is an important factor when justices are selected,[2] the evidence is clear that the behaviour of the justices is related to the party of the prime minister who appointed them. However, when combined with differences across issue areas, the data also indicate that philosophical differences among the justices do not fit the traditional liberal versus conservative continuum that seems to explain judicial divisions in the United States; rather, many of the justices have more complex policy preferences.

The analysis uncovered both continuity and change in the nature of the cleavages on the Court. In the pre-Charter era, conflict on the Court was structured by political party, region, and religion. In the post-Charter era, while divisions are still somewhat related to the party of the appointing prime minister, conflict is more often structured by gender. These results appear to confirm the early prediction of Justice Wilson that the appointing of female justices would make a difference. Moreover, the finding of substantial gender differences in the voting patterns of the justices highlights the political significance of the long strides made in Canada compared to much of the common law world regarding the gender diversification of the bench.

The empirical analysis of judicial votes on the Supreme Court was supplemented by interviews with the justices that explored their perceptions of the role of judicial attitudes versus legal factors in their decision making. Adherents of the attitudinal model would almost certainly discount any claims by the justices that they were constrained by the law. But what is impressive about all of the interviews with the justices is not their general claims that the law is important (though all of the justices interviewed for this project agreed it was) but what they say when they talk about the *process* of decision making. When asked about process, all described specific things they routinely did which were consistent with the proposition that they took the law seriously and which were inconsistent with expectations that one would derive from the unconstrained version of the attitudinal model. For example, every judge, without prompting, emphasized that he or she spent a great deal of time during preparations for oral argument attempting to master the legal arguments in the factums. Moreover, all justices asked their clerks to do additional research on the primary legal issues raised by the litigants, and especially to analyse precedents cited in the factums that the justices were not familiar with. Finally, all of the justices discussed the legal issues with their clerks prior to oral argument but only occasionally discussed the policy aspects of the case. None of these approaches to preparation appear to make a lot of sense for a justice who plans to make his or her decision solely on the basis of political considerations. Moreover, no justice mentioned asking a clerk to prepare legal justifications for a position he or she had already arrived at (which would be the rational way to utilize the talents of law clerks for a justice deciding purely on political grounds), and three of the justices stated that they never told their clerks which way they were leaning before the legal research was completed. They considered it important that those clerks approach the legal issues with 'a fresh mind.' Finally, several justices indicated that they switched sides moderately often after hearing the oral arguments. Such statements do not absolutely refute the attitudinal model, yet it is difficult to believe that a justice who was only concerned with whether a decision for the appellant rather than for the respondent was more consistent with his or her personal political position would ever be in doubt as to which way to vote after reading all the factums plus the lower-court decision plus a clerk's memorandum analysing the issue. In sum, then, the way the justices talk about their decision-making processes suggests that law and precedent do affect their decisions to at least some non-trivial degree.

On the other hand, all of the justices indicated that they believed that their personal attitudinal preferences affected their votes and opinions at least some of the time. They all admitted to that there were differences in 'judicial philosophy' and/or 'ideas about justice' among the justices, and they all appeared to understand that such differences were the basis for the splits on the Court on at least some issues. They freely admitted that their political attitudes do have some impact on their decision making, but there was also consensus among them that they are not focused solely on trying to shape the output of the Court to support their own political preferences. Thus, the interviews provide evidence that both political factors and the constraints of the law have substantial influence on the decisions of the justices. None of the justices appeared to accept the view that the Court is either a purely legal or a purely political institution.

Evidence to support the justices' conclusions that both legal and political factors influence their decision making was found in the analysis of the unanimous decisions of the Court (see chapter 8). If the decisions of the justices were driven primarily by their personal political preferences, then one would expect that they would be divided on most cases. Moreover, one would expect that the rate of division would have increased substantially after the Court gained control of its docket in 1975 and would have increased again after the adoption of the Charter of Rights thrust more politically salient cases onto the Court's agenda. However, the striking finding of chapter 8 was that there has been a high degree of unanimity on the Court throughout the thirty-four years examined. In virtually every year, more than 60 per cent of the decisions were unanimous, and overall, in both the pre-Charter and post-Charter eras, the rate of unanimity was approximately three-quarters of all decisions.

Such high rates of unanimity by themselves suggest that very often the outcome is not determined by the justices' political preferences. Further analysis in chapter 8 provided additional empirical support for the view that most of the unanimous decisions are not simply the product of political preferences.

The above empirical analysis is consistent with the views of the justices that in many unanimous decisions the final decision reflects a consensus reached after prolonged wrestling with the complexities of the legal arguments presented to the Court. Two themes emerged in almost all the interviews. First, the justices believed that unanimity was the end result of serious discussion and debate about the meaning of law and precedent for a particular decision. In addition, most of the justices suggested that informal norms of collegiality and respect for the opinions of colleagues often resulted in deliberate efforts to find compromise solutions that everyone on the Court could accept.

In sum, the views of the justices expressed in the interviews and the results of a series of empirical analyses of judicial votes and case outcomes converged in support of the view that the Supreme Court must be viewed as both a legal and a political institution.

A Moderate Court

A third theme that emerged from both the analysis of the data and the interviews with the justices was that once the Supreme Court of Canada is understood as both a legal and a political court, a political analysis of its recent history suggests that it is a politically moderate court. The moderate nature of the Court was evident in a number of separate parts of the analysis.

As noted above, in one sense the most basic political role of an appellate court is to determine a set of winners and losers in society. A truly conservative court might be expected to provide consistently high levels of support for business litigants against both governments and individuals and to support governments in criminal appeals and rights claims brought by individuals. A liberal court would presumably display opposite trends. An examination of the actual trends in who wins before the Supreme Court found neither of these extremes. Business litigants neither uniformly succeeded nor uniformly failed.

They won very close to half the time they appeared before the Supreme Court. Individuals were less successful than businesses but nevertheless were able to win in over 40 per cent of their appearances. The success rate of individuals appears to be somewhat higher in Canada than in the courts of a number of other common law countries. Moreover, these moderate patterns of outcomes were an aspect of continuity on the Supreme Court. While there have been minor year-to-year fluctuations, the overall rate of success for both individuals and businesses has remained remarkably stable since the early 1970s.

The political nature of the Supreme Court can also be assessed by examining the substantive policy positions supported by the Court and categorizing each as supporting either a liberal or a conservative position. Such an analysis (see chapter 6) indicated that overall, the Court's outputs have been neither predominately liberal nor predominately conservative. Overall, 44 per cent of the decisions have favoured a liberal outcome and 56 per cent have favoured a conservative outcome. Moreover, support for liberal outcomes has remained at a moderate level since 1970, never exceeding 50 per cent and never falling below 39 per cent. In contrast, support for liberal outcomes has varied widely on the U.S. Supreme Court, ranging from over 70 per cent during the Warren Court to less than half as much during some terms of the Rehnquist Court.

Similarly, the Supreme Court of Canada has been moderately active in its exercise of judicial review. The analysis in chapter 6 indicated that the Court struck down 31 per cent of the laws challenged and 39 per cent of the executive actions challenged on constitutional grounds. That is, the Court demonstrated its independence from the government by supporting a non-trivial number of constitutional challenges to government power, but still declined to exercise judicial review in the majority of opportunities presented to it. This moderate approach to the exercise of judicial review has characterized the Court even since the Charter. The Court supported Charter claimants in 38 per cent of the appeals brought to it. Thus, the Charter has clearly had an impact on the resolution of often politically salient cases, but in the majority of cases the Court has denied the efforts of those challenging the status quo through constitutional adjudication.

The Court might also be considered moderate owing to the absence of sharp partisan polarization in its decision making. As noted earlier, there are statistically significant differences in the voting trends of justices appointed by Liberal prime ministers compared to those appointed by Conservative prime ministers, and these trends have persisted since at least the 1970s. But the magnitude of those partisan differences has been quite modest – usually less than 10 percentage points. In contrast, partisan differences among the justices in the top appellate courts in the United States and Australia are sometimes two or three times as great.

Given these empirical differences in voting trends on the Supreme Court of Canada, it is not surprising that most Canadian justices have been perceived as relatively moderate by some of the most seasoned observers of the Court. A close reading of the newspaper coverage of new Supreme Court justices (see chapter 2) found that on a five-point scale, only 18 per cent of all newly appointed justices were perceived as at either the liberal or the conservative end of the political spectrum. More than 40 per cent were classified as moderates, and the rest were viewed as moderate liberals or moderate conservatives.

Finally, the high rate of unanimity on the Court is consistent with an understanding that it is a moderate court. All of the justices stressed in interviews that there was a high degree of collegiality on the Court along with an impressive willingness to compromise to avoid a divided Court. Several of the justices indicated that opinion writers are often willing to bargain with those initially opposed to the original draft in an attempt to reach consensus even when the writer has a majority in support of his or her position. One common result of such bargaining, according to several justices, is that the scope of the original opinion is limited in order to gain unanimous support. In the words of one justice, 'Opinions are sometimes "*fudgier*" … or more limited than the opinion writer initially preferred in order to obtain a unanimous decision.' Thus, in order to produce a unified court, the justices are often willing to accept a more moderate outcome than would have been produced had the majority insisted on its own political preferences.

A Democratic Court

The traditional view of courts is that they are inherently undemocratic. In most of the common law world they are not elected and are generally not viewed as democratically accountable either to the government officials who appointed them or to the broader public for the policy decisions they make. And most judges on the highest appellate courts come from a narrow, highly educated elite segment of society. To a considerable degree, all of these undemocratic features apply to courts in Canada. Supreme Court justices are appointed by executive officials with little public scrutiny, do not face any kind of periodic re-election or reappointment, have substantial independence that shields them from traditional notions of democratic accountability, and are certainly wealthier and more educated than the average Canadian citizen. Yet the analysis in this study suggests that there is a sense in which the Supreme Court of Canada can be understood as relatively 'democratic' compared to many other courts around the world.

Beyond electoral accountability and representation, there is another crucial component of democracy. Pluralist theories of democracy stress that the ability of a wide spectrum of people and interests to gain access to decision makers and to raise effectively their concerns for deliberation and decision is important for democratic health. In this respect, the Supreme Court of Canada appears to be more representative than either Parliament or Cabinet, though direct comparisons are difficult. Nevertheless, the findings of this study make it clear that ordinary people seem to have substantial access to the Court. In particular, the Court's agenda is heavily influenced by concerns brought by private individuals who are not connected to businesses or organized interests. This access to the Supreme Court is an important fact overlooked by critics on both the right and the left[3] who have attacked the Court as being 'undemocratic.' As noted in chapter 4, since the adoption of the Charter, more than half the cases heard by the Supreme Court have originated as appeals brought by private individuals. Thus it is private individuals, rather than business or government or organized interest groups, that have the biggest impact on the Court's agenda.

The analysis in chapter 4 also reviewed a series of studies of courts that have concluded that in most courts the 'haves' tend to come out ahead in litigation. This analysis was guided in large part by an extensive literature on what has become known as 'party capability theory.' Tests of this theory in a number of courts outside Canada, as well as in one earlier analysis by McCormick (1993) in Canada, have provided extensive evidence that in many judicial contexts, repeat player 'haves' tend to come out ahead in litigation.

These studies suggest that 'haves' win more often because they are likely to have favourable law on their side, superior material resources, and better lawyers, and because a number of advantages accrue to them as a result of their 'repeat player' status. Superior resources allow the 'haves' to hire the best available legal representation and to incur legal expenses, such as those associated with extensive discovery and expert witnesses, which may increase the chances of success at trial. In addition, as repeat players they reap the benefits of greater litigation experience, including the ability to develop and implement a comprehensive litigation strategy, which may involve forum shopping and making informed judgments regarding their prospects of winning at trial or on appeal (Galanter 1974).

Put another way, the legal system's impact on patterns of outcomes is that the elite or privileged segments of society and the well-organized sectors tend to win their court battles more often than less organized and poorer segments of society. In this sense, many legal systems have an impact that could be characterized as somewhat non-democratic. In contrast to these earlier studies, the analysis in chapter 4 indicated clearly that unorganized individual litigants tend to win more often in the Supreme Court of Canada than in many of the other national high courts that have been studied. Most notably, individuals have won more often in direct match-ups between individuals and business organizations.

The findings of this study also suggest that when the backgrounds of the justices selected to the Supreme Court of Canada are examined, the Court appears to be more representative than most high courts even if the justices cannot be said to mirror Canadian society. The justices are in many respects a highly diverse group. As noted earlier, custom and law have combined to ensure that the justices represent a geographical cross-section of the nation. This was true before the Charter and has been true since. Consequently, there is greater geographic representation on the Supreme Court of Canada than on the high courts of either the United States or Britain. Religion has also been important in Canadian society and politics, and the two main religious groups in the country (Roman Catholics and Protestant Christians) have been represented on a fairly equal basis on the Court since at least 1970.

The justices in the courts of all industrially advanced modern nations are of course more highly educated and tend to come from higher class backgrounds than the average citizen, and in this regard Canada is no exception. All recent justices have been university graduates and have received formal legal education. Thus, in terms of the overall level of education, the justices are of necessity part of the elite. Yet beyond the fact of their university education, the Canadian justices seem to have less elite backgrounds than the justices in many countries. The appellate courts in Britain have often been criticized for being composed overwhelmingly of the graduates of two elite universities:

Cambridge and Oxford. And to a lesser extent, the dominance of justices from a few elite 'Ivy League' schools has been a source of concern in the United States. But no such limitation to a small group of the most elite schools is evident in Canada. Instead, the justices have been recruited from a fairly broad cross-section of both law schools and undergraduate universities from across Canada. As the portrait of the justices presented in chapter 2 indicated, no law school has produced more than five of the most recent forty justices, with five different universities producing essentially the same number of justices. The justices are even more widely recruited from among undergraduate universities, with twenty-three universities represented by alumni who have served on the Court since 1970. No school has produced more than three justices in the same period.

The openness and diversity of the Supreme Court of Canada is even more apparent with regard to gender. The Canadian Court stands out among comparable common law courts when it comes to gender diversity. The first woman was appointed to the U.S. Supreme Court at about the same time as the appointment of Justice Bertha Wilson; yet since then, only one other woman has been appointed in the United States. In Britain, the first (and only) female Law Lord was not appointed until 2004, and only one woman had been appointed to the High Court of Australia before 2006. In contrast, since 1970 more women have served on the Supreme Court of Canada than the combined total of women serving on the top appellate courts of the United States, Britain, and Australia.

Conclusion

For much of its history the Supreme Court of Canada toiled in obscurity and was widely considered to have little relevance for the major issues of Canadian politics. But since the 1950s and 1960s, the role of the Court has been transformed. Today the Supreme Court of Canada is increasingly understood as an institution that plays a major role in shaping national policies. Few now doubt that the Court often appears centre stage in some of Canada's most dramatic policy debates. Nor is there any doubt that the Court will continue to play a major role in policy making in the foreseeable future. This study has attempted to provide an outsider's perspective to shed some light on the nature of that transformation and on the current role of the Court.

Many previous studies have provided normative critiques of the Court and its interpretations of the Charter of Rights. No attempt has been made in the current account to add to that already abundant literature. Instead, the focus has been on providing an empirical account of how the Court operates in practice and what the empirical reality of its decisional trends has been.

It was argued earlier that the current Court can be best understood in terms of four general themes that summarize the continuity and change that has characterized it since 1970. First, much of the transformation in the role of the Supreme Court was stimulated by the adoption of the Charter of Rights and Freedoms. The Court's agenda was certainly transformed by the Charter, and with that new agenda its policy-making role expanded dramatically. At essentially the same time as the Charter was adopted, the membership of the Court began a dramatic diversification with the appointment of more and more women. As the analysis above has shown, this simultaneous change – in the agenda of the Court and in its membership – has resulted in new cleavages in the Court's decision making. Second, while it is still fashionable in many circles to think of the work of courts as divorced from the often disdained world of politics, both the empirical analysis of the Court's decisions and the views of the justices expressed in interviews provide strong support for the thesis that one must understand the Court as a court of law *and* a political court. Acceptance of the idea that the Court plays an important political role leads to an analysis of the Court from a political perspective, and that analysis suggests that both before and since the Charter, the Supreme Court of Canada has been politically moderate. Finally, when the Supreme Court of Canada is compared to other courts in the common law world, one is struck by the extent to which it appears to be rather 'democratic' in ways that reflect Canada's diversity.

Appendix: Interview Schedule – the Supreme Court of Canada

Decision Making

1) Routine Criminal; 2) Charter of Rights; 3) Complex Private Litigation

I'm going to ask you to think about how you decided three cases. Each time, I'm going to describe a type of case that you see on the Supreme Court and I would like you to think about a particular case you remember that you've decided in the past year or so. I don't want you to tell me any specific details that would identify the case or the litigants; instead I'm going to ask you some general questions about how you go about deciding cases, but as you answer these general questions I want you to be thinking in your own mind about how you approached that particular case. OK?

1.1 Now first, I'd like you to think about a *routine criminal case*. Could you begin by telling me in your own words how you approached that case and how you made up your mind? What were the important influences on your decision? What was the process like? How many judges heard the case, how did the Court reach its decision and decide who would write the opinion?

1.2 Next, I'd like you to think about an important *Charter of Rights case*. Once again, could you begin by telling me in your own words how you approached that case and how you made up your mind? What were the important influences on your decision? What was the process like? How many judges heard the case, how did the Court reach its decision and decide who would write the opinion?

1.3   For the third case, I'd like you to think about a complex piece of *civil litiga-tion involving private litigants* (for example a contract dispute or a tort). Once again, could you begin by telling me in your own words how you approached that case and how you made up your mind? What were the important influences on your decision? What was the process like? How many judges heard the case, how did the Court reach its decision and de-cide who would write the opinion?

Now, if you can recall those same three cases, I'd like to ask you some specific questions about the way you and your panel reached its decision. The way I'd like to proceed is to ask about the specific factor, and then have you tell me sep-arately how you would answer for each of the three cases, so if there were dif-ferences in the three cases, you can point that out.

2   First, *how soon* in the process were you pretty sure how you were going to decide?
    a   criminal case
    b   Charter of Rights case
    c   Complex private litigant case

3   How would you characterize the *degree of discretion* you had in this case versus the extent to which you felt you were constrained to decide the case a specific way? Were you constrained just to decide the case in favor of one side with some freedom to decide how broad or narrow the ruling would be or the particular basis of the opinion, or did you feel that the ba-sic thrust of the opinion was also constrained? (FOLLOW UP – so would you say there was/was not a clear 'right answer'?)
    a   criminal case
    b   Charter of Rights case
    c   Complex private litigant case

4   How important were the *legal arguments* and discussion of precedent in the briefs? Did you go with the side that had the stronger brief?
    a   criminal case
    b   Charter of Rights case
    c   Complex private litigant case

5   What about *oral argument*? How much did it influence the way you de-cided?
    a   criminal case

b   Charter of Rights case
c   Complex private litigant case

6   How much of an influence were the *views of your colleagues* on the Court? Did you discuss the case before oral arguments? What type of communication was there after conference? Did the views of colleagues not hearing the argument affect your thinking?
a   criminal case
b   Charter of Rights case
c   Complex private litigant case

7   Was there much *bargaining* over the opinion?
a   criminal case
b   Charter of Rights case
c   Complex private litigant case

8   How constraining was existing *precedent* for the decision you reached in this case? Would the outcome have been different if a different size panel of court had heard the case?
a   criminal case
b   Charter of Rights case
c   Complex private litigant case

[Then we can code, like Kingdon did, factors that were spontaneously mentioned vs the importance attached to each when asked a specific questions]

Now let me shift the focus and ask you some more general questions not tied to the three specific cases we've been discussing:

9   First, I'd like to ask you about the way the court sets its agenda, that is, the way it decides petitions for leave to appeal.
a   Are there any important informal practices that modify in practice the formal rules?
b   What are the most important criteria for granting leave petitions? What are you looking for?
c   How much interaction is there between the 3 judge panels and the rest of the court? How autonomous are those panels?
d   What about the identity/reputations of either the attorneys seeking or opposing leave to appeal or the reputation of the judge below? (do you have a feel for the jurisprudence/leanings of most appeals court judges?)

10 What is the nature of the influence of interveners – especially those from interest groups?

11 The final topic I'd like to explore is the problem of maintaining coherence in the judicial hierarchy.
   a How effectively do you think the Supreme Court is in monitoring the courts below?
   b Are there particular courts (e.g., the court of appeals of a particular province) or particular judges below viewed as needing close scrutiny? (possibly mention 9th circuit in US)
   c Is there a problem with information asymmetry?
   d Do possible reactions from other political actors merit attention (e.g., the possibility of the use of the Notwithstanding Clause or legislative override of statutory interpretation or non-enforcement by the government)?
   e Is there much communication, especially informal communication, among judges on different levels or between judges and the government?
   f Are the policy preferences of judges or courts below known? If so, is there a tendency to 'give the benefit of the doubt' when a judge below makes a decision contrary to their normal political or jurisprudential leanings? (e.g., *a staunch Charter supporter rules against the Charter claimant in a case*)   .

Try Out Gravitational Theory?

1 informal processes that modify in practice the formal rules? How much discretion do judges have in setting the court's agenda? What are the most important criterion for selecting a case for review?

2 Decision Making Process: How do the justices go about making up their minds on docketed cases ? What is the role of the judges' clerks? How much interaction is there among the judges at different points in the process? Is there any informal pressure to reach consensus? What type of interaction is there between the justice chosen to write the opinion of the court and others Agenda Setting: What is the process for selecting cases for review? Are there on the court? What role does the Chief Justice play in decision making and opinion writing. How is the assignment of the court's opinion handled?

3   Influences on Decision: What proportion of the cases appear to have clear 'right' answers and how constrained do the judges feel on most cases? How much influence do legal arguments presented in briefs and in oral argument have on the final decision? How important are the individual preferences of the justices? Are there any external pressures on the court (public opinion, the government, the opinion of the bar)?

Maintaining the Judicial Hierarchy

How effectively are the judges able to monitor the courts below? Are particular courts (e.g., the court of appeals of a particular province) or particular judges below viewed as needing close scrutiny? Is there a problem of information asymmetry? Do possible reactions from other political actors merit attention (e.g., the possibility of use of the notwithstanding clause or legislative override of statutory interpretations)? Is there much informal communication among judges at different levels or between judges and the government?

Notes

Chapter 1

1 [1972] S.C.R. 150.
2 [1970] S.C.R. 160.
3 [1970] S.C.R. 175.
4 [1970] S.C.R. 201.
5 [2001] 1 S.C.R. 45.
6 Referring to federal minister of justice Anne McLellan.
7 *R v. Morgentaler* [1988] 1 S.C.R. 30.
8 *Globe and Mail*, 29 January 1988, page A1.
9 *Globe and Mail*, 29 January 1988, page A1.
10 *Globe and Mail*, 29 January 1988, page A11.
11 Direct quotations from the Court's decision received more than fifty column inches of space in the *Globe and Mail* and were followed by extensive commentary and elaboration by the paper's legal experts.
12 [1998] 1 S.C.R. 493.
13 *Globe and Mail*, page A4, 3 April 1998.
14 'Vetting the Judges,' *Globe and Mail*, 25 July 2005, A12.
15 One's political position undoubtably biases any attempts at generalization.
16 The funding for much of the data gathering for this project is part of a larger project funded by two grants (see acknowledgments). Additional support was provided by the Canadian Embassy in the United States, Canadian Studies Grant program, 'Decision Making in the Supreme Courts and Courts of Appeals in Canada and the United States.' For the NSF funding for my Appeals Court book, visit the United States Courts of Appeals Data Base, Donald R. Songer (Principal Investigator), NSF# SES-89-12678. These data can be found at: http://www.as.uky.edu/polisci/ulmerproject/databases.htm.

Chapter 2

1 These perceptions of public reaction to the nominations were shared by reporters from the *Globe and Mail* and the *Ottawa Citizen* interviewed by the author as well as by several career officials in the Justice Ministry.
2 The advisory committee had asked the candidates to supply copies of all of their opinions, speeches, and publications and had commissioned an academic specialist to analyse the complete record of each nominee.
3 Personal interview with Janice Tibbetts, *Ottawa Citizen*, 8 May 2006.
4 Personal interview with the author, 7 May 2006.
5 Personal interview with the author, 8 May 2006.
6 Interviews with Donald Songer in Vancouver, 14–17 June 2005. Interviews were conducted with the understanding that comments would not be attributed to specific justices by name.
7 For example, one of the two recent appointees from Ontario, Justice Charron, is considered a francophone, and little was made of this in either the Parliamentary hearing on her nomination or in the press.
8 *R v. Morgentaler* [1988] 1 S.C.R. 30.
9 For example, in the United States removal requires a separate majority vote in the House of Representatives followed by a two-thirds vote in the Senate.
10 See the formal regulations governing the operations of the Canadian Judicial Council at http://www.cjc-ccm.gc.ca.
11 In the following chapters, most of the tables present data on cases and their outcomes. These data cover the period from 1970 to 2003. However, given the important changes in the selection method discussed earlier in this chapter, the data on the justices serving has been updated through the end of 2006.
12 At the time of writing (early 2007).
13 Separate calculation, not displayed in table 2.4.
14 Justices with part-time appointments at law schools or who were listed simply as 'lecturing' at a law school were not included as having law school experience.
15 In the interest of parsimony, the list is not displayed.
16 The independent recoding of the newspaper ideology scores of the justices produced a 95 per cent agreement rate with earlier coding of Ostberg and Wetstein.

Chapter 3

1 A new section of the Criminal Code, 691(2), requires that there be a dissent on a question of law in the Court of Appeal for an automatic right of appeal

to the Supreme Court even when the Court of Appeal has reversed an acquittal at trial. From 2000 to 2006 the number of cases per year coming to the Court as appeals as of right varied between 12 and 17.

2 As a matter of right, provincial governments may similarly bring reference questions to the Court of Appeal in their province. These decisions may then be appealed from the Provincial Court of Appeal to the Supreme Court. The Supreme Court in recent years has been treating these appeals as appeals as of right even though it is not required to do so by the Supreme Court Act.

3 Since the justices were promised anonymity as a condition of the interviews, two conventions have been adopted in reporting the results. First, justices are referred to simply as 'Justice A,' 'Justice B,' and so on, and the masculine pronoun is used for all justices (even though both male and female justices were interviewed).

4 Three other justices spontaneously used the term 'fact driven' when describing the types of cases the Court was not interested in taking. Such cases tend to be of significance only for the specific litigants involved because whichever way the Court would decide such a case, the law would remain the same for future litigants.

5 In the summer of 2004 the author conducted interviews in London with seven of the Law Lords, applying essentially the same interview protocol as in the interviews with Canadian justices.

6 Before 1999 they were sent to the Registrar's Legal Service.

7 Leave applications contain records from the courts below, citations and/or copies of relevant precedent and other authorities, and a factum (similar to an appellate brief in the United States) that provides a written argument by counsel. Factums are limited to twenty pages, but the whole package supporting the petition is usually much larger (see Greene et al. 1998).

8 In the United States, all justices formally vote on all cert petitions brought to conference. Also, the decision rule is that cert will be granted, placing the case on the Court's docket, if at least four of the nine justices vote to hear the case.

9 The Charter was formally adopted in 1982, yet the first Charter case did not arrive at the Supreme Court until 1984. Thus, the analysis uses 1984 as the beginning of the Charter period.

10 For the analyses of issues reported in this chapter, criminal appeals are *not* counted as civil liberties cases even if there is an alleged violation of a Charter right that is considered by the Court in the resolution of the criminal case.

11 The time frames compared are slightly different because in the United States the terms of the Supreme Court run from October to June. In both England and Canada the court terms coincide with calendar years. The data

displayed for the United States are for terms rather than years, making the beginning and ending dates for the indicated periods a few months different from the analogous periods in the displayed data for Canada and the UK.

12 The database and its documentation are available to scholars at the Web page of the JURI project http://www.cas.sc.edu/poli/juri.

13 In the one year (1988) that the post-Charter proportion of rights cases did not exceed the highest total for the entire pre-Charter period, it was only one-tenth of one percentage point lower than the high for the pre-Charter period.

14 For the twenty post-Charter years (1984–2003) examined in this research.

Chapter 4

1 The columns in table 4.1 do not add up to 200 per cent because in many cases both the appellant and the respondent are from the same general category – for example, an individual is counted as participating in a tort case if the individual plaintiff is suing another private person or a corporation.

2 Figures based on the 2001 census.

3 We only included cases in which there was a clear 'winner' and a clear 'loser.' Cases in which there was a mixed outcome (e.g., appeal allowed in part and dismissed in part) have been excluded from the analysis.

4 The success rate of a litigant class when it appears as the respondent is not presented in table 4.8 but can easily be computed by subtracting the opponents' success rate presented in column 2 from 100 per cent. Thus, individuals had a success rate of 46 per cent when they appeared as respondents (i.e., 100 – 54.0 per cent).

5 See Songer, Sheehan, and Haire (1999, 819) for the U.S. data.

6 The pre-Charter period was defined as 1970–83 and the post-Charter period as 1984–2003 because, though the Charter was adopted in 1982, no cases raising Charter issues were actually decided by the Supreme Court until 1984.

7 The success rate of the federal government, as measured by its net advantage, did go down in the post-Charter period, but the success of the provisional government went up. More important, both changes were less than one percentage point.

8 In earlier versions of the model, controls were also added for two other issue types: other public law questions and private economic disputes. These were dropped from the final model because neither was statistically significant and because neither substantially affected the relative effects of the other variables in the model.

Chapter 5

1 On rare occasions, a decision will be made by a panel of six or eight justices, but this typically only occurs when one judge originally assigned to hear a case becomes unavailable through illness or death. If a panel with an even number of justices is evenly split, the appeal fails and the decision of the lower court stands.

2 Conversely, at least in the Lamer Court, if a case solely involves an interpretation of common law and is to be decided by less than the whole court, the chief justice typically leaves two of the Quebec justices off of the panel (Greene et al. 1998, 116).

3 The panel sizes noted in figure 5.1 and tables 5.1 to 5.3 refer to the sizes of the panels initially appointed by the chief justice. On occasion, a justice originally assigned to a panel will drop off the panel before it announces it decision owing to illness or death or some other unforeseen circumstance. Thus panels announcing decisions will on occasion have an even number of justices.

4 With the year 1975 itself excluded, because that year there was a mix of cases – some already docketed before the Court gained control of its docket, and some coming under the new leave-to-appeal rules.

5 Three executive legal officers to the chief justice also confirmed this preference of Chief Justice McLachlin to have the whole court sit whenever possible.

6 Interveners play a role that is essentially the same as that of *amici curiae* in the United States. Interveners are groups, government officials, or individuals that are not formally litigants in the case but that have a concern about the resolution of the case and/or the legal rule that may emerge from the Court's decision. In Canada, interveners may participate by submitting a factum for the Court's consideration and/or by participating in oral argument with the approval of the Court.

7 And the authors' observations of a dozen or so hearings confirm that when the justices speak during oral argument, the form of their participation is almost always a question.

8 There were interveners in only 49 per cent of Charter cases in 1996.

9 The right of appeal to the Privy Council in London was eliminated in 1949. Since that time, the Supreme Court of Canada has been the court of last resort and is no longer bound by British precedent.

10 *R v. Lavallee* [1990] 1 S.C.R. 852.

11 But even Justice E characterized the chief's expressions as 'gentle' pressure.

12 Example provided by Justice G.

Chapter 6

1 *Re: Resolution to Amend the Constitution* [1981] 1 S.C.R. 754.
2 *Vriend v. Alberta*, [1998] 1 S.C.R. 493.
3 *Morgentaler v. The Queen* [1976] 1 S.C.R 616; and *Morgentaler v. The Queen* [1988] 1 S.C.R. 30.
4 *Askov v. The Queen* [1990] 2 S.C.R. 1199.
5 *Canadian Wheat Board v. Hallet & Carey Ltd. and Nolan* (1950) [1951] S.C.R. 81.
6 *Murdoch v. Murdoch* (1973) [1975] 1 S.C.R. 423.
7 Note for American readers: as used by Canadian courts in their opinions, the phrase 'appeal allowed' is essentially equivalent to the American meaning of 'reversed.'
8 In some cases more than two Charter sections were referenced in these tag lines. In these cases only the first two Charter provisions were included in the analysis. In other cases, though one or more Charter provisions were mentioned in one of the opinions produced by the justices, no Charter provisions were referenced in the tag lines. These cases were not included in the analysis in table 6.9.
9 *R v. Brydges* [1990] 1 S.C.R. 1233.
10 *R v. Prosper* [1994] 3 S.C.R. 236.

Chapter 7

1 See also Maltzman and Wahlbeck (1996a, 1996b); Wahlbeck, Spriggs, and Maltzman (1998); Spriggs, Maltzman, and Wahlbeck (1999).
2 While it would be consistent with a strategic understanding of judicial behaviour to suggest that judges might also be constrained by external political forces from following precedent or other legally relevant considerations, virtually all studies of U.S. courts have limited their analysis to studying constraint on the expression of the judges' political preferences.
3 In one instance reported by Widner, the government of Uganda even executed the chief justice of the Supreme Court for that Court's failure to follow the government's dictates.
4 Cases in which there was no obvious underdog (e.g., a contract dispute between two corporations) are excluded from the analysis.
5 Antonio Lamer became chief justice on 1 July 1990 and left the Court on 1 June 2000.
6 Tate and Sittiwong also suggest that prior judicial experience and association with political groups also is related to judicial voting. However, secondary analysis suggests that there was too little variation in the measure

of political associations to make it a useful explanatory factor; also, preliminary analysis suggests that whatever power a measure of prior judicial experience had in the earlier period, it is no longer a significant predictor of
the justices' voting behaviour. Consequently, these two Tate and Sittiwong
variables were not included in the analyses reported in this chapter.

7 Since tables 7.6, 7.7, and 7.8 uncovered no relationship between any of these
three variables and the tendency to support pro-government outcomes in
other public law cases, no model of pro-government behaviour will be
attempted.

8 (1991) 2 S.C.R. 577.

9 (1993) 4 S.C.R. 695.

Chapter 8

1 E.g., a vote of 5–4 or 4–3.

2 Our calculation based on analysis of the Spaeth U.S. Supreme Court
database.

3 Since the justices were promised anonymity as a condition of the interviews, two conventions have been adopted in reporting the results. First,
justices will be referred to as simply 'Justice A,' 'Justice B,' and so on, and
the masculine pronoun will be used for all justices (even though both male
and female justices were interviewed) to prevent their identification.

4 Factums are what would be called appellate briefs in the United States.

5 For the post-Charter period, we also used a measure of Supreme Court
ideology devised by Ostberg and Wetstein (1998). Ostberg and Wetstein
adapted the measure developed by Segal and Cover (1989), which has
become the most widely used measure of U.S. Supreme Court ideology.
Content analysis of editorials and articles at the time of appointment for
each justice in the nine leading national and regional newspapers of
Canada produced a cumulative measure of the frequency with which new
justices were referred to as 'liberal' or 'conservative'; the result was a scale
running from most liberal (+1) to most conservative (-1). Using this measure of ideology produced results for the post-Charter period that are
virtually identically to those in table 8.2. Unfortunately, this measure is
not available for the pre-Charter period.

6 We counted as 'reversals' all cases in which the Supreme Court reversed,
vacated, or vacated and remanded the decision of the appellate court.

7 It is conceivable that such a liberal panel would make a conservative
decision to follow a very old precedent that reflected the median ideology
on the Supreme Court many years in the past. Such a decision could be

unanimously reversed by the current Supreme Court, consistent with the attitudinal model, only if the median justice on the Court that established the precedent was more conservative than the most conservative justice on the current Supreme Court. It is implausible that this scenario could account for more than a very small percentage of the unanimous decisions handed down by the Court each year.

8 For instance, there is no plausible reason to think that a panel of three moderate judges or three conservative judges will make a decision that is more liberal than the preferences of all of the justices on the Supreme Court.

9 E.g., the more liberal the most liberal member is when the Court reverses a liberal decision.

10 This prediction was investigated recently by Songer and Tantas (n.d.). They studied all appeals from three provinces (Quebec, Ontario, and BC) dealing with either criminal law or Charter issues that were heard by the Supreme Court from 1982 to 2000. The ideology of each appellate panel was measured by the proportion of times the median judge had supported a liberal position in cases not reviewed by the Supreme Court.

11 I.e., the percentage of all decisions that are unanimous (74.4 per cent) times the percentage of unanimous decisions with no concurrences (86.9 per cent) = 0.744 times 0.869 equals 0.646.

12 The justices showed little reluctance to admit that there was some variation in political perspectives on the Court and that these attitudinal differences produced divisions among their colleagues in some cases. In fact, not a single justice argued that political differences on the Court were irrelevant for their decision making. For example, Justice E expressed the opinion that his colleagues were not as sharply divided on political ideology as their brethren on the U.S. Supreme Court. Nevertheless, he suggested that attitudinal differences were evident in divisions on the Court in both criminal appeals (where the justices gave different weights to a 'public order perspective' versus a 'due process and fairness' concern) and on many civil rights issues. Similarly, Justice F suggested that the divisions on the court often reflected different attitudinal perspectives among the justices, but that one should not assume that those differences always fell neatly along liberal/conservative lines. For example, he observed that differences in 'family values' often cut across liberal ideology for some of the justices. Justice D, while not using the terms 'attitudes' or 'ideology' when discussing decision making on the Court, was convinced that disputes among the justices sometimes reflected differences in their 'sense of justice' in a given case and that these disputes were most apt to be sharpest in discussion on

the meaning of the Charter of Rights. Thus, while no justice used the term 'attitudinal model' when discussing decision making on their Court, all of the justices seemed comfortable with the idea that the attitudinal preferences of the justices affected their decisions in some cases.

Chapter 9

1 See Ostberg and Wetstein (1998) (using newspaper measures of ideology) and Tate and Sittiwong (1989) (using judicial attributes).
2 See McCormick and Greene (1990); Heard (1991); Morton, Russell, and Withey (1992).
3 E.g., see Mandell (1994); Morton and Knopff (2000).

References

Aldrich, John H., and Forrest D. Nelson. 1984. *Linear Probability, Logit, and Probit Models*. Los Angeles: Sage.

Allen, David W., and Diane E. Wall. 1987. 'The Behavior of Women State Supreme Court Justices: Are They Tokens or Outsiders?' *Justice System Journal* 12, no. 2: 232–45.

Anderson, Ellen Mary. 2001. *Judging Bertha Wilson: Law as Large as Life*. Toronto: University of Toronto Press.

Atkins, Burton M. 1991. 'Party Capability Theory as an Explanation for Intervention Behavior in the English Court of Appeal.' *American Journal of Political Science* 35 (November): 881–903.

Baar, Carl. 1988. 'The Courts in Canada.' In *The Political Role of Law Courts in Modern Democracies*, ed. Jerold L. Waltman and Kenneth M. Holland. New York: St. Martin's.

– 2002. 'Social Facts, Court Delay, and the Charter.' In F.L. Morton, ed., *Law, Politics, and the Judicial Process in Canada*. 3rd ed. Calgary: University of Calgary Press.

Balcome, Randall P.H., Edward J. McBride, and Dawn A. Russell. 1990. *Supreme Court of Canada Decision Making: The Benchmarks of Rand, Kerwin, and Martland*. Toronto: Carswell.

Baum, Lawrence. 1997. *The Puzzle of Judicial Behavior*. Ann Arbor: University of Michigan Press.

Beatty, David M. 1990. *Talking Heads and the Supremes: The Canadian Production of Constitutional Review*. Toronto: Carswell.

Becker, Theodore L. 1970. *Comparative Judicial Politics: The Political Functionings of Courts*. Chicago: Rand McNally.

Bevilacqua, F.M. 1990. *The Supreme Court of Canada: A Politically Legal Role*. Montreal and Kingston: McGill-Queen's University Press.

Brace, Paul, and Melinda Gann Hall. 1997. 'The Interplay of Preferences, Case Facts, Context, and Rules in the Politics of Judicial Choice.' *Journal of Politics* 59 (November): 1206–31.

Brenner, Saul, and Marc Stier. 1996. 'Retesting Segal and Spaeth's Stare Decisis Model.' *American Journal of Political Science* 40 (November): 1036–48.

Brodie, Ian. 2000. 'Interveners and the Charter.' In *Law, Politics, and the Judicial Process in Canada*, ed. F.L. Morton. 3rd ed. Calgary: University of Calgary Press.

– 2002. *Friends of the Court: The Privileging of Interest Group Litigants in Canada.* Albany: SUNY Press.

Bushnell, Ian. 1992. *The Captive Court: A Study of the Supreme Court of Canada.* Montreal and Kingston: McGill–Queen's University Press.

Camp Keith, Linda. 2002a. 'Constitutional Provisions for Individual Human Rights (1977–1996): Are They More Than Mere "Window Dressing?"' *Political Research Quarterly* 55 (March): 111–43.

– 2002b. 'International Principles for Formal Judicial Independence: Trends in National Constitutions and Their Impact.' *Judicature* 85 (March): 194–200.

Carp, Robert A., and C.K. Rowland. 1983. *Policy Making and Politics in the Federal District Courts.* Knoxville: University of Tennessee Press.

Carter, Lief H. 1998. *Reason in Law.* 5th ed. New York: Longman.

Cash, Colby. 2006. 'That Wasn't So Bad.' *National Post*, 1 March, A17.

Cook, Beverly. 1981. 'Will Women Judges Make a Difference in Women's Legal Rights? A Prediction from Attitudes and Simulated Behavior.' In *Women, Power, and Political Systems*, ed. Margherita Rendel and Georgina Ashworth. New York: St. Martin's.

Coyne, Andrew. 2004. 'A Purely Political Choice.' *National Post*, 25 August, A1.

– 2006. 'A Show Trial in Reverse.' *National Post*, 1 March, A17.

Danelski, David J. 1969. 'The Supreme Court of Japan: An Exploratory Study.' In *Comparative Judicial Behavior: Cross-Cultural Studies of Political Decision Making in the East and West*, ed. Glendon Schubert and David J. Danelski. New York: Oxford University Press.

Davis, Sue. 1993. 'The Voice of Sandra Day O'Connor.' *Judicature* 77 (November–December): 134–39.

Editorial. 2004a. 'Judge Abella's Views and Our Right to Know.' *Globe and Mail*, 26 August, A18.

– 2004b. 'To Let MPs Interview the Top Court's Nominee.' *Globe and Mail*, 21 February, A16.

Epp, Charles R. 1996. 'Do Bills of Rights Matter? The Canadian Charter of Rights and Freedoms.' *American Political Science Review* 90 (December): 765–79.

– 1998. *The Rights Revolution: Lawyers, Activists, and Supreme Courts in Comparative Perspective.* Chicago: University of Chicago Press.

Epstein, Lee, and Jack Knight. 1998. *The Choices Justices Make.* Washington: Congressional Quarterly Press.

Epstein, Lee, and Joseph F. Kobylka. 1992. *The Supreme Court and Legal Change: Abortion and the Death Penalty.* Chapel Hill: University of North Carolina Press.

Farole, Donald J., Jr. 1999. 'Re-examining Litigant Success in State Supreme Courts.' *Law and Society Review* 33, no. 4: 1043–58.

Flemming, Roy B. 2000. 'Processing Appeals for Judicial Review: The Institutions of Agenda Setting in the Supreme Courts of Canada and the United States.' In *Political Dispute and Judicial Review: Assessing the Work of the Supreme Court of Canada,* ed. Martin Westmacott and Hugh Mellon. Scarborough: Nelson-Thompson Learning.

– 2004. *Tournament of Appeals: Granting Judicial Review in Canada.* Vancouver: UBC Press.

Fouts, Donald E. 1969. 'Policy Making in the Supreme Court of Canada, 1950–1960.' In *Comparative Judicial Behavior: Cross-Cultural Studies of Political Decision Making in the East and West,* ed. Glendon Schubert and David J. Danelski. New York: Oxford University Press.

Gadbois, George H., Jr. 1969. 'Selection, Background Characteristics, and Voting Behavior of Indian Supreme Court Judges.' In *Comparative Judicial Behavior: Cross-Cultural Studies of Political Decision Making in the East and West,* ed. Glendon Schubert and David J. Danelski. New York: Oxford University Press.

Galanter, Marc. 1974. 'Why the "Haves" Come Out Ahead: Speculations on the Limits of Legal Change.' *Law and Society Review* 9 (Autumn): 95–160.

Galligan, Brian. 1987. *Politics of the High Court: A Study of the Judicial Branch of Government in Australia.* St Lucia and New York: University of Queensland Press.

Gold, Marc. 1985. 'The Mass of Objectivity: Politics and Rhetoric in the Supreme Court of Canada.' *Supreme Court Law Review* 7: 455–504.

Goldman, Sheldon. 1975. 'Voting Behavior on the United States Courts of Appeals Revisited.' *American Political Science Review* 69 (June): 491–506.

Greene, Ian, Carl Baar, Peter McCormick, George Szablowski, and Martin Thomas. 1998. *Final Appeal: Decision Making in Canadian Courts of Appeal.* Toronto: Lorimer.

Grossman, Joel B., Hebert M. Kritzer, and Stewart Macaulay. 1999. 'Do the "Haves" Still Come Out Ahead?' *Law and Society Review* 33, no. 4: 803–10.

Gunther, Lome. 2006. 'Bedrock Conservatives Scratching Their Heads.' *National Post,* 27 February, A14.

Hall, Melinda Gann. 1987. 'Constituent Influence in State Supreme Courts: Conceptual Notes and a Case Study.' *Journal of Politics* 49 (November): 1117–24.

Hall, Melinda Gann, and Paul Brace. 1992. 'Toward an Integrated Model of Judicial Voting Behavior.' *American Politics Quarterly* 20 (April): 147–68.

– 1994. 'The Vicissitudes of Death by Decree: Forces Influencing Capital Punishment Decision Making in State Supreme Courts.' *Social Science Quarterly* 75 (March): 136–51.

Hart, H.L.A. 1961. *The Concept of Law*. Oxford: Clarendon.

Hausegger, Lori. 2000. 'Panel Selection in the Canadian Supreme Court: Neutral Assignments or the Exercise of Power.' Presented at the annual meeting of the Southern Political Science Association, Atlanta.

Haynie, Stacia L. 1994. 'Resource Inequalities and Litigation Outcomes in the Philippine Supreme Court.' *Journal of Politics* 56 (August): 752–72.

– 1995. 'Resource Inequalities and Regional Variation in Litigation Outcomes in the Philippine Supreme Court, 1961–1986.' *Political Research Quarterly* 48 (June): 371–80.

– 2003. *Judging in Black and White: Decision Making in the South African Appellate Division, 1950–1990*. New York: Peter Lang.

– 2004. 'Structure and Context of Judicial Institutions in Democratizing Countries: The Philippines and South Africa.' *University of Aranello Law Review* 5: 25–56.

Haynie, Stacia L., Reginald S. Sheehan, and Donald R. Songer. 1994. 'A Comparative Investigation of Resource Inequalities and Litigation Outcomes.' Presented at the annual meeting of the Midwest Political Science Association, Chicago.

Heard, Andrew D. 1991. 'The Charter in the Supreme Court of Canada: The Importance of Which Judges Hear an Appeal.' *Canadian Journal of Political Science* 24 (June): 289–307.

Helmke, Gretchen. 2002. 'The Logic of Strategic Defection: Court–Executive Relations in Argentina under Dictatorship and Democracy.' *American Political Science Review* 96, no. 2 (2002): 291–303.

Hensley, Thomas R., and Scott P. Johnson. 1998. 'Unanimity on the Rehnquist Court.' *Akron Law Review* 31: 387–408.

Hogg, Peter W. 2006. 'Appointment of Justice Marshall Rothstein to the Supreme Court of Canada.' *Osgoode Hall Law Journal* 44: 527–38.

Howard, J. Woodford, Jr. 1981. *Courts of Appeals in the Federal Judicial System*. Princeton: Princeton University Press.

Ibbitson, John. 2004. 'A Good Day's Work and a Valuable Lesson for Democracy.' *Globe and Mail*, 26 August, A17.

Kawashima, Takeyoshi. 1969. 'Individualism in Decision Making in the Supreme Court of Japan.' In *Comparative Judicial Behavior: Cross-Cultural Studies of Political Decision Making in the East and West*, ed. Glendon Schubert and David J. Danelski. New York: Oxford University Press.

Kelly, James B. 2005. *Governing with the Charter: Legislative and Judicial Activism and Framers' Intent*. Vancouver: UBC Press.

Klein, David, and Stefanie A. Lindquist. 2002. 'The Influence of Jurisprudential Considerations on Supreme Court Decision Making: A Study of Conflict Cases.' Presented at the Political Science Research Workshop, University of South Carolina, Columbia.

Knight, Jack, and Lee Epstein. 1996. 'The Norm of Stare Decisis.' *American Journal of Political Science* 40 (November): 1018–35.

Knopff, Rainer, and F.L. Morton. 1992. *Charter Politics*. Toronto: Nelson.

Kritzer, Herbert M. 2003. 'The Government Gorilla: Why Does Government Come Out Ahead in Appellate Courts?' In *In Litigation: Do the 'Haves' Still Come Out Ahead?* ed. Herbert M. Kritzer and Susan S. Silbey. Stanford: Stanford University Press.

Kritzer, Herbert M., J. Mitchell Pickerill, and Mark Richards. 1998. 'Bringing the Law Back In: Finding a Role for Law in Models of Supreme Court Decision Making.' Presented at the annual meeting of the Midwest Political Science Association, Chicago.

Kuersten, Ashlyn, and Kenneth Manning. 2000. 'Women Judges on the Lower Federal Courts: Are They Different from Their Brethren?' Prepared for presentation at the 2000 Annual Meeting of the American Political Science Association.

L'Heureux-Dubé, Claire. 1991. 'Nominations of Supreme Court Judges: Some Issues for Canada.' *Manitoba Law Journal* 20: 600–24.

– 1997. 'Making a Difference: The Pursuit of a Compassionate Justice.' *University of British Columbia Law Review* 31, no. 1: 1–15.

Langer, Laura. 2002. *Judicial Review in State Supreme Courts: A Comparative Study*. Albany: SUNY Press.

Lawrence, Susan E. 1994. 'The Supreme Court and the Attitudinal Model: Introduction to the Symposium.' *Law and Courts* 4: 3

Lunman, Kim. 2004. 'Tory MPs Refuse to Accept Process of Selecting Judges for Top Court.' *Globe and Mail, 28 August*, A4.'

Maltzman, Forrest, and Paul J. Wahlbeck. 1996a. 'Strategic Policy Considerations and Voting Fluidity on the Burger Court.' *American Political Science Review* 90 (September): 581–92.

– 1996b. 'May It Please the Chief? Opinion Assignments in the Rehnquist Court.' *American Journal of Political Science* 40 (May): 421–43.

Maltzman, Forrest, James F. Spriggs, II, and Paul J. Wahlbeck. 2000. *Crafting Law on the Supreme Court: The Collegial Game.* New York: Cambridge University Press.

Mandel, Michael. 1989. *The Charter and the Legalization of Politics in Canada.* Toronto: Wall and Thompson.

– 1994. *The Charter and the Legalization of Politics in Canada.* Toronto: Thompson Educational.

Manfredi, Christopher P. 1993. *Judicial Power and the Charter: Canada and the Paradox of Liberal Constitutionalism.* New York: Oxford University Press.

– 2001. *Judicial Power and the Charter: Canada and the Paradox of Liberal Constitutionalism.* 2nd ed. New York: Oxford University Press.

– 2004. *Feminist Activism in the Supreme Court: Legal Mobilization and the Women's Legal Education and Action Fund.* Vancouver: UBC Press.

Martin, Don. 2006. 'How to Make a Judge Blush.' *National Post,* 28 February, A4.

Martin, Elaine. 1993. 'The Representative Role of Women Judges.' *Judicature* 77 (December–January): 166–73.

McConnell, William H. 2000. *William R. McIntyre: Paladin of Common Law.* Montreal and Kingston: McGill–Queen's University Press.

McCormick, Peter. 1992. 'The Supervisory Role of the Supreme Court of Canada: Analysis of Appeals from Provincial Courts of Appeal, 1949–1990.' *Supreme Court Law Review* 3: 1–27.

– 1993a. 'Party Capability Theory and Appellate Success in the Supreme Court of Canada, 1949–1992.' *Canadian Journal of Political Science* 26 (September): 523–40.

– 1993b. 'Assessing Leadership on the Supreme Court of Canada: Towards a Typology of Chief Justice Performance.' *Supreme Court Law Review* 4: 409–29.

– 1994a. *Canada's Courts.* Toronto: Lorimer.

– 1994b. 'Judicial Career Patterns and the Delivery of Reasons for Judgment in the Supreme Court of Canada, 1949–1993.' *Supreme Court Law Review* 5: 499–521.

– 1998. 'Birds of a Feather: Alliances and Influences on the Lamer Court, 1990–1997.' *Osgoode Hall Law Journal* 36 (Summer): 339–68.

– 2000. *Supreme at Last: The Evolution of the Supreme Court of Canada.* Toronto: Lorimer.

– 2006. 'The Serendipitous Solution to the Problem of Supreme Court Appointments.' *Osgoode Hall Law Journal* 44: 539–45.

McCormick, Peter, and Ian Greene. 1990. *Judges and Judging: Inside the Canadian Judicial System.* Toronto: Lorimer.

McCormick, Peter, and Twyla Job. 1993. 'Do Women Judges Make a Difference? An Analysis of Appeal Court Data.' *Canadian Journal of Law and Society* 8 (Spring): 135–48.

McInnes, Mitchell, Janet Bolton, and Natalie Derzko. 1994. 'Clerking at the Supreme Court of Canada.' *Alberta Law Review* 33: 58–79.

McKenty, Margaret. 2006. 'Commentary.' *Globe and Mail,* 23 February, A18.

Miller, Mark C. 1998. 'Judicial Activism in Canada and the United States.' *Judicature* 81 (May–June): 262–6.

Monahan, Patrick J. 1984. 'At Doctrine's Twilight: The Structure of Canadian Federalism.' *University of Toronto Law Journal* 34 (Winter): 47–99.

– 1986. 'The Supreme Court and the Economy.' In *The Supreme Court of Canada as an Instrument of Political Change,* ed. Ivan Bernier and Andrée Lajoie. Toronto: University of Toronto Press.

– 1999. 'The Supreme Court of Canada's 1998 Constitutional Cases: The Debate over Judicial Activism Heats Up.' *Canada Watch* 7: 4–5.– 2000. The Supreme Court of Canada in the 21st Century. Prepared for the Supreme Court Centennial Symposium, Ottawa.

– 2002. 'Does Federalism Review Matter?' in F.L. Morton, ed. *Law, Politics, and the Judicial Process in Canada.* 3rd ed. Calgary: University of Calgary Press.

– 2006. 'Commentary.' *Globe and Mail,* 22 February, A21.

Morton, F.L. 1997. 'To Bring Judicial Appointments Out of the Closet.' In *Globe and Mail,* 22 September, A15. Reprinted in F.L. Morton, ed., *Law, Politics, and the Judicial Process in Canada,* 3rd ed. Calgary: University of Calgary Press.

– 2002a. 'Judicial Recruitment and Selection.' In *Law, Politics, and the Judicial Process in Canada,* 3rd ed., ed. F.L. Morton. Calgary: University of Calgary Press.

– ed. 2002b. *Law, Politics, and the Judicial Process in Canada.* 3rd ed. Calgary: University of Calgary Press.

Morton, F.L., and Avril Allen. 2001. 'Feminists and the Courts: Measuring Success in Interest Group Litigation in Canada.' *Canadian Journal of Political Science* 34 (March): 55–84.

Morton, F.L., and Rainer Knopff. 2000. *The Charter Revolution and the Court Party.* Peterborough: Broadview.

Morton, F.L., Peter H. Russell, and Michael J. Withey. 1992. 'The Supreme Court's First One Hundred Charter Decisions.' *Osgoode Hall Law Journal* 30: 1–49.

Murphy, Walter F. 1964. *Elements of Judicial Strategy.* Chicago: University of Chicago Press.

Naumetz, Tim. 2004. 'Judges Review Dismissed as "Lip Service."' *National Post,* 26 August, A6.

O'Connor, Karen, and Jeffrey A. Segal. 1990. 'Justice Sandra Day O'Connor and the Supreme Court's Reaction to Its First Female Member.' In *Women and Politics* 10: 95–104.

Ostberg, C.L., Susan W. Johnson, Donald R. Songer, and Matthew E. Wetstein. 2004. 'The Nature and Extent of Attitudinal Conflict in the Supreme Court of Canada.' Presented at the annual meeting of the American Political Science Association, Chicago.

Ostberg, C.L., and Matthew Wetstein. 1998. 'Dimensions of Attitudes Underlying Search and Seizure Decisions of the Supreme Court of Canada.' *Canadian Journal of Political Science* 31 (December): 767–87.

– 2003. 'Acclimation Effects on the Supreme Court of Canada: A Cross-Cultural Examination of Judicial Folklore.' *Social Science Quarterly* 84 (September): 704–22.

– 2007. *Attitudinal Decision Making in the Supreme Court of Canada.* Vancouver: UBC Press.

Ostberg, C.L., Matthew E. Wetstein, and Craig R. Ducat. 2002. 'Attitudinal Dimensions of Supreme Court Decision Making in Canada: The Lamer Court, 1991–1995.' *Political Research Quarterly* 55 (March): 235–56.

Palmer, Barbara. 2002. 'Justice Ruth Bader Ginsburg and the Supreme Court's Reaction to Its Second Female Member.' In *Women and Politics* 24: 1–23.

Peck, Sidney. 1969. 'A Scalogram Analysis of the Supreme Court of Canada, 1958–1967.' In *Comparative Judicial Behavior: Cross-Cultural Studies of Political Decision Making in the East and West,* ed. Glendon Schubert and David J. Danelski. New York: Oxford University Press.

Perry, H.W., Jr. 1991. *Deciding to Decide: Agenda Setting in the United States Supreme Court.* Cambridge, MA: Harvard University Press.

Richards, Mark J., and Herbert M. Kritzer. 2002. 'Jurisprudential Regimes in Supreme Court Decision Making.' *American Political Science Review* 96 (June): 305–20.

Richardson, Richard J., and Kenneth N. Vines. 1970. *The Politics of Federal Courts: Lower Courts in the United States.* Boston: Little, Brown.

Roach, Kent. 2001. *The Supreme Court on Trial: Judicial Activism or Democratic Dialogue.* Toronto: Irwin Law.

Robertson, David. 1982. 'Judicial Ideology in the House of Lords: A Jurimetric Analysis.' *British Journal of Political Science* 12 (January): 1–25.

– 1998. *Judicial Discretion in the House of Lords.* New York: Oxford University Press.

Rohde, David W., and Harold J. Spaeth. 1976. *Supreme Court Decision Making.* San Francisco: Freeman.

Rosenberg, Gerald N. 1991. *The Hollow Hope: Can Courts Bring About Social Change?* Chicago: University of Chicago Press.

Russell, Peter H. 1969. *The Supreme Court of Canada as a Bilingual and Bicultural Institution.* Documents of the Royal Commission on Bilingualism and Biculturalism. Ottawa: Queen's Printer.

– 1983. 'The Supreme Court Decision: Bold Statecraft Based on Questionable Jurisprudence.' In *And No One Cheered: Federalism, Democracy, and the Constitution Act,* ed. Keith Banting and Richard Simeon. New York: Methuen.

– 1987. *The Judiciary in Canada: The Third Branch of Government.* Toronto: McGraw-Hill Ryerson.

– 1992. 'The Supreme Court in the 1980s: A Commentary on the S.C.R. Statistics.' *Osgoode Hall Law Journal* 30 (Winter): 771–95.

– 1995. 'Canadian Constraints on Judicialization from Without.' In *The Global Expansion of Judicial Power,* ed. C. Neal Tate and Torbjörn Vallinder. New York: NYU Press.

Russell, Peter H., and Jacob S. Ziegel. 1991. 'Federal Judicial Appointments: An Appraisal of the First Mulroney Government's Apointments and the New Judicial Advisory Committees.' *University of Toronto Law Journal* 41 (Winter): 4–37.

Samonte, Abelardo G. 1969. 'The Philippine Supreme Court: A Study of Judicial Background Characteristics, Attitudes, and Decision Making.' In *Comparative Judicial Behavior: Cross-Cultural Studies of Political Decision Making in the East and West,* ed. Glendon Schubert and David J. Danelski. New York: Oxford University Press.

Schubert, Glendon A. 1965. *The Judicial Mind: The Attitudes and Ideologies of Supreme Court Justices, 1946–1963.* Evanston: Northwestern University Press.

– 1968. 'Opinion Agreement among High Court Justices in Australia.' *The Australian and New Zealand Journal of Sociology* 4: 2–17.

– 1969a. 'The Dimensions of Decisional Response: Opinion and Voting Behavior of the Australian High Court.' In *Frontiers of Judicial Research,* ed. Joel B. Grossman and Joseph Tanenhaus. New York: Wiley.

– 1969b. 'Two Causal Models of Decision Making by the High Court of Australia.' In *Comparative Judicial Behavior: Cross-Cultural Studies of Political Decision Making in the East and West,* ed. Glendon Schubert and David J. Danelski. New York: Oxford University Press.

– 1985a. *Political Culture and Judicial Elites: A Comparative Analysis.* Vol. 1 of *Political Culture and Judicial Behavior.* Lanham: University Press of America.

– 1985b. *Subcultural Analysis of Judicial Behavior: A Direct Observational Study.* Vol. 2 of *Political Culture and Judicial Behavior.* Lanham: University Press of America.

- 1987. 'Subcultures and Judicial Background: A Cross-Cultural Analysis.' In *Comparative Judicial Systems: Challenging Frontiers in Conceptual and Empirical Analysis*, ed. John R. Schmidhauser. Boston: Butterworths.

Segal, Jeffrey A. 1984. 'Predicting Supreme Court Cases Probabilistically: The Search and Seizure Cases, 1962–1981.' *American Political Science Review* 78 (December): 891–900.

Segal, Jeffrey A., and Albert D. Cover. 1989. 'Ideological Values and the Votes of U.S. Supreme Court Justices.' *American Political Science Review* 83 (June): 557–65.

Segal, Jeffrey A., and Harold J. Spaeth. 1993. *The Supreme Court and the Attitudinal Model*. New York: Cambridge University Press.

- 1994. 'The Authors Respond.' *Law and Courts* 4: 10–12.

- 1996. 'The Influence of Stare Decisis on the Votes of United States Supreme Court Justices.' *American Journal of Political Science* 40 (November): 971–1003.

- 2002. *The Supreme Court and the Attitudinal Model Revisited*. New York: Cambridge University Press.

Sharpe, Robert J., and Kent Roach. 2003. *Brian Dickson: A Judge's Journey*. Toronto: University of Toronto Press.

Sheehan, Reginald S., William Mishler, and Donald R. Songer. 1992. 'Ideology, Status, and the Differential Success of Direct Parties before the Supreme Court.' *American Political Science Review* 86 (June): 464–71.

Smith, Miriam. 2002. 'Ghosts of the Judicial Committee of the Privy Council: Group Politics and Charter Litigation in Canadian Political Science.' *Canadian Journal of Political Science* 35 (Spring): 3–29.

Snell, James G., and Frederick Vaughan. 1985. *The Supreme Court of Canada: History of the Institution*. Toronto: University of Toronto Press.

Songer, Donald R., Sue Davis, and Susan Haire. 1994. 'A Reappraisal of Diversification in the Federal Courts: Gender Effects in the Courts of Appeals.' *Journal of Politics* 56 (May): 425–39.

Songer, Donald R., and Susan Haire. 1992. 'Integrating Alternative Approaches to the Study of Judicial Voting: Obscenity Cases in the U.S. Courts of Appeals.' *American Journal of Political Science* 36 (November): 963–82.

Songer, Donald R., and Susan W. Johnson. 2007. 'Judicial Decision Making in the Supreme Court of Canada: Updating the Personal Attribute Model.' *Canadian Journal of Political Science* 40, no. 4: 911–34.

Songer, Donald R., and Stefanie A. Lindquist. 1996. 'Not the Whole Story: The Impact of Justices' Values on Supreme Court Decision Making.' *American Journal of Political Science* 40 (November): 1049–63.

Songer, Donald R., and Reginald S. Sheehan. 1992. 'Who Wins on Appeal? Upperdogs and Underdogs in the United States Courts of Appeals.' *American Journal of Political Science* 36 (February): 235–58.

Songer, Donald R., Reginald S. Sheehan, and Susan Brodie Haire. 1999. 'Do the "Haves" Come Out Ahead over Time? Applying Galanter's Framework to Decisions of the U.S. Courts of Appeals, 1925–1988.' *Law and Society Review* 33, no. 4: 811–32.

– 2000. *Continuity and Change on the United States Courts of Appeals.* Ann Arbor: University of Michigan Press.

Songer, Donald R. and Julia Tantas. n.d. 'The Institutional Basis of the Attitudinal Model: Canada as a Test Case.' Manuscript currently under review.

Sossin, Lorne. 1996. 'The Sounds of Silence: Law Clerks, Policy Making, and the Supreme Court of Canada.' *University of British Columbia Law Review* 30, no. 2: 279–308.

Spaeth, Harold J. 1989. 'Consensus in the Unanimous Decisions of the U.S. Supreme Court.' *Judicature* 72 (February–March): 274–81.

Spriggs, James F., II, Forrest Maltzman, and Paul J. Wahlbeck. 1999. 'Bargaining on the U.S. Supreme Court: Justices' Responses to Majority Opinion Drafts.' *Journal of Politics* 61 (May): 485–506.

Supreme Court of Canada. 2000. *The Supreme Court of Canada and Its Justices, 1875–2000.* Toronto: Dundurn.

Swinton, Katherine E. 1990. *The Supreme Court and Canadian Federalism: The Laskin–Dickson Years.* Toronto: Carswell.

Tate, C. Neal. 1981. 'Personal Attribute Models of the Voting Behavior of U.S. Supreme Court Justices: Liberalism in Civil Liberties and Economic Decisions, 1946–1978.' *American Political Science Review* 75 (June): 355–67.

– 1993. 'Courts and Crisis Regimes: A Theory Sketch with Asian Case Studies.' *Political Research Quarterly* 46 (June): 311–38.

Tate, C. Neal, and Roger Handberg. 1991. 'Time Binding and Theory Building in Personal Attribute Models of Supreme Court Voting Behavior, 1916–88.' *American Journal of Political Science* 35 (May): 460–80.

Tate, C. Neal, and Panu Sittiwong. 1989. 'Decision Making in the Canadian Supreme Court: Extending the Personal Attributes Model Across Nations.' *Journal of Politics* 51 (November): 900–16.

Tate, C. Neal, and Torbjörn Vallinder, eds. 1995. *The Global Expansion of Judicial Power.* New York: NYU Press.

Tibbetts, Janice. 2006a. 'Supreme Court Pick Favors Restraint.' *National Post,* 28 February, A1.

- 2006b. 'Supreme Court Pick the First to Face MPs.' *Ottawa Citizen*, 18 February, A1.

Toharia, Jose J. 1975. 'Judicial Independence in an Authoritarian Regime: The Case of Contemporary Spain.' *Law and Society Review* 9 (Spring): 475–96.

Tremblay, Guy. 1986. 'The Supreme Court of Canada: Final Arbiter of Political Disputes.' In *The Supreme Court of Canada as an Instrument of Political Change*, ed. Ivan Bernier and Andrée Lajoie. Toronto: University of Toronto Press.

Ulmer, S. Sidney. 1973. 'Social Background as an Indicator to the Votes of Supreme Court Justices in Criminal Cases: 1947–1956 Terms.' *American Journal of Political Science* 17 (August): 622–30.

Wahlbeck, Paul J., James F. Spriggs, and Forrest Maltzman. 1998. 'Marshalling the Court: Bargaining and Accommodation on the United States Supreme Court.' *American Journal of Political Science* 42 (January): 294–315.

Walker, Thomas G., and Deborah J. Barrow. 1985. 'The Diversification of the Federal Bench: Policy and Process Ramifications.' *Journal of Politics* 47 (June): 596–617.

Wasby, Stephen L. 1993. *The Supreme Court in the Federal Judicial System*. 4th ed. Chicago: Nelson-Hall.

Weeks, Carly. 2006. 'Legal Experts Give Process Mixed Review.' *Ottawa Citizen*, 28 February, A3.

Weiler, Paul. 1968. 'Two Models of Judicial Decision-Making.' *Canadian Bar Review* 46: 406–71.

Weinrib, Lorraine Eisenstat. 1990. 'Appointing Justices to the Supreme Court of Canada in the Charter Era.' In Ontario Law Reform Commission, *Appointing Judges: Philosophy, Politics, and Practice* (Toronto).

Wetstein, Matthew E., and C.L. Ostberg. 1999. 'Search and Seizure Cases in the Supreme Court of Canada: Extending an American Model of Judicial Decision Making across Countries.' *Social Science Quarterly* 80 (December): 757–74.

Wetstein, Matthew, C.L. Ostberg, and Craig R. Ducat. 1999. 'The Bases of Conflict Underlying the Decision of Charter Cases in the Early and Late Dickson Courts.' Presented at the annual meeting of the American Political Science Association, Atlanta.

Wheeler, Stanton, Bliss Cartwright, Robert A. Kagan, and Lawrence M. Friedman. 1987. 'Do the "Haves" Come Out Ahead? Winning and Losing in State Supreme Courts, 1870–1970.' *Law and Society Review* 21, no. 3: 403–46.

White, Candace C. 2002. 'Gender Differences on the Supreme Court.' In *Law and Politics and the Judicial Process in Canada*, ed. F.L. Morton. 3rd ed. Calgary: University of Calgary Press.

Widner, Jennifer A. 2001. *Building the Rule of Law: Francis Nyalali and the Road to Judicial Independence in Africa*. New York: Norton.

Wilson, Bertha. 1986. 'Decision Making in the Supreme Court.' *University of Toronto Law Journal* 36 (Summer): 227–48.

– 1990. 'Will Women Judges Really Make a Difference?' *Osgoode Hall Law Journal* 28 (Fall): 507–22.

Woodruff, Judy. 2003. 'Sandra Day O'Connor: The Majesty of the Law.' In CNN Exclusive Interview, 19 May 2003.

Ziegel, Jacob S. 1987. 'Federal Judicial Appointments in Canada: The Time Is Ripe for Change.' *University of Toronto Law Journal* 37 (Winter): 1–24.

– 1994. 'Appointments to the Supreme Court of Canada.' *Constitutional Forum* 5: 10–20.

– 2006. 'A New Era in the Selection of Supreme Court Judges?' *Osgoode Hall Law Journal* 44: 547–55.

Index